T0266233

MANITOBA STUDIES IN NATIVE HISTORY

Manitoba Studies in Native History publishes new scholarly interpretations of the historical experience of Native peoples in the western interior of North America. The series is under the editorial direction of a board representative of the scholarly and Native communities in Manitoba.

MANITOBA STUDIES IN NATIVE HISTORY III

"The Orders of the Dreamed": George Nelson on Cree and Northern Ojibwa Religion and Myth, 1823

JENNIFER S.H. BROWN

ROBERT BRIGHTMAN

MINNESOTA HISTORICAL SOCIETY PRESS

©The University of Manitoba Press 1988
Fourth Printing 2004
Winnipeg, Manitoba R3T 2N2
Printed in Canada

Published in the United States by the Minnesota Historical Society Press, St. Paul 55102
   10 9 8 7 6 5 4

Cover illustration: The first page of George Nelson's sixty-page manuscript, written at Lac la Ronge in 1823. Reproduced with permission of the Metropolitan Toronto Reference Library, Manuscript Collection, the George Nelson Papers.

The pictographs were redrawn by Katherine Lipsett.

Library of Congress Cataloging-in-Publication Data

Nelson, George, 1786-1859
   "The Orders of the Dreamed": George Nelson on Cree and northern Ojibwa religion and
myth, 1823 / [edited and with commentary by] Jennifer S.H. Brown and Robert Brightman.
      p. cm. – (Manitoba studies in native history; 3)
   Bibliography: p.
   Includes index.
   ISBN 0-87351-224-3 (cloth)
        0-87351-370-3 (paper)

   1. Cree Indians—Religion and mythology. 2. Chippewa Indians—Religion and mythology. 3. Nelson, George, 1786-1859. 4. Indians of North America—Canada—Religion and
mythology. I. Brown, Jennifer S.H., 1940–. II. Brightman, Robert, 1950–. III. Title.
IV. Series.
E99.C88N45 1988
299'.78—dc19   87-35100
                                                                                                          CIP

The Manitoba Studies in Native History series is published with the financial support of the
people of Manitoba, through the Department of Culture, Heritage and Citizenship.

Manitoba Studies in Native History Board of Directors: J. Burelle, J. Fontaine, G. Friesen,
E. Harper, E. LaRocque, R. McKay, W. Moodie, G. Schultz, D. Young.

CONTENTS

viii   *Contents*

ILLUSTRATIONS

PHOTOGRAPHS

PICTOGRAPHS

MAPS

FIGURE

A Note About the Pictographs
The images which appear on the part title pages are renderings of ancient pictographs from the Precambrian Shield region of northern Saskatchewan. They were produced by the ancestors of the people currently inhabiting the area, the Rocky Cree, and were made as part of the ritual during which the individual encountered his *pawākan*, or guardian

spirit. The images portray spiritual beings, or the persons met during the vision quest.

Pictograph sites occur along the shorelines of many rivers and lakes in the Canadian Shield region of Saskatchewan, Manitoba and Ontario. The one shown in the frontispiece is the Hickson–Maribelli site north of the Churchill River in northern Saskatchewan. The drawings are smaller than the actual pictographs. The paintings themselves were made with anhydrous iron oxide, known commonly as red ochre, which is found locally in its natural state. The ochre was heated until the red colour had deepened to the hue desired; the resulting powder was mixed with oil, probably from whitefish, and applied to the rock. Over a number of years, the ochre would react with the rock surface until the organic medium had disappeared and only the red stained impression of the painted image remained on the rock face.

Ochre had sacred connotations for the people who produced these images. Ethnographic research conducted by Katherine Lipsett in northern Saskatchewan has shown scholars that the pictographs were made as part of the vision quest ritual. The images produced in the pictographs have not been definitively identified; however there is little doubt about the sacredness of the ritual and the sacred intent of the pictographs.

ACKNOWLEDGMENTS

We gratefully acknowledge the assistance and cooperation of several individuals and institutions in the preparation of this book. Several years ago, Sylvia Van Kirk shared with Jennifer Brown her discovery of the Nelson papers; and her researches and enthusiasm are bearing fruit as Nelson's writings progress into print, and as they are increasingly used and cited (e.g., McNeice 1984, Lytwyn 1986). The Metropolitan Public Library of Toronto, through Edith Firth, former curator of its rare books and documents, and Donald F. Meadows, director of the library, granted both staff assistance and photocopies, as well as permission to publish the text presented here.

Mrs. G. Lebans, Archivist of the Synod of the Diocese of Montreal, patiently went through the registers of Christ Church (Anglican), Sorel, to retrieve Nelson family entries scattered over a seventy-year period. Shirlee A. Smith, Keeper of the Hudson's Bay Company Archives, Provincial Archives of Manitoba, Winnipeg, and her staff, made possible access to and use of the Company's records relating to Nelson and Lac la Ronge. Without this assistance, our knowledge of Nelson and his contexts would have had serious gaps. In March of 1986, Jennifer Brown was able to visit the presumed site of Nelson's post at Lac la Ronge, thanks to the enthusiastic help of Katherine Lipsett of the University of Saskatchewan, Lois Dalby of La Ronge, and Tom McKenzie of Stanley Mission, Saskatchewan.

The Newberry Library, Chicago, Illinois, has been a fundamental source of support for this volume. While working on it, Jennifer Brown held a Newberry Library Associates research fellowship (fall 1982), and Robert

Brightman held a postdoctoral fellowship (1982–83) in the library's D'Arcy McNickle Center for the History of the American Indian. The Center granted work space and numerous other facilities to us. David R. Miller, its associate director at the time, was particularly helpful and supportive.

Maureen Gallagher of Parry Sound, Ontario, carefully prepared the first draft of the typed transcript. Our thanks for other assistance regarding specific points of information go also to Harcourt Brown (on French terms), David Pentland (on Nelson's Algonquian terms), and Wilson B. Brown, John Naples, and Anna Leighton (on botanical queries). Several friends and colleagues, including the readers, provided helpful advice and ideas on editorial, historical, linguistic, and other points; the responsibility is ours if we have overlooked or mishandled their suggestions. Final typing of much of our text was accomplished by Linda Gladstone at the University of Winnipeg, and we are grateful to the University for other support as well in the later stages of manuscript preparation. We also wish to express our thanks to the editors and staffs of the University of Manitoba Press and the Minnesota Historical Society Press for arranging copublication and thereby giving new life to the historic tie between Winnipeg and St. Paul. Special appreciation goes to Stan Cuthand and Maureen Matthews for their thoughtful contributions to our knowledge of Lac la Ronge and its history.

Robert Brightman's research with the Cree in northwestern Manitoba was supported by the Canadian Ethnology Service (Ottawa), the American Philosophical Society (Philadelphia), the Melville and Elizabeth Jacobs Research Fund, and the Smithsonian Institution (Washington, D.C.). The following persons provided information on traditional Cree religion which has been essential in interpreting Nelson's text: Johnny and Sarah Bighetty, Cornelius Colomb, Julien and Nancy Bighetty, Paschal Bighetty, Jeremy and Caroline Caribou, Sydney Castel, Luc and Caroline Dumas, Solomon Colomb, Antoine Bear, Henry and Angelique Linklater, Selazie Linklater, Jeremiah Michel, Jean-Baptiste Merasty, and Albert and Philomene Umfreville.

Finally, but not least, we must express our appreciation to George Nelson himself, in hopes that he would have approved our carrying out of his plans, never fulfilled in his lifetime, to publish his material. Acknowledgment of his contributions in documenting native North American religion and life is long overdue. This book may serve as a slightly late bicentennial commemoration of a writer too long ignored.

I

In the fall of 1807, John Lambert visited William Henry (Sorel) where the Nelson family lived. Although he found the town attractive with several stores and two churches, it did not appear prosperous. Many local men were voyageurs in the Northwest, leaving the cultivation of their farms to their wives and children (*Travels through Canada and the United States of North America, in the Years 1806, 1807, & 1808*, 2 vols., London 1816). Illustration from vol. 1, pp. 506–07, courtesy of the Newberry Library, Chicago.

Overleaf: NbNc-1, Hickson-Maribelli Site 2 Face xiv

INTRODUCTION

GEORGE NELSON

Background, Career, and Writings

Among Anglo-Canadian fur traders of the early nineteenth century, George Nelson stands out for his interest in the life and ways of the natives he encountered. His writings testify to his willingness to listen seriously and with a relatively open mind to what his Ojibwa and Cree associates had to tell him, and to his attention to detail and eagerness for accuracy. As a fur trade clerk, he served the XY Company (Sir Alexander Mackenzie and Company) from 1802 to 1804, the North West Company from 1804 to 1816 and again from 1818 to 1821, and the Hudson's Bay Company from 1821 (the time of its merger with the North West Company) until 1823. Yet while attending to business in an evidently competent manner, he also became a good observer and recorder of both the native and non-native people around him. His manuscripts are an invaluable and scarcely tapped resource on all the parties involved in the fur trade social sphere – and particularly on the Indians.

Nelson's papers are comprised of two major groups of materials: the manuscripts written during his fur trade service, and a body of reminiscences written between 1825 and about 1851, from two to twenty-eight or more years after he left the northwest. The document published here, which belongs to the first group, is, like the great majority of known Nelson material, held by the Metropolitan Public Library of Toronto, Canada.

In form, it is an untitled letter-journal, sixty foolscap pages in length, addressed to George Nelson's father, William. Internal dates and statements show that it was composed at intervals between March and early June 1823, while Nelson was serving as Hudson's Bay Company clerk in charge of Lac la Ronge (northeastern Saskatchewan), an outpost of Ile à la Crosse. The Lac la Ronge letter-journal is the last of his texts written in the Indian country, and the only substantial surviving manuscript concerning the final of his nineteen years of fur trade life.

Only one of Nelson's writings has previously appeared in print – his post-retirement reminiscence of his 1802-03 winter in the St. Croix River valley in northwestern Wisconsin (Bardon and Nute 1947). Some of the other papers bearing on the fur trade are being prepared for publication by Sylvia Van Kirk. The Lac la Ronge text includes relatively little about the fur trade, however, and because it stands apart as an ethnological contribution of high quality and great interest, we decided to annotate and publish it separately. This introduction portrays its author's background and career, and some of the contexts of his writing and thought. The text itself is reproduced in Part II. Part III, "Northern Algonquian Religious and Mythic Themes and Personages," places the document in a broad historical and ethnological perspective. In Part IV Stan Cuthand offers a personal commentary on Nelson's text, reflecting upon his own Cree heritage and his life in two worlds, and Emma LaRocque presents a native scholar's perspective on publishing historical documents.

Family and Childhood

Nelson spent his early years first in Montreal and then in a Loyalist community in Sorel, Lower Canada (now Quebec), about fifty miles down the St. Lawrence River from Montreal. His parents, William, a schoolmaster originally from South Shields, County Durham, England, and Jane Dies, were married in Sorel (or William Henry as it was then known) on 24 May 1785 (Nelson Family Papers 1765; Couillard-Després 1926, 141; Christ Church (Anglican) Registers 1787). Both had been among the many New York Loyalists who came to the Sorel area to escape the American Revolution. George, their eldest child, was born on 4 June 1786. He was followed by at least eight other children. The only two who found fame in their lifetimes were Wolfred and Robert, conspicuous for their roles in the Rebellion of 1837 in Lower Canada (Thompson 1976; Chabot, Monet, and Roby 1972).

George received, and evidently absorbed with success, a sound basic education; both the Lac la Ronge text and his other writings demonstrate considerable literacy and some familiarity with classical mythology and European intellectual currents. But on 13 March 1802, his father and the local notary set him upon a new course, drawing up a five-year contract to engage him in the fur trade as an apprentice clerk with the XY Company (Sir Alexander Mackenzie and Company), the firm which from the late 1790s to 1804 so vigorously challenged the North West Company for the fur trade beyond the Great Lakes (Archives nationales du Québec 1802). There were probably two reasons that William Nelson allowed George to take up this career at so early an age. First, George himself, infected by the examples of many other local youths who took up this adventurous life for what seemed a liberal salary, "was seized with the delirium" of their enthusiasm and campaigned to go (Bardon and Nute 1947, 5–6). Second, the fact that George as the eldest son had by that time six younger brothers and sisters in need of support may have swayed his father's views.

The Wisconsin Years

On 3 May 1802, George left Lachine, the fur traders' departure point near Montreal, in a brigade of six canoes to travel to the depot of Grand Portage on the southwestern shore of Lake Superior; then on 13 September he left there with three men to winter in northern Wisconsin (Bardon and Nute 1947, 6, 144). Nothing in his previous experience except hearsay from returned traders had prepared him for life in the fur trade and among the Indians, and he poignantly recorded his early homesickness and the trials of adjusting to so foreign a setting. Yet he remained open to contact with and involvement in his new world, gaining the Indians' acceptance and support, and even a tie of kinship. As he later recalled, "a mere stripling – how they laughed at, and pitied me alternately. A lad about a year older than myself, took a fancy for me, and treated me as a friend indeed: his father was well pleased, and adopted me in his family" (Brown 1984; see also Bardon and Nute 1947, 150).

In 1803, after a summer visit to Grand Portage, Nelson returned inland in mid-August, to winter in the Lac du Flambeau and Chippewa River areas of northern Wisconsin. Much travelling was necessary during this difficult winter, partly to avoid encounters with hostile Sioux, and partly because of food shortages. While under these stresses, Nelson had three

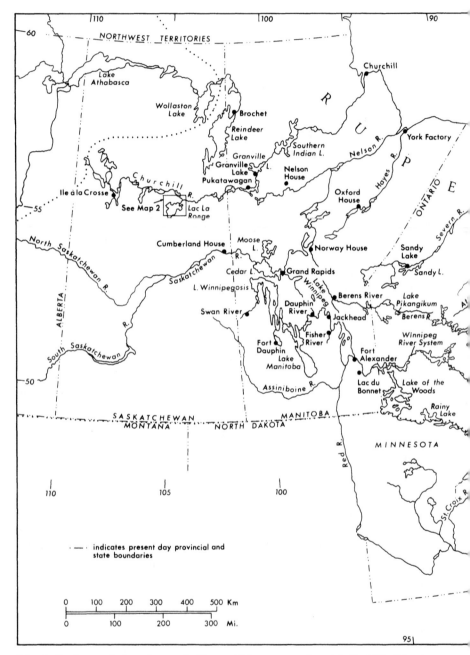

Map 1. Regions and places known to George Nelson or mentioned in Part III. (Map by Caroline Trottier)

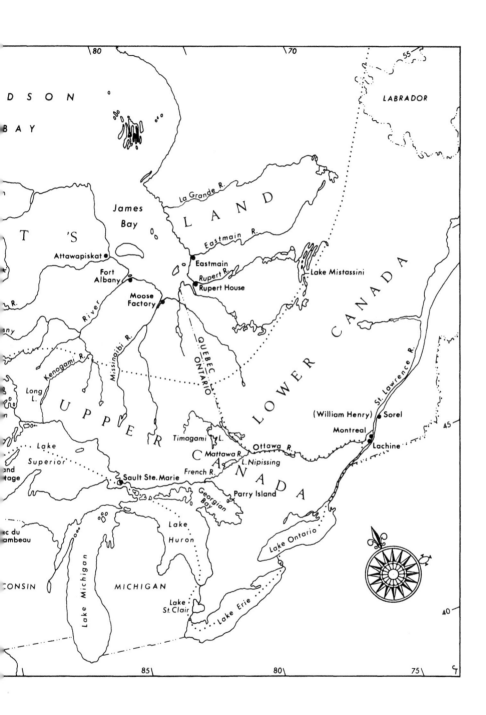

memorable experiences with Wisconsin Chippewa variants of the Northern Algonquian practice of conjuring as a means of seeking information and securing game, although use of the shaking tent, which he later found so common in more northerly areas, was absent in these instances. It is interesting that on all three occasions, Nelson and his men fostered or even initiated these activities, in empathy, it seems, with the Indians' sense that conjuring was, in the circumstances, as good and useful a coping strategy as any, and more satisfying than most.

The first incident was in early January 1804. Nelson became anxious when some of his men who were coming from another post did not arrive. His reminiscences record frankly, but with some introductory hesitancy, his successful application to a conjuror on this occasion:

I don't know whether I should relate a circumstance of conjuring that I had done by an old indian at this house. I had sent two men to our house above for rum. They had been gone 7 days beyond the time they thought they would be, and 3 days beyond what I expected. I therefore employed this old man, who, report said, never failed speaking truth, *His* way was after every body had retired to rest – *he* would have no Spectators. How he done I know not, probably it was inspiration, or vision in his dreams; but the indians said his *familiars* appeared to him, or told him, what he wanted to know. The next morning he told the people: "The men will be here by noon – they slept last night at *such a place*. They have had a great deal of trouble – they were near drowning, and are very hungry. But they are well, and bring the rum!" All he said turned out to be so correct that those who had been up, thought he had followed them (1825ff., 48).

By early February, both traders and Indians were in great need of food. The conjuring efforts that followed are described both in the Lac la Ronge letter-journal printed here and in Nelson's reminiscences. The latter (1825ff., 49–50) contain some vivid details that complement the account penned at Lac la Ronge:

Our indians frequently conjured, i.e., prayed and sang, and laid out all their most powerful nostrums, to kill bears, all to no purpose. How many appeals, what beating of drums, singing, smoking, &c, &c. Still to no purpose. At last *Le Bougon*, or Chubby, he who had killed the indian in the autumn, who was with us, said he would try. "I should succeed, I know, because I have never yet failed; but I have *polluted myself* [by killing] and I have no hope! What an event! How wretched am I now!" He was at last prevailed upon. "Well!" said he, "I will, possibly on your account, who have had nothing to do in that melancholly affair, I may possibly be heard!" At dark, he began, laying out and exposing all his nostrums, roots, herbs and dolls, to Pray (harangue), sing, beat his immense large drum, and smoke. He kept close to it the whole night. At Sun rise he gave a cry to attract attention, and accosted the others. "Old man," naming Le Commis [an Indian], "you will find a large Bear, after much trouble, in that wind fall, on the opposite Side of this creek. You, young man," to the Commis' Son, "you will follow your father's track till you have passed the two Small Lakes – you will see a Fir tree thrown down by the wind, beyond that is another windfallen tree, by the root of which you will find a young one, his first year alone. I also have one up this river!" And, if I remember right, he *gave* one to Le Commis' elder brother, who was with us. This is so strange, and so out of the way that I will ask no one to believe it. Those who will not believe the Gospel will still less credit this; yet **I say it is true**, believe who may. We had a Splendid feast at night, for they were very fat.

The third conjuring session was conducted by the traders themselves later that winter, after further food shortages for which Nelson, in retrospect, felt himself culpable, in his youth and inexperience: "we were still so improvident, and myself so thoughtless that we were literally always starving." Only partly in jest, Nelson and his men decided one hungry day "to imitate the indians' conjuring":

We speechified, sang, beat the drum, smoked and danced; Sorel, he who sang the best, imitating them, would run to the chimney yelling, "something shall be cooked in that place" – part indian, part french and English – "tomorrow, tomorrow, at latest, I smell it." The next day *Le Commis* brought us the sides of a moose he had killed! Sorel was frequently called upon after this, but he had lost his *influence* (1825ff, 51).

Nelson's second Wisconsin year, aside from these hardships and events, was also taken up by his involvement in an intimate native connection formed in the fall of 1803. His old Ojibwa guide, Le Commis (mentioned above), who was to lead Nelson to his wintering quarters, evidently hoped for an enduring trade and kinship tie with the young clerk, and presented him with his "very nice young daughter" whom he wished him to marry. Nelson put him off, citing the strictures of both his father and his employers, Sir Alexander Mackenzie and the XY Company, against such premature involvements. He later recorded the sequel: "The old fellow became restless and impatient: frequently menaced to leave me, and at last did go off. I sent out my Interpreter to procure me another guide. In vain – my provisions being very scanty, my men so long retarded, fear of not reaching my destination; and, above all the secret satisfaction I felt in being *compelled* (what an agreable word when it accords with our desires) to marry for my safety, made me post off for the old man. . . . I think I still see the satisfaction, the pleasure the poor old man felt. He gave me his daughter!" (1825ff., 35–36).

While Nelson clearly took pleasure in accepting the girl, the bond with her father had special importance. Indeed, as the conjuring incidents quoted earlier help to show, he found several times that winter that "our subsistence . . . depended entirely upon what the old man and his friends whom he kept with him, could procure us." But Nelson also became genuinely fond of Le Commis: "He was good, harmless, faithful, and his temper was so good that one could never discover when he was hurt but by a dejection of countenance and spirit, which yet soon gave way" (1825ff., 36, 40).

The summer of 1804 saw the end of that familial tie, however. On Nelson's return to Grand Portage, he was censured for his behavior and was obliged to send the girl away, a duty which he accomplished rather clumsily (Brown 1984). His posting to the Winnipeg district that season removed him permanently from the Wisconsin region.

The Wisconsin years made an indelible impression on Nelson's mind. He was at that time between the ages of sixteen and eighteen, sensitive and quick to learn. His progress toward eventual fluency in the Ojibwa language certainly began in this period. In remote inland settings where white companions were few and not necessarily congenial, and where Indian attentions and support were essential to his trade, Nelson found that his Indian ties were of great practical and personal value. Having an observant and inquiring disposition, he began also to learn about Ojibwa ways, which he found understandable and well suited to the conditions of northern life.

The Lake Winnipeg Period

The Lake Winnipeg phase of Nelson's career put him on familiar terms with the "Sauteux" (Saulteaux) or Northern Ojibwa of that area (cf. Steinbring 1981), and later acquainted him with the more northerly "Mashkiegons" (usually described by later writers as Swampy Cree) as they began to seek out the North West Company's trade. (On variants of terms for these Indians of the York Factory area and inland, see Pentland in Honigmann 1981, 227; Bishop 1981, 159.) No journal survives for the 1804–05 season spent at the mouth of the Red River, or for 1806–07; and that for 1805–06, spent at Lac du Bonnet on the Winnipeg River, is incomplete. Reminiscences written in the 1830s, however, help to fill the gaps, recounting, for example, local traders' reactions to the news of the merger of the XY and North West Companies in November 1804, following the death of Simon McTavish.

The 1805–06 journal, running from late August to early March, gives a good overview of seasonal activities and interactions with Ojibwa of the Lac du Bonnet area. Nelson once again became a kinsman of the Indians; his reminiscences note that, some time before November 1805, "The Red Breast [known in the journal as Red Stomach], a very good and sensible man, had adopted me as his Son." On various occasions, Nelson visited both Red Breast and his brother ("uncle" to the young trader) in their lodges (Brown 1984). In all, thirteen Indians and their families were named at one time or another as having trade ties with Lac du Bonnet in 1805–06.

When Nelson moved to the western Lake Winnipeg area in the fall of 1807, he became a part of increasing North West Company efforts in that area. By 1805–06 six NWC posts ringed the Lake Winnipeg basin: at Cross Lake to the north, Pike (Head) River (also known as Jack Head or Tête au Brochet) on the west shore, and Lake Folle Avoine (Rice Lake), Pigeon River, and Broken River on the east side, all subordinate to Bas de la Rivière (Fort Alexander) at the mouth of the Winnipeg River (Nelson 1805–06, 3 Jan. 1806; Lytwyn 1986, fig. 20). Nelson's new post lay just west and north of Jack Head, on the "River Dauphine" (Dauphin River), the waterway to the Fort Dauphin area and the outlet for Lake St. Martin and other lakes to the southwest.

Nelson's voyage to this place was marked by near disaster, and by the founding of a new and valued Indian tie. On 13 September 1807, while encamped at Tête au Chien (Dog Head), Lake Winnipeg, he was severely burned by the explosion of a keg of gunpowder. Immediate immersion in cold water and subsequent treatments with native remedies made from swamp tea and larch pine (tamarack) aided his recovery, as did the advice of Ayagon, the local Ojibwa leader in whose area Nelson was to be stationed. Ayagon urged Nelson to take a purgative to help remove the smoke particles and poisons from his system, and impressed the young clerk at the time by his "sound rational remarks" (1825ff., 194).

As a man of some seniority and influence both among his countrymen and in the fur trade, Ayagon became an important figure during Nelson's years on the west side of Lake Winnipeg. Although sometimes difficult to deal with, he became another adoptive father (see, for example, Nelson's River Dauphine journal, 2 August 1810) and a friend. Nelson appreciated in him the distinctive qualities of northern Algonquian leadership patterns: "He would only speak when there was occasion, but always to the purpose and expressed his ideas with ease and fluency; and when he had occasion to use his authority, which, by the bye, was very limited out of his family he would do so in such a manner as to convince all of what he was able . . . yet without giving offense" (Brown 1984, 226).

The years 1807 to 1812 afforded Nelson more continuity in both location and personal associations than did any other period of his fur trade service, and also allowed him to broaden his contacts with Indians. The journals record repeated encounters and trading with about fifteen to twenty named individuals and their families. Trade through the spring of 1809 was almost entirely with men whom Nelson identified as "Sauteux"–Ayagon and his associates. That June, however, the names of "Mashkiegon" Indians from farther north began to be mentioned with increasing frequency, eventually claiming as much or more of Nelson's attention than the Ojibwa. Their appearance reflected a regional domination of the North West Company over the Hudson's Bay Company at this time (Lytwyn 1986, 126-27).

The Mashkiegons (Swampy Cree) gave Nelson his first experience with the Cree language, and doubtless gave him a fund of knowledge and experience that was to prove useful during his year among the Crees who predominated in the Lac la Ronge area. Their arrival also gave him a basis for comparing two Indian groups and their languages and social relationships. In particular, he was struck by the good humour of the Mashkiegons, and by their determined cheerfulness in the face of adversity:

[In September 1809 at River Dauphine] I had all [Alexander] McDonell's indians, from the N. side of the lake. They were called Mashkiegons, from the word mash-Kieg, signifying a Swamp. Their language nearer the Cris [Cree] than the Sauteux, yet I in a short time acquired it from many of the words being derived from the same roots. A very peaceable and harmless set, extremely hospitable, social and gay, always singing, dancing, laughing and playing. They are so light hearted that in their greatest distresses and Starvation they cannot, it would seem, refrain from "cracking their jokes" on each other. Of course they were good natured, and always wished to please, and very seldom offended or wronged, maliciously. My old indians, the Sauteux had a contempt for them because they were too frivolous, and "had never faced an enemy." Yet they treated them kindly, carefully avoiding every word or gesture that might convey even a hint of disparagement. Still, the grave and solemn silence or taciturnity, yet quick penetrating eye and dignified demeanor of the Sauteux's, were of themselves sufficient to mortify these good people. I was afraid of a clashing, and warned the Sauteux's how much I should be displeased if they attempted to insult them. Man-nay-nag in-nung-gay! [Ojibwa mānēniminankē 'he would think badly of us'] replied they, i.e., surely we will not be so indiscreet – showing in that single expression how much they thought of themselves (1825ff.; 228).

Nelson's most enduring relationships, however, and the greater proportion of his record-keeping, were still centered upon the Ojibwa from River Dauphine southward to Bas de la Rivière where he regularly travelled to submit his fur returns. He was at that post in June of 1808 when rumors of Indian religious excitement and possible uprisings were circulating among the Nor'Westers who were meeting there. His descriptions of the movement clearly indicate that the Lake Winnipeg Ojibwa were being affected by the religious revitalization emanating from the Shawnee Prophet (Tenskwatawa) who had acquired numerous followers around the lower and western Great Lakes in 1806–07 (Tanner 1956, 147; Edmunds 1984, 75–83). Nelson's observations at the end of his 1807–08 journal and in his reminiscences (1825ff., 200–04) are a valuable documentation of the movement's manifestations in the northwest.

The summer visit to Bas de la Rivière in 1808 was also marked by another more personal event – Nelson's marriage to a cousin of the Ojibwa wife of his superior officer, or "bourgeois," Duncan Cameron (1825ff., 206–07). Although Nelson never named her or their children in his writings, the registers of Christ Church (Anglican) of Sorel identify them and record his attachment to them. His wife's background is recorded at the time of her baptism as Mary Ann on 29 July 1818. She was of the Loon Tribe of Indians (i.e., the Ojibwa Loon clan) on the north shore of Lake Superior – an origin suggesting that she and her kin, like many other natives of the time, were moving westward along the routes of the fur trade. Following his marriage, Nelson continued to serve as clerk in charge of River Dauphine, moving to the nearby lakeshore post of Tête au Brochet (Jack Head) for the 1811–12 season. His three eldest daughters were born in the Lake Winnipeg area, in 1809, 1811, and 1813.

A Decade of Changes

In 1813, Nelson was called away from these familiar grounds. His new post was Manitounamingan (near Longlac) north of Lake Superior – a much less peaceful location. Possibly his wife's connections with the area eased the transition. But the dominant theme of his writings in 1813–16, only fragments of which have survived, was the bitter competition with his local HBC rival and his resulting discomforts and insecurities (Van Kirk 1984). By mid-1816, the situation had led Nelson to decide to leave the fur trade. Recognizing that he would "have every other name but that of a brave man," he concluded in a letter to colleague William Morrison that July, "I cannot help it – I am tired of the Country" (Nelson 1816). By early October he, Mary Ann, and their four children were in Sorel; the two eldest daughters were baptized on the tenth of that month.

In the summer of 1818, Nelson reentered the North West Company, leaving his family in Sorel. The reasons on his part were evidently economic difficulties, but it appears that the company also sought him out as an experienced clerk needed in those days of opposition; Nelson mentioned both those factors in a letter he wrote to the company agents on 14 June 1820 (Nelson 1820). Perhaps he bargained to be allowed to return to familiar ground; in any case, he passed the 1818–19 season at the post he had left six years before – Tête au Brochet, Lake Winnipeg. Although disturbed at the apparent growing ascendancy of the Hudson's Bay Company in the area, he enjoyed renewing local ties.

The next June, however, he was obliged to leave Tête au Brochet for Moose Lake in the Cumberland district to the north. His journal of 6–7 June 1819 records his final departure and his regrets. Before he left, his friends invited him to watch the initiation of two men and a woman into the "Meetaywee" (Midewiwin or Grand Medicine Society) brotherhood – a ceremony with a long subsequent history at this place (Hallowell 1936, 47; Steinbring 1981; 252). He much admired the dancing and speeches, "having now a far better idea of their *Theology*, and understand their language also much better than I did 13 years ago when I saw them the first time." As he made his farewells to the Indians, he was "happy to be able to say that they all, even to the women expressed much uneasiness about my not returning. – This is a great consolation to me in spite of all" (Brown 1984, 204).

The following two years at Moose Lake (1819–21) were not easy. Feeling the pressures of the closing phase of HBC/NWC rivalry, Nelson also became increasingly unhappy at his employers' lack of appreciation for his services. The coalition of the companies brought momentary hope that a new regime might yield better rewards; instead, it soon became clear that the great surplus of manpower in the combined concern was to lead to the demotion or dismissal of many experienced employees. Nelson was kept on for two more years, having the charge of dry goods at Cumberland House in the winter of 1821–22 (Van Kirk 1984).

The Lac la Ronge Phase

In 1822, Nelson was transferred from the Cumberland district to that of Ile à la Crosse where he took charge of the HBC outpost on Lac la Ronge, a large lake lying just south of the Churchill River (see Map 2). The area, although new to Nelson, had seen intermittent fur trade activity for forty years (Wilson and Light 1980, table 1). Peter Pond had visited it in the late 1770s and had wintered at Lac la Ronge in 1781–82; HBC surveyor Philip Turnor had travelled the Churchill River in 1791–92; and Simon Fraser had been at the lake in 1795–96. More recently, Nor'Wester Benjamin Frobisher (d. 1819) had represented his company at the lake, having built the house in which Nelson was to reside (see below, "Conjuring at Lac la Ronge, June 1823"). The precise location of Frobisher's and Nelson's post has not been absolutely confirmed, but it probably stood on a slightly known archaeological site on the northeast shore of the lake opposite the southeastern shore of Kenderdine Island (Wilson and Light 1980, 84–85). A modern visitor to the site finds it largely overgrown, with a gentle southwestward slope to the water's edge. A few hummocks and depressions remain as clues to long-vanished structures.

In its geography and zoology, Lac la Ronge was a relatively familiar environment for a trader long accustomed to the central Lake Winnipeg basin. Subarctic in climate, it has a short cool summer between its mean last and first frost dates of 26 May and 7 September (Richards and Fung 1969, 52, 57). Maps of surrounding soil and forest types and geology vividly show its boundary-zone location, between the coniferous forests and the "rock knoll and basin" landscape of the Canadian Shield to the north and east, and the mixed woods of the Saskatchewan Plains that stretch to its west and south (ibid., 4, 46, 76, 92). Its ecological border position is expressed in several features of Nelson's text. Moose, bear, and beaver were by far the most frequently mentioned animals. Yet the "Buffalo" appeared in the conjuring tent as a fairly frequent Plains visitor, being a somewhat intrusive figure whose utterances were in a different language (as described below in "Other Beings"). The outpost's mix of fur trade products also reflected this borderline position; in 1824, they comprised nearly thirty-two packs of furs, a box of swan quills, and nineteen bags of pemmican, according to the Ile à la Crosse journal (HBCA B.89/a/7, p. 116).

The Lac la Ronge journal for 1822–23 has not survived. An unsigned account book for 1822–24 attributed to Lac la Ronge (HBCA B.106/d/16),

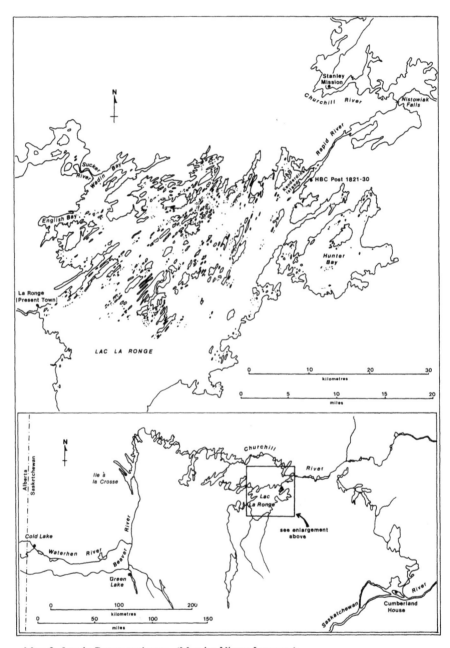

Map 2. Lac la Ronge and area. (Map by Victor Lytwyn.)

however, and the journal and district report of George Keith, the former Nor'Wester who was the "bourgeois" or district officer for the Ile à la Crosse district for that outfit (HBCA B.89/a/5; B.89/e/1), shed some light on the local residents and conditions, and on Nelson's activities in that period. Keith's report, written in July of 1823, characterized the populations around the three posts under Keith's charge – Ile à la Crosse itself, and the outposts of Cold Lake to the south and Lac la Ronge to the east. It indicated that Nelson's relations at Lac la Ronge were mainly with Cree Indians and with "halfbreeds." The "Cree tribe," consisting of sixty-five men, seventy-six women, fifty youths and boys, and forty girls, resorted principally to Cold Lake and Lac la Ronge; the "Northern" (Chipewyan) Indians, who were not enumerated and may have been in an inferior social and economic position (Jarvenpa 1982,285), were said to limit their trade contacts to Ile à la Crosse (HBCA B.89/e/1, fo. 2). Although Keith in September of 1822 criticized the Cree as "a dispicable, indolent and improvident people" (HBCA B. 89/a/5, fo. 8), his views had moderated by July 1823. They had, he then claimed, a "much more lively and engaging disposition" than the Northern Indians. The authority of their chiefs, he thought, had started to decline during the period of fur trade rivalry. Certain heads of families retained power and influence, but "more by means of gentleness and persuasion than presumption or assumed claims" (HBCA B.89/e/1, fo. 2).

The account book for 1822–24, assuming it is correctly attributed, serves to underpin and yet modify George Keith's observations. Chipewyan Indians were evidently not at Lac la Ronge in the fall or winter of 1822–23. But in April of 1823 and thereafter, nine apparently Chipewyan names appeared in the ledger. Six of them were kinsmen who had previously traded at Deers Lake (HBCA B.106/d/16).

Nelson would have lacked the language skill and the time to become well acquainted with these new arrivals, and their presence does not emerge in his 1823 text. We may assume, however, that he knew well the fifteen or so Cree who were listed in the accounts from October 1822, on, although this letter to his father (unlike his journals) does not name the Indians he met. Unlike the Chipewyans, the Cree had traded locally; they brought no debits from elsewhere. Seven had debits brought forward from the North West Company; five had balances owing to both "the late NW" and the "old HBC" (HBCA B.106/d/16, 1822–24).

Families of mixed descent were numerous in the area, a fact congruent with Nelson's frequent letter-journal references to "halfbreeds," and with the appearance of a large local métis Cree fur trade workforce in subsequent decades (Jarvenpa 1982, 286). In the fall of 1822, dependents at the posts in the district totalled sixty-one women and children under the age of fourteen at Ile à la Crosse, twenty at Cold Lake, and nineteen at Lac la Ronge (HBCA B.89/a/5, fo. 12). Nelson's own native family was in Sorel at the time. Retired, deceased, or transferred traders, mainly of North West Company background, had left behind ten sons and fifteen daughters under the age of fourteen, presumably in the care of other families. Benjamin Frobisher, who died of exposure when escaping HBC imprisonment in 1819 (Masson 1889–90, 2:179–220), and whose haunting of his old Lac la Ronge residence in skeleton or *pākahk* form is mentioned in Nelson's text ("Conjuring at Lac la Ronge, June 1823"), left a girl and a boy both aged less than seven in the district (HBCA B.89/e/1, fo. 4).

Aside from these dependents, a good many men of mixed descent were working at the posts or trading as Indians, and also serving, in some instances, as Nelson's informants and as active participants in Indian rituals and social life. The account book of 1822–24 named a few trading Indians whose names suggest mixed descent; "Joseph Paul's You[st] Son" (c.f. Masson 1889–90, 2:189, 208–10), for example, appeared intermittently between October 1822 and May 1824. The "Baptiste" to whom Nelson referred in his text ("Sexual Sorcery" and "Love Magic," below) may have been an HBC native employee, Baptiste Paul (HBCA B.89/a/7, p. 60). The extent to which Nelson's "halfbreed" informants put their own imprint on his data, emphasizing, for example, conjuring and love magic rather than animal ceremonialism, needs to be considered. These people were clearly close to Indian life. But "halfbreeds" and Indians might differ in their interpretations and emphases (see, for example, "The Sun; Nelson's Dream" versus "Sickness in Spirit Form").

Company records help to trace Nelson's own movements and activities during the outfit of 1822–23. In the summer of 1822, he accompanied the Cumberland brigade to Fort William on Lake Superior. In August he returned inland, spending the night of the 22nd at Fort Alexander or Bas de la Rivière (HBCA B.4/a/5, fo. 9). The pace of his journey was evidently slower than some expected, for on 28 August, George Keith recorded his disappointment at having to leave Cumberland House before Nelson's arrival. Keith left behind a man to guide Nelson to Lac la Ronge and a letter "acquainting him with his appointment and urging in the most pressing manner the necessity of his making every possible dispatch" (HBCA B.89/a/5, fo. 3). On 8 October, Keith finally received word that Nelson had arrived at Lac la Ronge after a thirteen-day trip from Cumberland House (ibid., fo. 9).

On 10 December, Keith heard from Nelson that company affairs at Lac la Ronge were "in as prosperous a state as could be expected." Nelson sent to Ile à la Crosse a horse and mare described as unmanageable, requesting a "horse that is broke in" and a cart. And he forwarded "a quantity of Iron works to be repaired and forged" (HBCA B.89/a/5, fos. 15–16).

A short document among some miscellaneous papers in the Nelson collection shows, however, that Nelson's mind during the winter was also engaged by topics other than the fur trade and the Indians. Three foolscap pages dated 17 January 1823 and seemingly intended for his father launched into observations on and criticisms of the French revolutionary calendar promulgated in 1793, and went on to deplore the tendency of reformers to set aside too casually old and valued symbols – in particular, the Christian cross with its many functions in both religious and secular life. The discourse was stimulated by Nelson's having at hand a volume of the *New Quarterly Review and British Colonial Register* (August 1812, no. 3, London), which contained reviews of two books, one by John Brady and one by Richard Grier, on these topics. The text concluded with a request that his father purchase these works for him, "as should it please God to take me Home again, I shall study them as they both deserve" (Nelson 1823, 7–8).

Keith visited Lac la Ronge from 23 to 27 January 1823. He expressed general satisfaction. "Mr. Nelson showed us much attention," and company affairs appeared on the whole "to have been conducted with a proper attention to system and economy." One comment, however, might not have squared with Nelson's own perceptions of his fur trade life; Keith wrote, "In the article of the mess Mr. Nelson appears to have been pretty much inclined to epicurism; but this is no more than might have been expected from one who has been for some years back at least, accustomed to comparative luxurious living" (HBCA B.89/a/5, fo. 20).

In his March report, Nelson felt it necessary to warn Keith of probable disappointment in his winter's trade. A letter Keith received on 27 March gave "a very forlorn account of his [Nelson's] prospects for the ensuing returns, proceeding apparently in a great degree from the poverty of the Country" (HBCA B.89/a/5, fo. 25). When, however, Keith and Nelson met at Rapid River on 13 June, travelling outward with their furs, Keith was gratified at Nelson's success: "The returns of Lac la Ronge are more considerable than I expected and exceed those of the preceding year by one Pack" (ibid., fo. 35).

While Keith travelled on to Norway House, Nelson headed south with the brigades for Fort William, stopping at Fort Alexander on 19–20 June 1823 (HBCA B.4/a/5, fo. 3). To judge by remarks near the end of the Lac la Ronge text, he evidently did not know until he reached Fort William that he, like so many of his contemporaries, was not to be rehired, although he must have suspected that it could happen. The end of his fur trade career was succinctly announced in the final entry in his company employment record, dated 1823: "£125 English River. Good Clerk and Trader no employment for him. Canada" (HBCA A.34/1, fo. 55). We may surmise that Nelson was able to hand-deliver the Lac la Ronge letter-journal to his father, although he had not counted on doing so.

Nelson's later life in Lower Canada was not happy. Like numerous other retired fur traders, he experienced poverty and illness as he tried to adapt to lifestyles and occupations from which he had long been isolated. His efforts at farming and in other enterprises, such as potash, found no great success. His life was saddened by familial burdens and losses. Three children had died during his 1818–23 fur-trade service – two daughters, and an infant he never saw. Of eight children born to Nelson and his Ojibwa wife, Mary Ann, between 1809 and 1829, only one daughter survived past 1831 and into adulthood. Mary Ann, with whom Nelson solemnized by Christian rite their seventeen-year fur-trade marriage in the Sorel Anglican Church on 16 January 1825, died in November 1831. For Nelson, the writing of his reminiscences, the final fragment of which is dated 1851, was probably one of the greater pleasures of his life, as he looked back with nostalgia at the more lively and stimulating, if often arduous, days of his career in the Indian country. He died in 1859, aged seventy-three.

Interpreting the Indians: Nelson's Frameworks and Dilemmas
As he wrote about Indian religion and legend in the spring of 1823, Nelson

was completing his nineteenth year of living close to a variety of native communities. His text demonstrates the depth of his knowledge about and empathy with these people. Yet it also reveals conflicting frames of reference in his own mind. Most of the time, his intent was simply to give truthful accounts of people and events. But when questions of explanation and interpretation arose, there were no easy answers; there was no ready way to reconcile the differing frameworks that Nelson carried in his mind, given the inconsistencies of his background, inclinations, and experiences.

The interpretive framework that seemed to dominate most of his writing was pragmatic and reflective of his own observations "in the field." Viewing the natives in context and on their own terms insofar as he could, Nelson sympathized with their needs and concerns, and saw their cultural and social arrangements as appropriate to those concerns. Conjuring practices, for example, served as expressive, dramatic, and even humorous means of communicating with and manipulating a harsh environment. The Indians' language, Nelson wrote at Lac la Ronge, was also adapted to their needs – being, as he conceived it, straightforward and without the euphemisms or affectation that came with the elaboration of social distinctions.

Nelson's remarks on such topics as language show, however, that another interpretive framework impinged upon the pragmatic–experiential one. A passage dated 16 April 1823 expressed his hope of recording Indian life with sufficient detail and insight that readers can "form a proper estimate of man in his *natural* state." Later in the text ("Affinities and Origins"), he made clear his disagreement with those writers who argued that the Indians are "from a different origin with ourselves, i.e., Adam." Although he did not elaborate on these points, his phrasing indicated his exposure to eighteenth-century Enlightenment thinking, and specifically to the intensifying debates between monogenists and polygenists about the question of a unitary origin for all mankind (Stocking 1987, 26–27, 49), which he had doubtless heard about from his schoolmaster father. Some of his North West Company superiors also broadened his reading opportunities. Most notably, Charles O. Ermatinger, by introducing Nelson to the numerous historical works in his personal library in the summer of 1806, "gave me a taste for this truly delightful employment which I have ever since strongly loved" (1825ff., 73; on Ermatinger, see McNeice 1984). The fur trade northwest was no place to find the newest books or the best libraries; as noted earlier, Nelson's reading matter at Lac la Ronge included a periodical already eleven years old. But during their often considerable periods of enforced idleness, some traders took pleasure from whatever reading was available – old or new. Nelson, writing to an educated father in Lower Canada, looked for ways to relate his experiences to ongoing intellectual currents and discussions, insofar as he knew about them.

Upon the foundations of his own observations on one hand and Enlightenment concepts of monogenesis and the natural man on the other, Nelson in his later writings built a superstructure that was intensely personal, yet echoed certain other currents of contemporary thought to an extent probably not known to him. Enlightenment thinkers such as Adam Ferguson, Condorcet, John Millar, and William Robertson had built upon "man in the state of nature" a schema of evolutionary progress – history as the story of human advancement (Harris 1968, 29–35; Pearce 1967, 82–88). Nelson was far less certain, far more ambivalent about the virtues of progress and civilization. As he accumulated more and more evidence about and personal injury from the pretensions, corruption, and injustices that he found rampant in white society, he increasingly articulated the same kinds of critical comparisons of white to Indian as had certain French writers from the sixteenth century on (Dickason 1984, 192–93), and as did the radical primitivists of the late eighteenth to mid-nineteenth century – Hector St. Jean de Crèvecoeur, Philip Freneau, the transcendentalists, and others (Marshall and Williams 1982, 187, 213, 222; Pearce 1967, 136–50). Unlike most of these writers, however, he could build his case on ethnography; almost two decades of firsthand observations gave him numerous examples to cite in favor of Indian lifestyles, wisdom, and morality. Looking back on his fur trade years, he appreciated the absence among the Indians of "those subtile distinctions of society into classes of First, Second rate, &c." He recalled with pleasure an early conversation with Indians in Wisconsin: "the old men told me that all was in common before we came in amongst them to put an imaginary value upon their furs . . . they consider every man equal, since every man comes into, and goes out of, the world in the same way – there is no precedency known but such as are acquired by the *practice* of the virtues" (Brown 1984, 203).

This primitivist outlook brought Nelson into tension with another weighty portion of his cultural baggage – his Anglican Christianity. There is no questioning his religious commitment and sincerity; but it is equally certain that his juxtaposition of Indian virtues and qualities, as he perceived them, to the supposed enlightenment of Christian civilization posed some interpretive difficulties. Diverse methods of resolving the tension occurred to him at different points in his writings. One solution was to explain Indian virtues with reference to the idea that all peoples carried Christian knowledge in their hearts and might sometimes express it unwittingly. Thus, deeply affected by an Ojibwa naming ceremony he attended in May of 1809, he later recorded his admiration that these Indians "without the Slightest, most distant instruction in the knowledge of Divine truths, should still have such ideas of human obligations and express them with such beautiful Simplicity and not infrequently with a Sublimity of expression that would do honor to many of our clergy. These things Show, as St. Paul says the knowledge of the Lord in our hearts &c, &c" (1825ff.,223).

If Nelson believed that the Lord was a hidden or implicit presence, however, he also believed that the Devil sometimes manifested himself among Indians. Undesirable features of Indian behavior and morality could be attributed to his evil influence. Similarly, the means that Nelson (and many another Christian) found to explain supernatural occurrences such as those in the conjuring tent was to see in them the agency of the Devil.

At other times, Nelson simply presented Indian moral values as ideal in every respect except in their lack of a Christian point of reference. Recalling both the expressiveness and the content of native oratory, for example, he wrote, "The exhortations to their children much pleased me – they were truly edifying. There was nothing of course in them relative to the atonement by our Saviour, but their discourses were full of strong argument, beautiful comparisons and allegories, and most pathetic appeals to the understanding as well as to the feeling. . . . I have been astonished many a time by their shrewd remarks, the justice and correctness of their notions" (1825ff., 50).

Alternatively, Nelson sometimes emphasized "civilized" man as decadent – the greater sinner for having been offered enlightenment and having lost or rejected it. This view, expressed most vividly in one of his last reminiscences, left him perhaps the greatest scope of blending the European primitivists' idealism with a critique of his own society, all seemingly cast within an implicit framework of the Fall of Man:

I am forced to say, that so far as regards intellect, uncultivated, as a people, they are far, very far our Superiors. Many, no doubt, will deny this, and few, perhaps none of *us* will relish it, but let all such reflect well, consider and compare *all* things – the many advantages we have to instruct ourselves, to improve our minds, to extend our knowledge; how reason, knowledge, religion, common sense, and experience of itself, nay, every day's circumstance shows what weak and silly creatures we are, how incumbent it is on us to curb, at least our passions – yet how many excesses, or follies at least, do we every day commit. . . . The indians are savages and barbarous; but our wars – our courts of law also shew a catalogue of crimes never Surpassed and seldom equalled by those we so complacently call Barbarians (1825ff., 288).

This passage was as close to a final synthesis as Nelson ever came. The ethnographer/primitivist/Christian trinity of voices within him could never achieve full harmony or reconciliation.

More complete assessments of the diverse currents in Nelson's thought and speculation await a fuller analysis of his writings as a whole, and their placing in the broader spectrum of English Canadian exploration literature (Warkentin 1983). For the present, the Lac la Ronge text, written at midlife and serving as a vivid finale to Nelson's writings in the Indian country, furnishes rich insights into this fascinating and complex individual, providing, among other things, a sampling of his confrontations with the interpretive dilemmas in his own mind, and more broadly, those of the period in which he lived. The concluding pages speak for themselves, as Nelson faces at first hand the power and mysteries of Indian conjuring and then, fearful for his Christian integrity (and also recollecting his father as audience), seeks to maintain or regain a personal religious and intellectual equilibrium deeply shaken by the experience.

EDITORIAL PROCEDURES

George Nelson's handwriting in the document presented here is consistently legible and his spelling, although at times idiosyncratic or reflecting some Francization (medicine/medecine, agreeable/agreable), has required almost no emendation for clarity. The published text thus represents as close a facsimile of the original words and letters as we have been able to achieve. Original capitalizations, underlinings (here italicized), word breaks, and abbreviations have also been retained; ampersands, however, have been rendered as "and," except when Nelson wrote &c for *et cetera*.

In the matter of textual breaks and punctuation editorial intervention was required. Nelson, like many another fur trader, was perpetually anxious about running out of paper, and his minimal paragraphing reflected this concern. To increase his text's clarity and to increase its conformity with standard printing conventions, both his dialogues and subject transitions have been appropriately indented.

Since the manuscript was a first draft, never polished for publication, punctuation was often casual or missing, quotations unclosed, and so on. With due care not to distort meaning, quotation marks, commas, periods, and other appropriate marks have been introduced where needed. No ellipses occur since there are no omissions from the text, but Nelson himself sometimes embellished a textual break with dots or short lines, here printed as long, closed ellipses..... Occasionally he set off a passage in square brackets; these have been converted to parentheses, and the use of brackets has been reserved for our in-text editorial emendations.

The original manuscript contained no subheads, and many subject transitions were too abrupt or obscure to be adequately announced even by paragraph indentations. As editors, we have done our best to devise titles that faithfully reflect both the intent and the content of the passages that they demarcate. The exercise of doing so suggested that Nelson was a more organized writer and thinker than he himself thought. Although he chided himself for digressions, for beginning a story in the middle, or for being too readily interrupted, he in fact followed through rather consistently on his stories and themes, and sometimes organized discussion of a topic with much success. His presentation of the windigo complex is particularly clear and well structured, as well as perceptive. The beginning and the end of the manuscript have a symmetry, intended or unintended: Nelson began it with a secondhand account of conjuring at Lac la Ronge in December 1819, and concluded with a firsthand description of a conjuring session in which he participated in June 1823, just before his departure. The process of editing the text, in sum, has not simply been a matter of establishing and carrying out mechanical procedures; it has been a means of getting to know Nelson himself rather better than we did before.

An attempt has been made to phonemicize Cree and Saulteaux (Ojibwa) words recorded by Nelson using the orthographies employed by Leonard Bloomfield (1946), except that his double vowels are written here with macrons (¯) as in more recent works on Cree (for example, Wolfart 1973). The symbol ð ("edh") represents the voiced dental or interdental fricative

in English "them" or the voiced stop in English "den." The symbol
č is equivalent to English "ch" as in "church"; in Cree the sound is usually
closer to English "ts" as in "cats" and is represented by c. The symbol
š is equivalent to English "sh" as in "she" or "wish". Cree and Ojibwa
terms for some of the animal beings mentioned by Nelson have been taken
from the standard dictionaries of these languages, respelled in Bloomfield's
orthography. These are not necessarily the same words that Nelson would
have heard from the Saulteaux in the nineteenth century – there is no dictionary of the Saulteaux dialect of Ojibwa – but a high degree of correspon-
dence is probable. Other Cree terms were recorded by Brightman in the
ŏ or Woods Cree dialect (popularly called the "th" dialect) of northwestern
Manitoba; this is closely related to the (Western) Woods Cree dialect spoken
at Lac la Ronge (cf. Pentland 1978), but in Nelson's day š was still distinct from s (e.g., šīsīp 'duck', modern sīsīp) and ē (as in French "été")
had not yet become ī (as in French "fini").

II

The first page of George Nelson's sixty-page manuscript, written at Lac la Ronge in 1823. Reproduced with permission of the Metropolitan Toronto Reference Library, Manuscript Collection, the George Nelson Papers.

Overleaf: NbNc-1, Hickson–Maribelli Site Face xxvii (detail)

GEORGE NELSON'S LETTER-JOURNAL

[To Mr William Nelson, William Henry (Sorel), Lower Canada]
[Composed between March and 6 June 1823, at Lac la Ronge]

The following few Stories or Tales will give a better notion or Idea of the religion of these People than every other description *I* am able to pen, and as their *history* is read with interest, I am persuaded these poor Pages will be found equally deserving attention. I give them the same as I received them and leave every one to make his own remarks and to draw his own conclusions.

[Conjuring at Lac la Ronge, December 1819]
My Interpretor, a young half breed, passed the winter of [18]19–'20 with the Indians and gives this account. One day shortly before Christmass he was out with an elderly man, a chief of this place, a hunting. Suddenly he [the chief] stopped as to *listen*, apparently with great eagerness and anxiety, upon which after allowing a sufficient time the Int[erpreter]r asked what was the matter?

"Listen, and you'll hear."

"I have listened," says the Int[erprete]r, "but hear nothing, and it is surprising that you who are deaf should hear and I not."

"Ah! a white man is thy father and thou art just as *skeptical*: doubting and ridiculing every thing we say or do till when it is too late – then you lament, but in vain."

After this the Indian became much down-cast and very thoughtful for several days; and as if to increase his anxiety or rather to corroborate the husband's questions, his wife said that one day she also *heard*, tho' the other women that were with her heard nothing, and an altercation ensued. His uneasyness increasing too much he was forced to have recourse to *their* only alternative in such cases, i.e., *une Jonglerie* as the french term it; that is, conjuring.

One of their party, another half-breed abandoned many years since by his Father and leading an indian life, was applied to: he is reputed a *true man*; i.e., never lies. Out of respect to the other he was induced to consent, but much against his will; "for I am much afraid that some of these *times they will carry me off.*" He was prepared, and entered with his *rattler*, shortly after which the box [conjuring lodge] and the rattler began to move in the usual brisk and violent manner. *Many* [spirits] entered, and one asked what was wanted that they had been called upon. The indian from the outside of the frame (for only the conjuror alone and ~~stark naked~~ enters) inquired if there was not some evil spirit near from whom he had ~~much~~ everything to dread?

"No," replied the same voice, "*all is quiet*, you trouble yourself with vain phantoms."

"What then is the meaning," asked again the Indian, "of those sudden flashes of light I sometimes see in the night?"

"What?" rejoined another voice from within. "Hast thou attained unto this age and never yet observed this;" and then laughing, continued, "it is always the case during this *moon* (December) and if you doubt me, for the future observe attentively and you will find it to be the case."

This satisfied him for the time, he became cheerful and assumed his wonted ways. But not for a long time – he soon relapsed, and after some days applied again to the conjurer. When he [the conjuror] had entered his box or frame – a number again entered and one of them enquired why they were called for? The conjuror said [the reason]. "What?" says he, i.e., the Spirit, "again! Thou art very skeptical – dost thou not believe? Now thou art fond of, thou wantest to be haunted, well, thou shalt have thy desire."

At these dreadful words, which were uttered in an angry and reproving manner, every soul was struck with terror; but as if to give some consolation assured him that that spirit had but just left his *home*, and coming on very slowly would not be up with them till *such a time*, a little prior to which they were ordered to conjure again, when they would be told what to do. This was no pleasant information to the conjuror who never

undertook this job but with the greatest reluctance, nay indeed, even sometimes horror: However, he neither, poor creature, had no alternative. At
the time appointed he entered again, every thing being prepared. After
the preliminary demands or questions &c, "Yes," replies one of the *spirits*,
"that which thou dreaddest *is* near, and is drawing on apace."

"How shall we do? What shall we do?" exclaimed the indian. At last
one of them, who goes by the name of the Bull or Buffaloe* (thro' the
conjuror, for he alone could understand him his voice being hoarse and
rough, his uttering thick and inarticulate) asked the indian if he remembered
of a dream he made whilst yet a young man?

"Yes," replies the indian – "I remember perfectly – I dreamed I saw
one just like yourself, who told me that when advanced in life I should
be much troubled one winter, but by a certain sacrifice and a sweating
bout I should be relieved; but I have not the means here – I have no stones."

"You are encamped upon them," rejoined the *spirit*, and at the door
of your tent are some."

"Yes, but," says the indian, "the dogs have *watered* them, and they
are otherwise soiled."

"Fool, put them in the fire; will not the fire heat, and make them change
color and purify them? Do this, fail not and be not uneasy – we shall go
four of us (spirits) and amuse him upon the road, and endeavour to drive
him back."

At this the Interpretor burst out laughing and exclaimed, "sacré bande
de Bêtes and do you believe all that d--d nonsense?"

"You doubt too," says a voice addressing him (the In[terpreter]) from
the inside: "go out of the tent and listen, you'll see if *we* lie."

He did indeed go out to some distance and after awhile heard as a distant hollow noise, which increased till it became considerably more distinct and then vanished as a great gust of wind, tho' the night was mild,
calm, clear and beautifully serene – it even startled the dogs.

"Mahn!" (an indian term or exclamation signifying haste), said the
spirits from within, "*they* have turned him off the road, as soon as the
noise was heard, but he will not turn back, or go home: he is *sent* after
you by another indian who conjured him up from out the Deep (i.e., the
bottom of some flood). But be not too uneasy; if those four will not do,
there are yet a vast many of us, so that between us all we *shall* drive him
back: we will perplex and bewilder him: surround, torment and tease him on

*This and other personages are explained and discussed in the Dramatis Personae section,
pp. 107ff.

every side: but he is of a monstrous size, ferocious and withal enraged against you: the task is mighty difficult. Observe! See how beautifully serene the night is – if we succeed, the sky will change all of a sudden and there will fall a very smart shower of snow attended with a terrible gust of wind. This will happen between day light and sun rise *and is his spite*, all that will remain in his power – he'll then return to his home."

The Int[erpreter], tho' he laughed at all this and could not bring himself to credit it, yet swears that he heard the rumbling noise, *on their road*, and seemingly far off: the indians gave implicit faith to all – and the conjuror did not know what to believe. "There is something," says he, for my *Dreamed* or *Dreamers* have assured me of it, but *I* don't know what to say – however, most assuredly tomorrow morning we shall have the snow." This *snow* both comforted and depressed the poor indian very much, seeing the weather was then so beautiful and so destitute of all the usual signs of bad weather. It did snow – it came as foretold, quite suddenly, and as suddenly became fine again.

In the ensuing morning the Indian begged of the Interpretor to chuse one of the longest and straightest Pine (Epinette [prob. spruce]) trees he could find of the thickness of his thigh; to peel off all the bark nicely, leaving but a small tuft of the branches at the tip end – this they painted cross-ways with bars of vermillion and charcoal, alternately the whole length, leaving however some intervals of undaubded – and about 5 or 6 feet from the Ground, fastened a Pair of artificial horns, representing those of a Bull, and decorated with ribbon.

He also (the Indian I mean) made the sweating hut, and in short done every thing as directed, after which he (the indian) became to resume his wonted cheerfulness and contentment. However, once more he was obliged to have recourse again to the Conjuror, from hearing another rumbling noise. "Thou fool," answered the spirits: "wilt thou never have done tormenting thyself and disquieting us – that rumbling noise proceeds from the ice in a Lake a long way off – it is only the ice – be therefore peaceable – I shall advertise thee if any ill is to happen thee." —— The flashes of light, or those sudden glares that the indian inquired of the Spirits, is, as they told him, lightning, which always happens in the month of December and they laughed at his having lived so long without observing it before.

The Conjuror had lost his smoking bag one day that he was out a hunting and as it contained his only steel and not a small part of his winter stock of Tobacco &c, he was very uneasy, and hunted several times for it. They [the Indians] having told the Interpretor often how kind and charitable and indulgent those *spirits of the upper regions* were, and he, desirous of Proving them, told the Conjuror to send for his bag. He asked, "which of you will go for my bag that I lost? He that brings it me, I shall make him smoke."

"I will go," said one – they heard a fluttering noise, and soon after, they heard the same fluttering noise and the rattler move, and down fell the bag by the Conjuror, covered with snow. "How stupid thou art," said the Spirit, naming the Conjuror, "thou passedst over it and yet did not see it." It was a long time since the bag was lost and the distance was several miles.

Another one could not kill with his Gun, owing to its being crooked, or some other cause – however, he attached the fault to the Gun. The first time, I believe it was, that this half-breed conjured, the People on the outside hearing many voices speak as they entered, at last they stopped at one whose voice and articulation was different from that of the others: "Who is that one just now entered?" said those outside.

"It is the Sun," replied the Conjuror.

"Ha! Well, I am happy of it," said the indian, "is it not *he* who says himself able to repair Fire-arms (Guns), and do anything with them he pleases? – ask him (addressing the Conjuror) if he will not have compassion on me and put my Gun to rights, that I also may kill – I am walking every day and frequently shoot at moose, but always miss."

"Hand it me," said a voice from the top of the conjuring frame. The Gun was given to the Conjuror. "It is loaded," continued the voice, "shall I fire it off?"

"You may, but take care you hurt no body," replied the indian. The Gun was fired, and shortly after handed back to the owner. "Here is your Gun – you will kill with it now," said the Spirit. Both this business of the Gun and smoking bag took place, the first time, I believe, the man conjured.

[*Dreaming to Conjure and Predict*]

There are but few individuals (i.e., men) among the Sauteux or Cris or Crees who have not their medicine bags – and [are not] initiated into some ceremoney or other, but it is not *all* of them who can conjur. Among some tribes, most of them can; and among others again, there are but very few. Nor is it every one of them that tells *all truth*, some scarcely nothing but lies, others again not one falsehood, and this depends upon their *Dreamed*, sometimes, but I think may be equally imputed to their own selves, i.e., Presumption, ignorance, folly, or any other of our passions or weaknesses. But to become conjurors, they have rights [rites] and ceremonies to Perform and go through, which, tho' apparently simple and absurd, yet I have no doubt but fully answer their ends. Any Person among them wishing to dive into futurity, must be young and unpolluted, at any age between 18 and 25, tho' as near as I can [tell] born between 17 and 20 years old. They must have had no intercourse with ~~any of~~ the other Sex – they must be chaste and unpolluted. In the spring of the year they chuse a proper place at a sufficient distance from the camp not [to] be discovered nor disturbed. They make themselves a bed of Grass, or hay as we term it, and have besides enough to make them a covering. When all this is done – and they do it entirely alone, they strip stark naked and put all their things *a good way off* and then return, ly on this bed and then cover themselves with the rest of the Grass. Here they remain and endeavour to *sleep*, which from their nature is no very difficult task. But during whatever time they may remain, they must neither eat or drink. If they want to Dream of the Spirits above, their bed must be made at some distance from the Ground – if of Spirits inhabiting our Earth, or those residing in the waters, on the Ground. Here they ly for a longer or shorter time, according to their success, or the orders of the Dreamed. Some remain but 3 or 4 days, some 10, and I have be[en] told one remained 30 days without eating or drinking, such was the delight he received from his Dreams! When I laughed at this, the man was vexed, and the others not a little hurt.

   The first thing they do after their return to their friends is to take a good drink of water, smoke the Pipe; and after that eat, but as composedly as if they had but just risen from a hearty meal. Their *Dreamed* sometimes order them to make a Feast; and not uncommonly tell them where to go, where they will find the animal whose flesh is to be served up (i.e., always boiled) &c. They sometimes lie in one Posture, and sometimes in another, i.e., their head to some one of the Cardinal Points. Some have the most pleasant dreams imaginable; others indifferent. When they are to live to a good old age (!!!) they are told – "You will see many winters! Your head will grow quite white"; or, tho' you shall never see your head white, yet you shall live till you are obliged to make use of a stick, and long after" – "You shall die old, very old, respected and regretted." If they are to die young..... "Thou shalt see the years of a young man"; and so on of the other ages, as well of the manner of life they shall have; and the language is not very dissimilar to that of our version of the Bible. But that stile [style] seems to me to be the language of Nature which *I* always find the more charming the more retired the *speaker* is from the Pompous, bombastic walks of high life, which, tho' they furnish us with more ideas, *I* do not think adds much to the beauty of the language.

[*The Spirits, their Shapes, and their Songs*]

As I have said before, the purpose of these Dreams is to dive into futurity. Every thing in nature appears unto them, but in the Shape of a humanbeing. They dream they meet a man who asks them (after some preliminary conversation of course), "Dost thou know me? (who or what I am)?"

"No."

"Follow me then," replies this stranger. The indian follows – the other leads him to his abode and again makes the inquiry – the answer is perhaps as before. Then the Stranger assumes his proper form, which is perhaps that of a Tree, a Stone, a fish, &c, &c. and after rechanging several times in this manner, till such times as the 2nd becomes perfectly to know him, then this stranger gives him to smoke, learns him *his* Song, &c, thus addressing him: "Now don't you remember my Song?.....Whenever you will wish to call upon me, Sing this Song, and I shall not be far – I will come and do for you what you require."

They know many of *these spirits* as soon as they see them (in their dreams) by the description the other indians have given to them – some, however, they know from their Nature. When the *Snow* addresses them – he they know, because he is perfectly white. The *Ice* also. The Sun and Moon from their beautifull brilliancy and the elegance of their abode. The Houses of the two last being uncommonly neat and handsome, such as those of the white (i.e., Civilised).

[*The Supreme Being*]

The Principal amongst all these [spirits], and every thing in Nature appears at least to some of them, is the Supreme Being, whom they term Weesuck-ā-jāāk (the last a's being pronounced as in, all, hawk, &c; the first as ale, bail, &c), i.e., by his Proper name, his common name, Key-shay-mani-*to* (this is among the Crees Nation) which signifies "The Greatly charitable Spirit." [But see Nelson's correction below, under Skepticism, Belief, and Innovation.] He is uncommonly good and kind, addresses them and talk[s] to them as to children whom he most tenderly loves and is extremely anxious for. Thus far every thing is very well, and is perhaps a better *idea* than many of the vulgar christians can give; but on the other hand again their Mythology, or stories relating to him, are many of them absurd and indecent in the highest degree: reducing him to the level of his creatures, and not unfrequently making him their dupe; but become so by such vile, such abominable deception as I doubt to be equalled by the most absurd and romantic of the arabian Tales; for there are many of these Tales the author durst not publish for the obscenity and indecency. There are some obscene passages also in these tales (of the indians) but not more than might be expected from a people yet in a perfect state of nature, as to their mental Powers, to our eternal shame and scandal. This one they love, they love him a great deal, and are by no means afraid of him, because he always addresses them, "My Little Children, &c," and all the rest of his character is of a piece with this.

[Old Nick (Key-jick-oh-kay)]

The Next one is Old Nick [English term for the Devil]. Him some term "Key-jick-oh-kay" (the J being pronounced soft, as Git, or Gil, in french, for *I* know of no English word where properly speaking the J is of any use and has the sound seemed intended by it) or "Key-jick-oh-*kaiw*." I cannot at present give the proper signification of this name, for I am not sufficiently acquainted with the language, but it appears to me as to mean "he who made the Day or Skies or resides in the Sky," &c. This one they represent wicked, and terrible, inexorible to the highest degree; always plotting evil, and endeavouring to circumvent the rest of the creation; is always jawing and bawling; but when the other appears he orders him in a peremptory manner, "hold thy Tongue; Get thee hence, thou deceiver; thou ill-liver." But these words are uttered in such an authoritative and commanding tone that the Indians themselves are quite astonished, to see one who is so uncommonly kind and indulgent to them in every respect; so tender and affectionate, even in the choice of his words, assume so suddenly and with so much authority so much Power over one whose name alone they never utter but with the greatest dread and horor. Their Horor of the Devil is so great, that no one ever utters it but when unavoidable; and if thro' inadvertancy or ignorance one of their children should mention it he is severely reprimanded by all who hear.

[*Other Beings*]
There is also the Sea Serpent, a monstrous animal and has much Power; the Mermaid (or Sea Man), the Water Lynx, or rather Tyger – a dreadful character this last, who keeps all the Inhabitants of the deep in the Greatest Subjection – there are however one or two who contend with him; and sometimes he is reduced to the necessity of compounding with them. The Great Turtle, and many others. They have their abodes in the Deep, but perfectly dry and comfortable. Each one of these, and indeed all of them have their stories or Mythology; some I forget intirely, and others remember too incorrectly to mention at present.....When any one conjures, if he is a renouned *Medicine* Man, *they* all appear, and Speak to him, mostly in his own language, some few excepted as the Pike (or Jack fish) who speaks french; the Sun and Moon, both speak English; the Bull or Buffaloe is an unknown or at least strange language; but all perfectly intelligible to the Conjuror.

[*The Sun; Nelson's Dream*]
I am quite astray – leaving the proper thread of my story to follow one of its branches – I ought to have said that the Sun when he appears to an indian, he is seen in the Heavens, as an Indian (i.e., a Man) "*Walking on the Wind.*" His dress is of a variety of colors and handsome. I had a dream ~~in the month of February~~, the latter part of which I shall relate to you as it is perfectly descriptive of the manner or form in which the Sun appears [but see Nelson's correction, below, under Sickness in Spirit Form]. I related it the next day to some of my half-breeds, when one of them replied; "What a pity! Had you now forborne for a few days mentioning *this*, he would have appeared again to you; and then you would have had a fine opportunity of learning (from the fountain-head, as we may say) how it is the indians come to perform those things the white will never credit": and he continued that it was precisely the form he [the Sun] assumed when he appears to the indians.

In my dream I thought we were travelling a road from which some of

38   Part II

our Party had the utmost to dread from the ambush of an indian who could
transport himself to what place he pleased. As we were walking I happened
to look above and was much struck with the appearance of a man walking
in the Heavens. His dress was that of a neat *Southern* [Cree] Indian, composed mostly of red and yellow, but also of a few other colors: The Garters
of his leggings were also Neat and handsome and had a tuft of swans-
down that had been Powdered with vermillion, attached to the [k]not, on
the back part of the leg. To his shoes were attached 2 long Swan quills
inclosing the foot thus with a tuft of down at each end and in
the middle of both sides, all Powdered with vermillion – with these quills
and down, and the down on his Garters buoyed him up in the air. I addressed
[him] in broken Cree – he answered in the same broken accent; upon my
second address I though[t] he did not understand more of that language
than I did myself: The Sauteux seemed to me his proper tongue and I was
glad of having an opportunity of speaking that language; so I the third
time addressed him in it, asked him from whence he came, whither he
was going, &c, &c. He was very hi[gh] insomuch that the others thought
it preprosterous in my addressing him – that he could not hear from that
distance. Upon this, he came down and talked with us – saying he was
an ambassador &c. Such is the habillement, and manner in which the Sun
shews himself.

   The Thunder also appears to them, in the Shape and form of a most
beautiful bird (The Pea-Cock).

[*Roots and Herbs*]

Roots and herbs also (this ought also to have come in afterwards), i.e.,
such as are medicinal, appear, and teach their votaries their respective
Songs – how they must do, what ceremonies they must perform in taking
them out of the Ground, their different applications, &c, &c. But these
roots, herbs, &c (medecins), tho' they appear in their Dreams, they do
not shew themselves in the Conjuring Hut, box, or frame, that I learn.
They are sent, as appears, by Wee-suck-a-jaak, "to teach indians their
use and virtue," &c, without which "they would be very ill off, whether
to heal or cure themselves, or expell the charms by which other indians
may have bewitched them," &c. And tho' they are acquainted with many
of these roots &c, the use and virtue of some of which I can no more doubt
than those used by the Faculty in the Civilised world, yet they tell me

there are several which they use to different, and some to diametrically opposite purposes.

[*The Manner of Conjuring*]

Their manner of conjuring is this – in the first place a number [of] straight poles of 2, or 2 1/2 ins. diameter and about 8 or 9 feet long are prepared, i.e., cut, branched and Pointed at the lower end – they seldom require so *few* as four, commonly 6 or 8, these are planted in the Ground from 12 to 20 or 24 ins. deep in an hexagon or octagon form, inclosing a space of 3 feet diameter, more or less – these Poles are secured by hoops, 3 or 4 in number, and well tied to each pole, so that none be able to move without the rest. This Hut, square, box, or frame, whatever it may be termed is covered with skins, an oil cloth, or some such sort of thing. The Conjuror is bound hand and foot, not as if he were a man going to *pry* into futurity, but as a Criminal, i.e., a *mere*, pure Devil, and one whom they intend never to loosen, so barricaded and cross-corded is the creature, sometimes all crumpled into a heap. He is tied only with his Cloute on him and thus thrust into the hut, underneath, i.e., by raising the lower covering – his "she-she-quay" [Ojibwa šiššīkwē 'rattlesnake': probably a metaphor] or rattler with him. Some of them sing on entering, others make a speech. Here they remain, some several hours, others not 5 minutes, before a fluttering is heard. The rattler is shaked at a merry rate and all of a Sudden, either from the top or below, away flies the cords by which the indian was tied *into the lap of he who tied him.*

[*The Spirits Enter: Their Names and Natures*]

It is then that the Devil is at work – Every instant some one or other enters, which is known to those outside by either the fluttering, the rubbing against the Skins of the hut in descending (inside) or the shaking or the rattler, and sometimes all together. When any enter, the hut moves in a most violent manner – I have frequently thought that it would be knocked down, or torn out of the Ground. The first who enters is commonly Meek-key-nock (the Turtle), a Jolly Jovial sort of a fellow, who, after disencumbering his votary, chats and jokes with those outside and asks for a pipe to smoke &c. There is a good deal of talking inside as may be supposed from the number of folks collected in so small a space. To some renowned characters, all the spirits appear. The Thunder also frequently comes but he is desired to remain outside as he would break all. It is reported that he once entered and split one of the Poles into shivers. The Flying Squirrel also enters – he is no liar, but you must take everything he says as we do our Dreams, i.e., the opposite: his nature is such that he durst not tell the truth but in this ambiguous manner, otherwise the conjuror would soon after die. I do not know that the Skunk ever comes, but the Wolverine (Carcajoux) does and he is known immediately by his stink, which occasions no small merriment at his expense, on the outside.

The *Loon* also enters – he is known by his usual cry – "nee-weah-wee-wey" [Cree *niwīwīwin*, Ojibwa *niwīwīw* 'I want to have a wife'], repeated commonly 3 times as he does when in the water. And this too occasions a great laugh, for these four syllables, which form the most common cry of that bird in the *Spring* of the year, as every body may observe, *are* also 3 words in the Sauteux and Cree languages, which signify, "I want to marry! I want to marry!"

"What! and will you never have done marrying? – you were marrying all last Summer and still want to" – will some outside say, and every one has his word to put in.

Hercules also comes in – he is perhaps as much revered by these people as ever he was by the Spartans or Athenians. His name is Strong Neck (and every body knows how strong Hercules was) – he does not seem over fond of Jokes – and when the other Spirits announce his coming all those on the outside must cover their heads and not look up; for it appears that he cannot come *invisible* as the others do, or will not, but still does not chuse to be seen.

Once upon a time his arrival was announced, and every body was ordered to cover themselves, so as not to see (this, and all such like orders are commands sent to the Conjuror, and which he (being inside) must *Promulgate* to those on the outside). There was one young Buck, however, who wanted to shew himself superior to these orders and divert his freinds, [and] would not cover himself. Hercules entered – and at that time, as at all others, he was not in too good a humor. Some altercation ensued and, "I am Strong Neck," said he.

"Poh!" says the young man at last, "the neck of my os-Pubis indeed is strong!" This raised a most violent laugh, but the young man was lost – he disappeared from amongst them, and was never again heard of. Since *that* time they are rather more cautious.

Some of the *Ancients* also enter – they are called "O-may-me-thay-day-ace-cae-wuck," i.e., *Hairy breasts* such as the Ancients are said to be. These are great boasters – they recount the exploits of their younger days, apparently with the greatest satisfaction; say, "I used to do so and so on such occasions – I never shot a moose or Buffalo, but pursued them on my feet, and ripped them open with my knife, &c." But this is only *wind*, for no sooner do other powerful ones enter, but these chaps seek to secret themselves.

The Sun enters – speaks very bad English at the offset, but by degrees becomes to speak it very easily and fluently. He is Gun Smith and watchmaker, or at least can repair them. When he is entered there is commonly a beautiful clear light visible, through the covering. He neither does not admit of too much familiarity, but is still good natured and condescending.

The Pike or Jack fish also enters; as the Sun, they also speak (French) badly enough at the offset. When there are 2 or 3 on the outside who can speak french and address him together, merely to perplex and bother him, he laughs at their folly and says, "you may talk 20 or 100 of you together if you chuse, yet are you not able to perplex me – come as numerous as you chuse, yet are there many more of us *Pike* than you frenchmen" – he is very familiar too.

The Bull or Buffaloe is understood only by the Conjuror, his voice being hoarse and rough – his language quite foreign. The Conjurer must interpret when any thing is wanted of him. As is his voice, so are his manners – however, he will joke a little too; but let them beware not to let drop anything in a sarcastic or contemptuous manner as to his power or knowledge of the future, for he takes it up and reproves in a very tart manner; and in a way too that conveys no comfortable ideas to any one present, for they all endeavour to excuse it by saying it is only a joke. "I know jokes too; and can laugh, and understand the nature of laughing as well as the best amongst you, but such language is unbecoming and I will have no more of it."

A half-breed one time, *because his father was a french man*, thought he might go any lengths he pleased with him (the B[ull]) – he replied very warmly thus: "How durst thou doubt anything I say – knowest thou not how clearly and distinctly objects are discovered and seen in a plain, from an eminence; and my abode is in the regions above – I see every object as distinctly as you see at your feet, doubt then no more, and never hereafter call our Power to question."

"Aye!" replied some of the other spirits. "We not only see *all that you do, however secret and hid you think yourselves*, but we also hear every word you utter."

"If that indeed be the case, tell me, where now are and when will be here, my father's Country men [i.e., Canadian traders]?" (The conjuror had been employed to tell what the people were about as it was long since the time they were expected, and ought to have arrived, had elapsed.)

"Wait! I shall go and see" – and shortly after, he returned. "They are now all asleep at such a place – the weather will be calm tomorrow, and tho' the distance is great, yet will you see them tomorrow night, for they are as anxious as yourselves."

Another one said, "since then ye Spirits pretend to know every thing and are vexed when we call any of your saying in question – come tell me – how long shall I live? Shall I yet see two more winters?"

"Ha!" (laughing replied the same voice) "two winters? I see you all yet alive two winters hence, every soul that sets here and considerably more; and some of you I see crawling with old age!!!"

With some of the Spirits as I've already said the by standers (or setters rather for they are seated on the Ground, round about) are very familiar. The Turtle is one of them, he is very humersome, and their jokes with him were such (for I've heard this myself) as I should have been ashamed to hold even with a bawd – it was pure ribaldry. But they durst not doubt him when he speaks seriously; for he is very powerful and makes himself respected when he thinks it necessary.

"Who is that, now speaking?" said one of the indians (this I was told).

"It is Mehkenack," said the Conjuror.

"If it be him, prove it – take him in your hand and show him to us."

Now the conjr. was a very great medicine man – he took the turtle upon his hand, raised the covering of his *box*, and called them to look. Every one was astonished at his beauty – he was very small, scarcely more than 2 ins. long. When all had gazed enough the Conjurer drew him in. The Turtle was very quiet while out, but as soon as he got in exclaimed, "Oh! how afraid I was when I saw the children look so eagerly – I was afraid some of them would have attempted to take me in their hands and let me fall, perhaps in the fire," and laughed heartily.

The Bear is a rough beast and makes a devil of a racket. Towards the latter end master Keyjickohkaiw, that old Serpent, Satan, enters: his arrival is announced – all hands are greived, for then the conclusion is soon to take place. He makes every thing fly again, kicking up his own (i.e., the Devil's) racket, jawing and blab[b]ing, scolding and giving the lie to and abusing all hands: The indians are hurt and displeased, but durst not say any thing – they must swallow all quietly, and then it is that the Conjuror most dreads for his own *bacon*. This however does not last very long, for Weesuckajaak (the Supreme Being) [but compare "Skepticism, Belief, and Innovation," below] enters last. As soon as his coming is announced Nick begins to sneake, but still *en maitre* – Wee[suckajac]k enters, Nick *jaws*, silence is imposed, Nick still troublesome, at last the Word comes authoratatively and away *he* flies. The indians are uncommonly fond of Weesuckajack – he commonly speaks to this effect: "My Little (i.e., Grand) Children, I am very indulgent and kind, I am very charitable, and love you much – a great deal more than you imagine. You must not live ill, nor make a bad use of your power and knowledge for I hate that; hence it is I command Nick in that authoratative manner; because he is wickedly inclined – mischief and destruction are in his nature – he greives at any good he sees: take ye heed, beware of him for he is ever on the watch to destroy you." When *Charly* [cf. old Brit. term, "Charley," night watchman, here in ref. to Weesuckajack] enters after some abuse he calls out, "Get ye hence, get ye hence, what are ye doing so long from your home: off with ye immediately"; and rubs up and down the Skins that form the covering lest any should be hid. Thus he sends off all the Spirits, who, as they *fly* off, as well as when they enter, give this frame a terrible shaking. It may be supposed what sort of a shaking he gives as he comes and goes, and how he shakes the rattler; for they all shake the rattler on entering. When Weesuckajaak goes off, all is done.

[*The Conjurors' Power*]

Some conjurors are so powerful that the *hut* they enter, must be doubled; that is two rows of Setts of Poles one on the outside [of] the other; and each row fastened with good strong hoops well tied, after which the outer and inner row are also fastened – thus arranged, they seem to be beyond the Power of any 3 or 4 men to move, yet when the Spirits enter it sets a-going with a motion equal to that of a single pole indifferently stuck in the Ground and violently moved by a man. I have never seen any of these double ones, but twice or thrice saw the others, whilst the conjuror was in. Some time afterwards, when they were off, I shook them with both hands and with all my strength but the motion was nothing like that of the Conjurors. I have been told that those who enter these Double ones are so powerful that almost all the Creation comes to see them, and they are shaken with uncommon violence. This motion the Conjurors say is produced by the concussion of the air; i.e., the Spirits come and enter with such velocity that it is the *Wind they Produce* which occasions it. The conjuror is all the while seated Peaceably in the bottom (on the Ground) of his hut.

Some of them to shew their Power have had small sticks of the hardest wood (such as produces the wild Pear,* and of which the Indians make their arrows, and ram-rods &c for Guns) about the size of a man's finger, made as sharp pointed as possible, and dried, when they become in consequence nearly as dangerous as iron or bayonets. Some have 18, 24, more or less, tho' seldom less than 18, planted in the bottom of their hut – they are about 12 or 14 ins. out of Ground. On the Points of these Sticks is the conjuror placed, sometimes on his bottom, at others on his knees and elbows; and here he remains as quietly and composed as if he were on "a bed of Roses"; and when he comes off no marks of injury appear, tho' he entered naked, only his Cloute about him, and of course the Cords with which he is tied. "Their familiars (their Dreamed, or those who appear to them in their dreams and Promise them their assistance and Protection) support them so that no injury happens them!!!"

[A Cree Myth, 1823: The Birth of Wee-suck-a-jock and Mi-shaw-bose]
March 29th. I feel but very indifferently disposed to write, but I am on the eve of an accumulation of business and may not, after a few days, have the necessary time, so that I shall risk.

A Couple of days back I have been conversing with a Cree (indian) who by *peace-meal* gives me the following account of their mythology. The North (wind), apparently one of the oldest of created rational beings, thus addressed his daughter, his only child, "My daughter! be very careful and remember that anything you do, or wherever you go, on turning yourself,

---

*Anna Leighton suggests this is probably *Amelanchier alnifolia* or Saskatoon berry. See Leighton 1985: 28.

turn *always in the same direction with the Sun*, and *never in a contrary direction.*" Now women are a compound of Perverseness, obstinacy and curiosity; and withall forgetful enough too, sometimes. This Girl one day [when] she was chopping fire-wood, without thinking of her father's admonition, in going to another tree, [she] turned ~~herself~~ round to the right, in a contrary direction to the Sun, and instantly fell to the Ground and died. The time she used to take up in this occupation being expired, her Parents became very uneasy, and after some search found her on her back, dead, and her belly swoln to an enormous size. The father and mother, on each or opposite sides, contemplated her situation with great grief. At last the Father arose, stood up, and made a long speech, praying to "The Father of Life" to have mercy and compassion on his child. His speech was not ineffectual: the Girl was delivered of a Boy, and shortly after, of another. The Elder was called Wee-suck-a-jock, the younger "Mi(or Mee)shaw-bôse." After this the girl recovered and became as aforetime.

These two young men immediately attained "man's estate," i.e., to manhood, &c, and became hunters. The younger of the two one day was in pursuit of a Grey or rein Deer (carriboeuf) after which also pursued a wolf. The Deer having thus no hopes of escape fled to a rock on the edge of the waters and plunged in. Mishabôse and the Wolf followed: but they all three became a prey to the Michi-Pichoux, or Great Lynx, i.e., water Lynx, water-Cat, or water-dog. Wee-suck-a-jack was very uneasy for his brother, was anxious to revenge his death, but scarcely knew well how. At last one day seeing a Kings-fisher hovering in a certain spot [he] addressed him thus: "My younger Brother! What art thou there looking at?"

"I am looking at Mishabôse, your brother, lying in the bottom of the deep, drowned" &c.

[*The Battle of Weesuckajock and the Water Lynxes*]
After some further conversation, Weesuck discovered the means of avenging himself. He accordingly set to work and made himself a *large Canoe*, on board of which he embarked the Moose, Deer, Bear, otter, Beaver, muskrat, wolf, &c, &c, and repaired to the place where the Sea Lynxes used to resort to sleep; this was a fine pleasant place on the Land. Here he observed several of them and began his work. It is not related how many he did kill, but the waters upon their death came rushing upon him

in a violent torrent; as he expected this, he had bro't his canoe near hand, but before he reached it, after killing his enemies, he was already knee-deep in the water; however, he got safely on board, but in his hurry forgot to embark a little earth.

Now the waters swelled immensely, and in a very short time the highest land was covered and Weesuckajock was tossed about by the wind and waves. It appears that he had not the foresight either of taking with him a sufficiency of Provisions for he became very hungry, and thus expressed himself to his crew. After some time he saw something on the water, very large and moving towards him. He thus addressed it, "Who or what art thou, my young brother?" (for he being the first born, always addressed the rest of the creation, whether animate, inanimate, or rational or not, as his *younger Brothers*) "and whither art thou going?"

"Why! my Elder (brother) I am a *water Lynx*, and am sent by [my] *Confreres* in search of Weesuck and to destroy him."

"Aye! is it so indeed? And how or with [what] instrument do you intend to destroy him?"

"I have a large and very strong Iron-tail, with which if I smite his Canoe he must perish!"

Weesuckajock, seeing his danger, tho't to get off by duplicity and dissimulation and thus continued: "Indeed you must have a very extraordinary *tail*, my Younger [brother]; come near, and let me see it, how it is made &c." The Lynx drew up, presented his tail, Weesuck took hold as to look on it and placed it on the Gunnel of his canoe and with a stone cut it off saying, "now go to thy friends, and tell them how Weesuck has served thee." He retired doubled quick, grieved, ashamed, and not with a little pain.

"Ha!" said the water Lynxes on perceiving the situation of their companion, "ha! Weesuck is cunning, and too powerful; we must destroy him for our own safety. Come, now, who amongst us will volunteer and go to destroy that enemy of ours?" They at last pitched upon an enormous Beaver and thus addressed him at his departure. "Go thou our Brother, and destroy that mutual enemy of ours, be not afraid of him for he is not worthy of fear; but still be cautious, for he is very artful."

Weesuck descryed him also, and the same addresses and compliments passed as with the first. "And how do you intend to destroy Weesuck?"

"With my teeth."

"Well then, do come near and let me see them." The beaver drew up
and shewed his teeth: Weesuck put his hand on his head and while exclaim-
ing, "What terrible teeth! – how immensely broad and sharp – they are
like large axes!," he with the other hand took up a large stone and with
a dreadful blow broke them all in his head. "Now go thou too to your
friends and tell them how Weesuck hath served thee." Indeed the Beaver
did go, sniffling and blowing and yelling. The Lynxes were astonished,
and durst no more attempt anything at him.

[*The Making of the Land*]
His situation however was very disagreeable, very uncomfortable, and
what added to it was his want of food. He thus addressed his companions
one day: "Come now, we very reprehensibly forgot to bring earth with
us, and who knows how long this will continue? Which of you all will
endeavour to get a little earth for me out of which I shall try to make *Land*
for us to live on? – whoever will go shall be amply rewarded." They all
said it was very deep, and there was scarcely any hopes. Then he said
to the Otter, "Go thou my *younger* (brother) and if thou diest in the attempt,
I shall restore thee to life and make thee immortal." Saying this, he tied
a long leather thong to his tail and sent him down: he found the otter was
dead, hauled him up in to the canoe, rubbed him dry and blowed in his
nostrils, when he revived.

Then he sent the musk rat: "Come my little brother, go thou, thou art
small and very active, art fond of water, and goeth to great depths – thy
reward shall be as that of the otter." The rat was secured with a thong
also and down he went. Weesuck found he was dead, hauled him up, and
was extremely happy to find he had some earth in his little paws and mouth:
he restored him to life as he did the otter, and sent him down again. When
he bro't [him] up his mouth [was] as full as it could hold and a good deal
in his *hands* which he held pressed to [his] breast.

Now Weesuck took this earth and made a ball of it, and blew in it a
considerable time and sent off the Wolf to make its circuit to see if it was
large enough. After four nights he returned and thus spoke: "My Elder,
the earth is indeed Large and beautiful; but our number now is small: when
we increase it will be too small for us; we will all be upon top of each
other (i.e., we will be in each other's way &c), and if you make man as
you contemplate, it will be much more so."

Weesuck then blew it out again and once more sent the wolf. He was 8 nights absent, and reported it still too small. Weesuckajack then blew it out for a long time and sends the wolf again. But before he went off he said, "My Elder, the Earth must now be very large, and I shall possibly be too much wearied to make its circuit: I shall travel, and if I find any thing to assure me of its being large enough I shall *howl*, which will be a sign to you; and whatever place may suit me there will I make my residence."

After several nights absence they heard him howl, wherefore they all concluded the Earth was sufficiently Large. Weesuck then *blessed* the others and sent them away telling them to multiply "and be good, not vicious or ill inclined, nor secret or hide themselves too much from *my* little brothers" (the human beings which he was about to create) "when they might want to eat" &c, &c.

[*The Making of Human Beings*]

Now after this he became very lonesome and bethou[gh]t himself of making Indians, i.e., human beings. He in consequence took up a stone and fashioned it into the form of a man; but whilst at this work it struck him that by forming them of so strong and hard a substance that in time when they would become to know their nature, they would grow insolent and rebellious and be a great annoyance to each other and of course also would never die. "This will not do, I must make them of a more weak and fragile substance, so that they may live a reasonable time and behave as becomes human beings." Upon this he took up a handful of common Earth and made the form of a man, and blew into his nostrils *the breath of life*.

The Moon formed the Female, as Weesuck did the male, hence the reason of the Periodical return of their sickness with that of the moon, "as also among the Sluts" (Bitches).* Hence also all women are forbidden when they go out from the calls of nature, and that *one* in particular, to look at the moon while thus employed. Those who are thus forgetful, ignorant, or obstinate immediately find the effect by the return &c.....I should have said that he bruised the stone to Pieces, altho' a great part of it was already formed.

---

*In Nelson's time, "slut" was a synonym for "bitch" or female dog (Oxford English Dictionary).

For the white (I believe it was the Moon again) he made a Partner for him of one of his ribs and another piece, which he wrapped in a handkerchief and laid beside him saying, "this, by the time thou risest, shall be a full grown woman and shall be thy companion" &c.

[*The Son of Weesuckajock (Nay-han-nee-mis, cf. Stories of him, infra)*]
After all this done, he made a seperation in the Earth, one part of which was a beautiful plain meadow Ground, and the rest woody; and then set off travelling in the Earth. He took a partner to himself, by whom he had a son. This son got to man's estate, but had a great aversion to the female Sex, which gave his Parents a great deal of anxiety: all their trouble, all their remonstrances were to no effect. At last the father betho't of a plan in which he was sure of success. He transformed himself into a most beautiful woman, and when the Son was returned from his hunting, "Well, Son!" said the Mother, "here is a young and handsome woman we have procured merely for thee; does she please thee?" Her *charms* were so great the young man immediately became extremely fond of her. But this, in the end, became the source of much trouble to both Parents and of disgrace to the father particularly. The mother became jealous and vexed on her son's account that he should so be imposed upon, and done many shameful things to her husband.

Here follows a train of Stories the most indecent, shameful and sometimes obscene, that one can well imagine. But these people are yet, so far as regards their faculties, in a state of Nature. Every thing appears reasonable and natural and must be very gross and palpable indeed when they do not give credit to them. Their language is also that of nature, and they speak out what they think – they do not use circumlocution to avoid an indecent term, nor have they flourishes to embellish their discourses; and their speeches, to my taste, at least, are far more pleasing and natural than those strained and laboured compositions we meet with amongst ourselves. But this is not the place for these discussions.

[*Sickness in Spirit Form: A Lac la Ronge Cree Account*]
April 4, 1823. There is a sick indian with me whom I have been obliged to feed with his whole family all winter, not being able to endure the cold on his lungs, and in a manner deserted by his friends. To get as near the truth as I can possibly do in all things relating to their mythology, I

frequently converse with him on these subjects; and when *"not forbidden by his Dreamed, or familiars"* [he] is explicit enough. A few nights back he thus informed me upon the several questions I proposed. The one that I saw in my dream, as above related, *is not the Sun*, as my half-breeds told me. The Sun is dressed like a Gentleman, i.e., a short coat, waist-coat, short breeches, stockings, boots, a hat and a beautiful feather stuck in it. He speaks English &c, and the rest as mentioned above. But the one I mentioned above, is Sickness, or the Plague. There are four of them: two walking in the air as I mentioned and two *in* the earth; i.e., in the bowels of the earth at a certain moderate distance from the surface, perhaps in the same *proportion* as those who are above. The indian thus relates of him: "When I was a young man, he appeared to me, and told me his name was Sickness; and that every time a *general* sickness was to take place amongst us he would come and forwarn me. See: Four winters ago (in 1819) after we had taken debt in the fall and were proceeding each of us to our hunting Grounds he appeared to me one night and said, 'I am come to tell you to get out of the way of all *Large waters* (i.e., Lakes and rivers) and pitch off immediately into the woods: Be cautious also and select proper ground for encamping; never pitch your tents in Large high woods, particularly of the Pine kind, chuse *low woods* to encamp in and never look up to Gaze lest I see you see and you be smitten. Keep off, aways from Large waters, for I am on a circuit round the earth: I shall follow the travelling waters (i.e., the routes or roads usually frequented or navigated) and smite all those I there find with sickness: in the interior, or to one side I shall not go. Tell this to the indians that they keep out of the way.'" It was that year that the *Measles* made such havock in some places.

He thus continued: "This last fall (in December) I saw him again – he told me he was on another circuit and intended making a large selection, passing thro' the plains and coming down again this way. He said he would pass ~~just~~ when the leaves would be rather large (about the 20th June, in these parts) and told me as before to admonish every body to keep out of the way of *large waters*, trees, &c, &c. 'It is not my doings, nor is it my choice that I thus *prowl* thro' the earth,' said he, 'but I am sent and cannot resist.' Now we will be again this spring visited with some sickness, but I cannot tell which – it is a breaking out in the flesh &c and his appearing to you (i.e., me) is a sign that he will certainly pass."

I then asked him if he intended telling the other indians of it. "I shall tell my Elder (brother), but not the others, for they won't believe me." He was very diffident: he wanted to communicate to me all he was told, but said he durst not lest he should injure himself, by exasperating the other (i.e., Sickness) and being *enigmatically* forbidden! "He told me," continued the indian, "as a sign that two of our number should die this winter, one a small one (and *he* is dead, naming to me a child that died about that time, tho' very distant then from him) and the other a full grown person – whom he is I know not, but *one must die!*"

[*The Spirits' Gifts and Demands*]

These chaps seldom appear (in dreams) less than 4 times, but commonly 6 times, and each time in a different form till the last, when he *makes himself known* and ever after appears (or rather appear) in the same uniform manner. It is then, after they have made themselves completely known to their votaries, that they communicate their power &c, &c, &c, and teach their *songs*, which tho' in their dreams, are so indelibly imprinted in their memories that they are never forgotten. For every one of these spirits, Genii, demons, phantasies, or whatever you may please to term them, have each their *Song*, which they communicate to their votaries, as well as explain also their power. Hence it is, that when any one amongst them has dreamed of a certain of number, commonly a good many, 20, 30, or perhaps a thousand, that they can *conjure* when they please; for these, like the guardian Genii in the fables, keeps always near them, and protect them from *too* much injury from the evil machinations of some of the mischievous ones. Indeed, from what I can learn, there are but few of these *familiars* but do evil to their votaries if they (the votary, i.e., the indian) neglect performing the regular annual, or perhaps more distant periodical sacrifice; and this sacrifice, their *familiar* tells them what it is he expects.

[*Encounters with Pah-kack (Skeleton)*]

A few days ago, in the night between the 31st March and 1st April, this indian was sleeping in an old house I sent him to, when at a late hour in the night he was pulled most violently out of his bed; so that his wife that was lying beside him awoke and with difficulty kept him down, tho' he also struggled himself to make his *Familiar* leave his hold: and the house shook violently. The next day he sent me his wife to ask a little grease to make a sacrifice (i.e., burnt offering*). I gave her a little, and the husband came the same evening to sleep with us. Upon enquiry he told me thus. "It was a *Skeleton*: he *was* displeased with me because I did not make him my usual offering and yet he knows that I am *pitiful*, that I cannot move to hunt myself, but am beholding to others for every mouthful I and my family eat; but they are wicked when they think themselves neglected or abandoned, and think nothing of carrying off an indian and throwing him in some distant place, dangerous precipice, or other place where he must perish if not succored by some other more kind one."

"Some years back," continued he, "I went out one night in the fall to hunt moose. I had tied my Canoe very securely in the rushes and there was waiting alone to hear the moose either come to the Lake, or cry after the Dam, for it was in the rutting season" (and the indians commonly go out in this manner at that season, for the Buck has a certain cry which he makes at that time either to call the female, or as with the domestic cattle to exult, as one might think from their capers). "I all at once heard far a-head of me cries of heh, heh, heh (or hayh, or haih) sudden, quick, coming in the air and directly towards me. 'Oh! now,' said I, 'I am gone!' Indeed he came – I *cringed* and laid myself as low in my Canoe as possible; but he came straight to me, took me up and threw me in the water, all the time crying, 'he! he!' I then endeavoured to take out my *fire-bag*; but this he would not let me do. Having then no alternative, I was obliged to make for the shore as well as I could, he all the time crying in the same manner just above my head, as if he intended absolutely my death. However, I reached the shore, tho' with the greatest difficulty. Then I took some dry grass which I rubbed and bruised till it became soft and put it under my arm pits and crumpled myself into a small heap and remained till the sun began to warm when I swam back to my Canoe. He kept hovering over me all night and untill the Sun was pritty high, always making the same cry; tho' when he found me so benumbed with cold on my debarkation he laughed, 'ha! ha! ha!' &c, &c."

Today (April 4th) he asked me for a needle and thread to sew the sleeve of his Capot, which this *Ghost*! had torn in his endeavours to carry him

---

*God forgive me the comparison, which by the bye is not meant to ridicule, but is really the case. [*G.N.*]

off the other night. Whilst he was sewing, "how he has vexed me," said he, "by tearing my old Coat, but I am afraid of him."

He related me another story of *them* as follows. "I went out one time a hunting beaver with a friend of mine: it was a long distance from our lodges – we killed 6 Beavers, and slept out. I awoke in the night and was much astonished to observe a man seated on the opposite side of the fire, resting his head on both hands, with his elbows on his knees apparently in a very pensive, sullen manner. He had but skin and bone – not the least particle of flesh: and this one had hair on his bony head. I gently pushed my friend and told him to look at *that stranger*. We were both extremely agitated in consequence of our fear, and were at a loss what to do. Having no alternative, I arose; conceiving he came to ask for something to eat I took a Beaver, cut it in two, and offered presented him the half of it: he did not deign to look at it – I was much afraid. I then bethought of cutting it into mouthfuls, which after presenting him I threw into the fire – thus I did with the whole; and when done, he arose and walked off peaceably in the *air*."

This sort they term Pâh-kàck, i.e., Skeletons, or such as die of hunger: or some that die extremely lean whether from the consumption or other sickness. Those, i.e., many of them, when they have nothing but just the mere skin and bone remaining, some of them in this situation disappear from the Earth and go to reside with all those who have already departed in that distressed state. This band or congregation have a head or chief. Their color is commonly green, tho' sometimes black; and it is extremely uncommon when one has any hair, being bald – as if a blown bladder. They sometimes are heard in the day, and the noise is sometimes as of a quantity of dried bones rattled or shaken in a forcible manner in a kettle; and sometimes as above related making that some monotonous but frightful cry of heh! heh! very quick and with an abrupt termination.

[*Sacrifices and Feasts for Pah-kack*]
The sacrifice they offer to these is Grease, generally a large bladder full, and of the best kind. All the natives present are invited. Tobacco of course goes before every thing else. He who makes the feast, or his assistant, most commonly lights, or fills rather, the pipes of all who smoke, but when it is light it is first presented to that quarter where *these* are supposed to reside (I believe in the N.W. or West) then to the cardinal points

– then to the (bladder of) Grease which is put in a dish fit to contain it and covered with down. Some of them have a small board about 20 or 24 ins. long, flat, painted with red earth, and a head made to it, of the same piece, and flat as the rest. At a certain distance below the neck, as we might suppose the Shoulders, other small pieces made in the same form and about 3 or 4 ins. long are stuck in each side at short distances, reaching to the ground – the lower end being small, and the head end would bear some resemblance to the ribs or arms were there not so many, by their being somewhat in a hanging form. After smoking and some speeches, in which these Ghosts are addressed, he who makes the feast, *waves* it 3 times crying, "he! he!," very loud for a good many times, and then presents it to this board, which is intended as a representation of the Pah-kack, desiring *him* to accept it, and be propitious and merciful to them, neither to injure them nor their *little ones*. Then he dances 3 times round the tent (in the inside) and when he comes to the 4th time, the one seated next him (in the direction of the Sun) rises. He makes a point of offering it twice to the one who rises, who in his turn *does* as if he was going to receive it; and the 3d time it is thrown into his hands: this one makes a double turn upon his heels and dances or *trots* once around the tent, and the next him, seated, rises to take it in his turn, with the same ceremony, till all have passed. Then it comes into the master's hands again who reperform[s] the same ceremonies once more – puts down the grease, cuts it up, and shares to every male or widow present, in proportion to their numbers (i.e., the families they may have).

[Pah-kack Feasts at Lac la Ronge]
Shortly after my arrival here this last fall [1822] they invited me thro' compliment to two of these feasts. I went both times merely to have a better opportunity of making my observations, which are as above, as near as I can bring them. But my mind was too much disturbed with reflections which soon became so melancholy that I had nothing to bestow on what was going on. "Poor unfortunate creatures!" I often exclaimed to myself – "Ye are desirous, nay anxious to perform your duties to your maker, but know not know. If you only knew how he abominates this ceremony which you perform with so much devotion, how soon would you cast off all your superstitions, and rather live without any religion at all, and risk all upon chance, than perform sacrifices, for aught I know,

to demons!" I shall not here enter upon these reflections further, suffice the above; for they are too long, too frequent, and besides I wish to sacrifice the little paper I have remaining to such others things as I have, and which I think may not be uninteresting to you. Had there been but their speeches, and the ceremonies, I should not perhaps have thought so deeply. But their cries of he! he! and ha! ha! &c, so repeated and vociferous, that I was struck with a certain horror and thought that half of the devils in hell had entered the throats of these men to give *me* an idea of their Pandemonium below. Good God! what a miserable reflection! but how much more so the occasion leading to it.

[*Medicines and the Abode of "Esculapius"*]
Notwithstanding they some times *Dream* of roots (medicines &c) there is a certain place according to their notions consecrated to *Esculapius* (and perhaps Appollo also, conjointly). It is depicted as a most heavenly abode, so delightful. He (Esculapius) resides in a mountain in the bowels of which is his house – it has 6 doors, but so mysteriously constructed that no soul whatever, besides himself and his *inmates*, of whom there are a great number (of Every Nation and language) can open them. The Lock apparently is in the form of a screw, or Spiral, and is opened on the inside, but only to such as Escu. deems worthy of admission. These doors open *to* different quarters, the house being immensely large, and as above mentioned, in the bowels of [the] mountain. *In* this residence is of every medicine useful in life, such as do not *vegetate*, i.e., minerals, fossils, &c, &c. These are shown to the votary; he is instructed in their use; the manner of preparing and mixing them; the ceremonies, i.e., songs and sacrifices &c, &c, to be performed in their application, taking of them up, or in instructing *others*; because it is not every *Indian* that is favored with these Dreams.

The mountain is of a moderate size, and there issue from it 40 Rivers which fall into a Lake not far from the *base* and situated in a beautiful plain. This Lake is shallow and has some handsome sandy shoals, and in the borders of (in the water) it grow beautiful *rushes*. The water in every one of the rivers is of a different color, no two being alike, one is Black, another white, red, Green, blue, *ash-color*, &c, &c. *In* the latter grow herbs and plants of a vast variety, as also their nature. In the sides of the mountain are of every herb and plant that grows in any part of the world whatever. When any one of them (of the Indians I mean) is thus favored, he appears first at these rivers, when the head or chief of the mountain comes out, accost[s] him in a freindly manner, and after some conversation he is introduced into the interior of the house, where he is astonished to find people of every nation and language in the earth. But if I can form a right opinion, there are but few of each language. They are seated in Four rows, their seats being something like those of a Theatre, semicircular and rising a little one above the other. These are all Doctors; and it is their business to instruct the *votary* in the object of his mission &c. They have a great quantity of medecines already prepared, of such as are produced in the bowels of the Earth, such as minerals, stones, shells &c, &c, and most, or many of these, are hung up in the house. Here he is taught how, and in what manner, to prepare these, as also the Songs and sacrifices &c, appropriate to each different one or sort. When on the outside, or out-of-Doors, he is shown all the roots, herbs, plants &c, and is taught the respective song (of each) or of any particular one, or number, or such as only grow in the climate he inhabits. Both the songs and the Plant, herb, &c, are so indelibly imprinted on his mind (or memory), tho' he had never seen them before, or should not happen to meet with any of them for years afterwards, yet on his first view, he immediately recognises them, and every circumstance that had been instructed him, as if he had passed a regular apprenticeship. This may seem very extraordinary, if not indeed absurd, to people unacquainted with them, but still it is no less a positive fact.

These rivers, i.e., waters, are of different colors, so also is the *rapidity* of each stream; some of them moving in a turbulent and awful manner as the rapids and eddies at the foot of large falls; some moving in large majestic waves like the swells of a large and deep Lake agitated by the wind; and some in a beautiful smooth current, down which the *canoes* are scarcely perceived to move. These are the tokens or signs or emblems of the manner of *our* lives, here below, so far as regards to health and sickness, and of course their description requires no further explanation.

In some of those rivers grow herbs or plants which, themselves, as well as their roots, are a rank, deadly poison, more or less; and their effects, when any Demon-Spirited wretch employs them as instruments of vengeance, tho' I have known none to carry off the object *immediately*, yet have a most melancholy baneful effect; some of them exactly similar (in their effects) to *Lunar Caustic* [silver nitrate, a cauterizing agent poisonous in large doses], and oftentimes with an additional humiliating effect. (But more of this hereafter.) And some deprive the object of every one of his senses but that of feeling – a melancholy instance of this I saw in the Spring of 1813 [i.e., in the Lake Winnipeg area] and sufficient of itself to *emeliate* [emolliate] an heart of adamant! Sometimes Esculapius will not instruct his votary in their use, satisfying himself with telling them they are bad *medecines*, or perhaps not mentioning them at all. To others again, he explains every *circumstance* &c, relating to them; but with a *most strict* injunction never to employ them at his *Peril* "unless you wish to die: I teach you all these things because I love you, and know your heart to be compassionate: but *mind my words*, if ever you employ them with an ill or evil *view*, thou shalt die. Other *indians* as well as thyself love life – it is sweet to every body; render it therefore not a burden or a disgrace; and I *hate* those who thus abuse my confident affection" &c, &c.

They are also forbidden sometimes as strictly, and for the same reasons, instructing others in their use. Notwithstanding this great love and cautious diffidence of Esculapius, there are other malignant Powers who teach them and encourage their use – hence those distressing objects, I cannot here for the want of Paper, speak of.

What I have mentioned of minerals &c, which from their description are indeed really such, i.e., minerals &c, yet I cannot take upon myself from my slender knowledge of their language and *technical* terms, to *assure* you that they are prepared after *our* manner, i.e., by Chemical processes. Mercury, sulphur, saltpetre or nitre, &c, I do not know that they have; but there being french, English, German, and from the description, Greek and Hebrew Doctors, among the number, I should not suppose it preposterous in concluding that they have them all in the same way as ourselves. But from what I can learn it is *Stones*, that is, some particular kinds of them, that are most used, such as talk [talc], pumice stones, and of various other kinds. These they are shewn how to reduce to Powder, and with what water, i.e., out of which river (or color'd water if you please) the water is taken to mix up those Powders. With the roots and herbs &c, it is different – *they are boiled* &c. These *stones* (for they are most commonly denominated by them) are held in very great repute by them; tho' many of those that have been shewn me as possessing wonderful virtues I considered as very common and foolish, or at least harmless things.

Here! I am again digressing, which is everlastingly the case with me when not in the *humor* of scribbling. I should have mentioned first (Because as you may see, I have begun *this* story in the *middle* instead [of] at either of the two ends) that when they want to dream of these things, as well as of any other particular thing, they must fast, and lay down to sleep, keeping their minds as free as possible from any other thoughts whatever, and wholly bent and employed on that particular one alone. I also should have observed in the proper place that the door the votary is introduced [into] is exactly in the middle of these rivers, there being 20 on each side of the door. The use, intent, &c, &c, of the other 5 doors, I never thought to enquire, and must leave you to guess as well as myself till such times as I can get this matter explained.

[*Songs: Their Transmission and Uses*]

Their songs are delivered in *Notes*, impressed or drawn on bark, in the form of hierlographics, and thus taught, and being hierlographics (and not very dissimilar to those anciently used by the Egyptians; nay indeed, I have reason to think from what I have seen of both, that any *Learned* man being perfectly acquainted with the one could trace a great deal in the other; but this opinion I hazard from my own ignorance) no two are alike, it therefore requires time to learn them; that is, any *one* of them: for those notes are not like ours, *marked* with regular bars &c, so that one Gamut serves for all; but with them, each one may be said to be itself a Gamut.

However, I have reason to think that they are regular and uniform; for many years ago, when I was still scarcely more than a boy [i.e., probably in northern Wisconsin 1802–04], I rem[em]ber throwing away the contents of one of these medecine bags in which there were several strips of Bark covered with these Notes. An indian happened to be by – he took one up and with the Point of his knife placing it on one of these began to sing, moving the knife regularly as children do when they begin to learn their a, b, c. This surprised me a little at the time, for the indian was a stranger and had but lately arrived from his own lands that were several hundred miles off. After laughing at and ridiculing him as is the custom with us, I asked how he could make them out?

"The same," said he, "as you do to *reckon* (i.e., read) your *papers*. See, this one is (meant for) the *Thunder*; that, the Earth, &c, &c; but I only know a few of these songs: the possessor of this bag knew a great deal – he was a great Medecine man, i.e., Doctor" &c.

As far as I can learn, every different root, herb, plant, mineral, Spirit (or whatever you may please to term this latter) have each their respective songs; and which they must sing, were his voice like that of a choked Pig, when he employs them for one of themselves, or learns them to another. When they sing, those of their *familiars* who instructed this Song, whether to the one who sings, as having learnt it from himself (i.e., Familiar) or having been handed to him; he is said to attend, invisibly, of course, and perform that which he promised this (medecine, supposing it is one) should effect. (This is a long and complex job, and I doubt much if I can get thro' with it without more of my blundering; but I shall risk blunders, omissions and repetitions.) Hence it is they always sing when they attend on a desperately sick person, amongst themselves, tho' very rarely when they administer to the white.

When any one is very sick, and that they be *called upon*, or perhaps, tho' rarely, ordered, in their dreams, by their familiars, they sing, blow, and suck, alternately, and with such violence that one would think they wanted to blow them to the d--l, or swallow them down their throats; but no, it is to force in the medecine, of which they have generally a mouthful, masticated into a pulp, or something near *Salve*, sometimes: the suction business is to draw out the Devil; i.e., the medicine, bone, stone, iron, brass, stick, or whatever they imagine it is that occasions the disease. If the complaint lies in any particular part, to that part it is they apply themselves most, and sometimes *only*: supposing the hip, knee, &c., for there they imagine it is a worm or maggot gnawing them. But if the complaint is universal, that is, the whole system be sick and debilitated, it is then the pit of the Stomach and the temples; rubbing sometimes the wrist, the palms of the hands, and opposite the heart. This is very frequently done, and in the intervals the songs and rattler together, and often a short speech or prayer to that one of their *Familiars* whom they think will be most propitious on the occasion, or *he* from whom they hold such, or such instruction, &c.

These songs are a dull monotony; for tho' they have a few variations and are hi[gh] and low, and the transition sometimes so very sudden that it requires a particular command of the throat to sing them; and to *me*, so difficult that I should I believe require a 7 years apprenticeship even with Esculapius (but I believe it is *Pluto* or *Pan* who teaches the songs) himself, for me to learn them, and there is certainly no musick in them; tho' some few that I've heard many years ago, passing a winter with them, I found pleasing enough; but perhaps more from the *solemnity* with which all was going on was I struck, than any thing else: indeed we had great reason to be solemn, for we were dreadfully pinched by hunger.

[*Conjuring against Starvation, Wisconsin, 1804* (*cf. Nelson 1825ff.: 49–50*)]

When oppressed thro' starvation, they have a variety of ceremonies which they perform; and tho' the songs be different, as also the *ceremonies* themselves, still are they intended to answer the same purpose. I shall endeavour to describe a couple to you from which you may form a pritty just idea of the rest. It was the latter end of Jan[uar]y or beginning of Feb[ruar]y 1804, four of us, only *white* people mind, were pitching off, or rather flying off from our house we had built in the fall on account of *the* enemies [Sioux, cf. Nelson 1825ff.: 47]. We had a small stock of dry Provisions and speared a few fish once or twice, but there were so many of us that we were soon bro't to short commons, as the *strip* of country we were then going thro' contained no other animals but a few strag[g]ling Bears; but these animals at *this* season could not be found notwithstanding all the exertions of our hunters.

One evening on my return to our lodges one of the women told me that the oldest man of our band, a great Doctor, or conjuror, as we frequently denominate them, said that if I were to pay him half a carrot (1 1/2 lbs) tobacco, he would conjure and be assured of success, for it required payment. Tho' I suspected there was a trick in this, I did not hesitate, but gave him his demand. The first night their songs and ceremonies were as usual. "Tomorrow, my *familiar* tells me we shall get a Bear." All the hunters returned at evening, *mais tous à blanc*. The second night, the rattler, songs, speeches, smoking, and medicine bags opened: "tomorrow we will assuredly get something." But the same as the day before. The third night, the same, but every thing conducted with a sort of awful silence and solemnity that surprised me a good deal. I was harassed with constant walking, weak thro' hunger, and tired with their *Bêtises* as the french say; but the manner of their conduct kept me that time from growling. "Oh! now tomorrow, indeed, we shall not fail – we shall certainly eat flesh; for the old man is a great conjuror and well liked: he prayed to the *master* or giver of *Life* and his Dreamed have promised him success." But we got no more than before.

In these conjuring boutes – they make no use of drums, but instead of that had cut a small hollow tree of maple, about 5 feet long and scraped it out after splitting so that it resembled a semicircle – or stove pipe split down. This *hollow* board had been well dressed, i.e., reduced to about half an inch in thickness and well polished: there were to the best of my memory four men seated taylor fashion and held a small stick about 3/4 ins. diameter and about 15 (ins.) long, in each hand: with these they beat time to the tune and another moved or shaked the rattler in the same manner. All this, however, was to no purpose.

There was another indian in company with us, but *tenting* by himself (and his family). This indian who was very fond of me would frequently call me in and give me a share of what he had, to eat. "Well!" said he, "what success have your great men?"

I answered I did not expect much.

"No," replied he, "they did not go the right way to work – had I not polluted (spoiled, as he said) my person last fall," attending to an indian he had then killed [cf. Nelson 1836: 37], "I should *try*; and I believe that my familiars would be *charitable* to me: however, I shall let them go on till they are done, after which I shall make a trial: perhaps on *your accounts* they may shew me their wonted attention."

I took this as wind, but as he spoke in so very *earnest* (si naivement) a manner, I concealed my sentiments. The second night after the others had finished – he began a little after dusk. But what a difference between them! He had an immense large drum, as large [as] those among the military, and stretched hard: upon this he beat time, but very hard, to accord with his Songs which were as loud as he could bawl: at certain intervals also he used only his rattler, but with as much violence as he could.

Thus he continued alternately singing, praying (or making speeches) and smoking, till broad day light. When he began, we thought the fellow was mad or only jesting; but the indians of our lodge reproved us. At Sun rise he came out of his lodge, and made a long speech, in which he told one to go one way and a second another, and himself by another route.

"Thou," addressing the first one, a young lad – "thou wilt soon find thy (bear): but thou," addressing the father, "on thy way on thou wilt pass very near, but will not see him: Thou'lt search a long [time] and return giving up all hopes: but when come to this thou must return again and between *this* thy last track and the first one thou shalt make this morning, thou'lt see him in his nest. As for me, I shall have much trouble to get mine."

I heard him speak, but not understanding sufficiently the language, the women explained to me. I need not tell you how *we* laughed at the poor Devil; and so went off hunting *Ivy* [Ojibwa *pīmākkwat*; Nelson's description in 1825ff.: 49 shows that this was *Celastrus scandens* (bittersweet); cf. also Jones 1965] which had been our support for a long time: but in the evening we found all that he predicted, perfectly verified. This I assure you is a fact, and will maintain it notwithstanding every thing *skeptics* (excuse the term) or those unacquainted, or but superficially so, with these people may say: and I am also certain that he had no previous knowledge of their being there; for there was plenty of snow and there were no other tracks but those of these 2 hunters, and we had pitched *up* the river that day.

But here I am digressing: to return therefore. I am altogether out of the regular track that I had proposed to myself at my first setting off: my time is to[o] short, and my memory to[o] bad, to read over the whole, so as to resume the regular course. The remainder shall be composed of *fugitive Pieces*. Indeed the nature of some of them being a *compound* will not admit of their being *treated* of but in *sections* if I may use the term. The first therefore, lest I have not time to *enter* all, I shall speak of is The Soul!

[*The Soul*]

This seems, to me, at least, a most extraordinary and incomprehensible thing – yet from the different sources which I have received it, and the manner of relation, serves but more and more to perplex. Whether it is really and absolutely the soul, or some other *principle* on which the very existance depends I cannot say; but something it is lodged apparently in the Heart or breast, that on these occasions flies off and leaves them; and at the very instant of its exit it is perceived, and occasions such a derangement of the whole system, and particularly of the faculties as very soon to deprive the object of life, but primally a total want of sense, such as we suppose the Soul *endows* us with.

I shall here relate you one of many stories of the kind verbatim as I received it. It was from an indian of course. He told me that one summer being on a visit rather to a distant part of the country (perhaps 2 or 300 miles) he fell in with one of his acquaintances, who (as often happens between strangers, particularly to such as come from the Southward) asked to purchase *medecines* of him. "I had but a small quantity and only of 4 Sorts or kinds: he being very anxious for them, I sold them *all* to him: He was not satisifed – he must have more tho' I positively assured him I had given him the last. Then he menaced me, and said I should feel the effects of his resentment arising from my avarice and *uncharitable* spirit. Knowing his disposition, I returned to my friends, intending to be as far out of his way as Possible.

"One night in the winter he conjured – I was fast asleep (and several hundred miles off) and never thought more of him: but he called upon his Familiars and demanded my Soul (!) – *it was taken* to him; but just as it was on the eve of entering his conjuring hut I perceived it and sprung from my bed in the most dreadful agonies and convulsions insomuch that two men holding and pulling of me with all their might, and also had the assistance of the women, could not keep me quiet: I was constantly spring-ing forward, rushing hither and thither and absolutely (i.e., totally) deprived of my faculties for I have not yet the least knowledge of what I was doing, so great was my horor in observing this conjuring tent.

"At last a friendly spirit interfered and forbad the conjuror at his peril to do any thing to my soul, but allow it to return immediately. He was afraid for his own life and durst not disobey – he let *it* go. I cannot tell you how happy I felt and so easy – the distance was great indeed – but I soon flew back and re-entered my body; when I became entirely composed. But I had been so dreadfully agitated that I found myself in a profuse sweat, my whole frame so shaken, debilitated and weak, that for several days I could not move but with pain. 'Heh!' said I, 'what a narrow escape!' The other indians asked what ailed me? I told them where *I* had been – they would scarcely credit; but in the ensuing summer upon enquiry they found it true; and were now fully convinced that this Power doth lodge with indians!"

They represent the soul as being small: not very dissimilar in size and shape from the yolk of a large Hen, or duck, Egg: some of them very hard, and others again much more soft and tender: some are easily *kept* and bruised, but others are with difficulty taken and continually in motion; but all are extremely impatient of restraint – cannot bear it; and confine-ment is death to the body from which it has issued.

Some conjurors possessing sufficient power, and influence, take a soul, if they want to destroy the body (in the conjuring box or tent) and wrapping it in a piece of leather, rub and bruise it between both hands till they destroy its subtility or subtilty. As soon as it comes within view of the conjuring tent its agonies are terrible as also those of the body, however distant that may be; but as soon as its motion is destroyed the body dies likewise.

Others again, take it and put it in a Jappan'd Tobacco box, and tie the lid or cover securely tied with a *woman's Garter*, from whence if not loosened by some one it can never escape – any other lashing is not, anything near, so completely effectual as this: reflect and you will guess immediately the reasons they give. As I do not know Latin, and you don't understand indian I must suppress this and many other things. Others again take a different method, thus: But by-the-bye, this has but very little relation to the Soul.

[*Soul-darting*]

I shall therefore refer it till afterwards and give you another Story as received from a Canadian an eye witness. He was passing the winter with the indians and one night the head man of the tent he lodged in gave a feast. He was in the habit of doing it and was himself apparently a good and peaceable man, but not to be trifled with by other indians. Every thing being prepared, the guests were just going to eat when the feast-man's mother dropped suddenly as if dead: every one was struck with consternation. They had recourse to their medicines, songs, rattlers, &c, as usual; at last he fell to sucking his mother in one of her temples; suddenly they heard something *crack*: the indian drew back, his mother arose perfectly recovered and all become well. However, that which occasioned the *crack*, the indian took out of his mouth, wrapped carefully up and gave it to his wife to put in a tobacco box, which she did: it had all the appearances of a *Bean* (un[e] fève) – the wife wanted to tie the lid but the husband said there was no necessity – they resumed their meal.

But the old woman was not long in possession of her senses. She very soon relapsed, and as instantaneously as at the first. "Ho!" exclaimed the indian, "the *Dog* is off." They looked into the tobacco-box but nothing was found. They continued conjuring 3 nights, and the last especially, the man told me he thought the devil was amongst them from a certain kind of indescribable noise in the air, round about their tent, and the sudden flashings of light. This was Powder (Gun powder): they had carefully thrown out all the fire, thrown a great quantity of snow and water on the hearth, and then put fresh Earth upon it – it was perfectly dark in the lodge, there being no other light than what is usually emitted from the heavens: upon this hearth of fresh earth they would throw some Powder and then retiring to the bottom of the tent would say, "come! let me see if I be a manito?" – then singing &c, off the Powder would fly! They continued this way 3 nights but all to no purpose: The old woman yet lived 2 years but never spoke &c.

He said (the indian) that this *bean* was "the Soul or Spirit of another indian, then at a vast distance, which he darted at my mother to render her pitiful and miserable; but I shall make the Dog suffer." However, after this, the Canadian enquired why he did not revenge himself and kill him. "No," said he, "that won't do: he has got back his Soul it is true, and I cannot get it again, yet I might easily kill him if I chuse, but this won't do – he is somewhat justifiable, for I took both his wives from him." There are many other instances of a like nature but different in the proceedings, that I do not recollect sufficiently to commit to Paper.

[*Sorcery for Protection and Revenge*]
Now again for the other way. If an indian has a spite against another and is induced to it for the preservation of his own life, or from motives of revenge, he takes the following plan or method. He takes a piece of leather and cuts it into the shape of his *enemy*; and if he wants him to die speedily he places a little *Powdered medecine* opposite the heart, or upon it. This medecine is I believe a root, and very inflammable; he holds a small spark of fire *near* it – it immediately *explodes* and that part of the leather on which *it* was becomes burnt and shrivelled: when he performs this, he generally utters words like these, "Let the Heart of *such a one* become like this Leather, let it shrivel and die within him!" If it is a leg, an arm, the head or any other particular part, or parts, or even the whole body, it is the same and the words also; unless he doth not wish for the death; then he will say, "Let *such a part* become lame, useless, ulcerous," &c, &c, according to his disposition; and that part, or parts, become thus affected according to his wish.

"But how is it possible that such things can be? Do you really think that an insignificant root of no apparent power or virtue whatever can effect such things?" Thus I would frequently question, and their answers with little variations [were] universally the same:

"Yes, most certainly; it is not the root alone, but with the assistance of that one of his Dreamed that is most powerful, and most fond of him: he! you white people you know not; you are consummately ignorant of the Power of our Great medicine men. Many things might I tell you much more surprising – but you do not believe these trifles, how much less, then, those you do not know?" What then is to be done! how do with, what say, to a people so blind, so infatuated!

[*Sexual Sorcery*]

They have some roots that are dreadful in their effects – Being a female, I think I should prefer immediate death. They have some that have the same effects as *Lunar Caustic* [silver nitrate]. They use them thus. During the time of their "Seperation" (i.e., menstruation) they endeavour to give them to smoke, which is never refused – there is some of this root mixed with the Tobacco. Once smoking is sufficient – a few months after, their complexion begins to change – and at last becomes of a *nasty* black with abundance of hair growing out on the face; and if these women were to shave, I verily believe their beards would become as bushy and thick as those of any man whatever. In performing this, they must also utter words thus: "Let the one for whom I intend this, and who shall smoke of it, become black and hairy; and become as ugly and rejected as she is now fair and searched for!" Sometimes they mingle it with their food or the liquor they drink: there is more than one kind of this dreadful root, one of which I was shewn, but have forgotten, there being 2 or 3 others resembling it – it is like many others a perennial herb, and hath some resemblance to the long or tall Thistle.

To return: when the subject, or object, discovers that she hath been thus dealt with, which they sometimes do a few weeks after, they may be restored, for there is an *antidote* to it; but I have never known one instance of this, tho' a dozen of the others I have. Some handsome, fair complexioned young females refusing the importunate sollicitations of an abandoned, vicious, revengeful wretch, becomes the victim of her *coyness*; and 2 or 3 years after, I have positively not known them and could scarcely believe my Eyes ——

There is of another kind and which is very common, whose effects is an extraordinary *vacuation* of blood, and in a few days would occasion death. A half breed I lately had with me, the Son of a man who many years ago was a servant of yours,* being not of an extraordinary good moral character finding his sollicitations rejected with scorn became jealous and very anxious to revenge himself. He applied to an old indian, but in so cautious a manner that the indian gave him of the root without suspecting and told him how to use it. He pulverised it, and mingled it with a little vermillion and then watched his opportunity, which occurred, I believe, the ensuing morning. In our *out*-Posts we have no temples dedicated to Cloacinda [i.e., privies, ref. to Lat. *Cloacina*, "cleanser," surname of Venus], and besides, the females here are ashamed to *sacrifice* at them: he therefore could not miss his opportunity – he watched, and after she entered he went and soon found the place by the *Smoke*: here he sprinkled some of this Powder which he took in a quill, pronouncing, "Let me see blood issue from the same place *this* hath done – I want to see blood."

Scarcely two hours after, the woman, who was married and of course so much the less bashful, said, "what is the matter with me, I have been just now out and want to go again." You may suppose her astonishment seeing the time of the natural return was scarcely half elapsed, but how much more so finding it issue far beyond anything she had ever known. This continued till very late in the day and the beast was watching to see if it would answer. He went in to the house on pretence of a friendly visit, and remarked how *Pale* she was – the mother told him, "my daughter has been bewitched and could you not do something to ease her?"

He became extremely uneasy in his turn: he went out and passing by the place she went to he easily discovered, notwithstanding her precaution, of what dreadful consequences it would be if not timely attended to. He was afraid she would die before anything could be done. However he went to the old indian, and speaking in a most sympathising strain,

---

*The only HBC employees in the Ile à la Crosse district records who appear to fit Nelson's descriptions here and infra ("Love Magic") are Paul Paul, a voyageur from William Henry (Sorel) where Nelson's family lived, and Baptiste Paul. Paul Paul had been in the fur trade for about twenty years. Baptiste, described as "native," was presumably his son (HBCA B.89/a/7, p. 60, 1823-24).

asked him if he could not administer something to stop that extraordinary issue.

"Why!" replied the old fellow – "that root I gave you the other day is its own antidote – give her the length of her middle finger to *eat* and it will stop quick enough."

He did not chuse to tell the indian that it was this that had occasioned it lest he should be punished by him in his turn; but artfully conducting his discourse got more from him, [and] administered it to the woman, muttering in himself, "Let this blood cease, I have seen enough of it" – and she was soon healed! I done all I could to make him confess it, without coming to the point; but he never would: he satisfied himself by assuring me with the most solemn asseverations that it was the case; "and if you doubt it," continued he, "you may make the experiment – you need be under no apprehensions whatever, for on giving her of the same root to *eat*, it will stop."

This root, when masticated and applied when reduced to pulp, but better when pulverised, stops the blood immediately on application to any wound – "how *profusely soever it may flow*." It is very astringent, and somewhat hot.*

[*Hunting Medicine*]
Another herb, I believe it is the (wild) Carroway [caraway], i.e., which we commonly denominate aniseeds – at least the smell and taste much resemble that, and its stalk bears a very great resemblance to the wild mint, as well as the leaves and flowers.‡ I *suppose* this is the one meant, because they tell me the taste and smell are delicious.

This root, and all its appurtenances (i.e., stalk, leaves and flowers) is of wonderful effects in various *things*. I shall give you some of the stories relating to it as I received them. "I was living out with *such* an indian, and we became reduced to *short commons* – one day he (the indian) took a piece of bark and drew upon it 3 moose – and put some of this *medecine*

---

*Although firm identification of this root is impossible, compare Leighton's description (1985, 25) of the east-central Saskatchewan Cree use of baneberry (*Actaea rubra*).

‡Anna Leighton suggests that this is *Agastache foeniculum* (Pursh) Ktze. or giant hyssop. See Leighton 1985, 26.

upon the heart and head of each; then he fastened a piece of sinew to it and told me to fasten it to a small stick that had been stuck *slant-way* in the Ground. 'Now,' said he, 'let me see if this will do: oh no! I am afraid it won't; but I'll try – if it answers, the bark will dance!'

"I laughed at his idea" (a half breed told me this) "and so did one of his sons: however the son told me that he had seen his father do so before, and that he killed every time. 'Stop! let us see how he will go on,' said the Son.

"The father began to sing (and if *I* remember right, beat the drum also) – shortly after, the bark began to move, and as the old fellow raised his voice so did its motion increase, till at last it began whirling round with great violence, sometimes one way then another till it was wound up close to the stick, when it began changing sides – sometimes *upon* and sometimes *below* the stick. He ceased: began to talk with us and saying he was afraid it would not *answer*. This he did 3 times, and the bark moved every time with the same violence. Now he desired in the beginning that if his *familiar* would have compassion on him, he would render these 3 moose foolish: that they might not be possessed of their usual cunning &c.

"The next day we went out – the old man, his son and myself, a hunting – we were hungry – we walked till late in the day and finding no tracks I proposed our return, but he told me we ought to proceed; for in the low ground beyond a small ridge then near in sight of us, 'we may perhaps find some tracks. I am never deceived when I am answered (i.e., my bark dances).' We soon reached this low Ground and shortly after heard a noise: jumping, running and breaking of Sticks. 'Ah! here they are,' said the old man: 'see how their *head* is turned! What a noise they make – how they play – they are foolish.' We killed them all. If you doubt me, ask any of the indians, and see if they won't all tell you that *he* does so when he wants to kill."

[Love Medicine]

Another story: for *love potions*, or philters, are also composed of this. "There were several young men (half-breeds) of us together and also some young women, who came with us to await the arrival of their husbands from Fort William at *that* place. Two of our party wanted to pay them a *visit* in the night and I endeavoured to dissuade them, but to no purpose: they [the women] began bawling out on purpose to awake every one near and shame us; for we were lodging by ourselves, and then took good cudgels and pursued them into our place: *we* enjoyed this confusion of the others, tho' partly at our own expenses.

"One of them then addressed me, 'come B[a]pt[tiste], this bitch has vexed me – I know you have *good medicine* – give me some of it that I may laugh at her in my turn.'" (I must tell you that one of them I have known many years back was, and is still, a *bitch*, i.e., according [to] the indian acceptation (as well as our own) of the term; and the man is the same one I mentioned little above, at the conclusion and beginning of pp. 30 and 31.)*

"I gave him some with the *directions* – he returned again very soon after (in the same night) – found her asleep – he then rubbed her forehead, opposite her heart, the *pit* of the Stomach, and the palms of both hands. Then he awoke her.

"The next day, as my comrades were desirous of revenging themselves, they broached the conversation publicly and had the laugh in their turn: the women had the *best* at the offset, but as they could not deny the other charges they became extremely confused and vexed: a quarrel ensued but my comrades exultingly told them, 'we can turn and twist you *now* about our fingers as we please.' And they did too. For the women both *giving suck* at that time thought it was their children that were handling them, as they used but *one* finger, and gently."

The other story is thus: A man that I have with me at present, "in consequence of some *slips* of his *Rib* had frequent, and some severe quarrels with her – she began to hate him and wanted to go with her *Par-amour*: the husband tho' vexed and confused *did not want* to lose her: he began by soothing, coaxing and caressing her, but she always bawled out as loud as she could that every body might hear, tho' it were at midnight, 'thou white dog, leave me alone, why art thou fumbling at me?' The more she became averse the more he coax'd and she bawling out, "don't *slabber* me' every time he attempted to kiss her – and she was watching a fair opportunity to slip off to her lover (an indian).

"At last he lodged his complaints to me, and asked if I could not *assist* him. I gave him some of this *medecine* with the usual directions and told

---

*See note, p.67, "Sexual Sorcery," on "Baptiste."

him as soon as he had executed all properly to come away and leave her, and not return to her for a couple of days so that in her turn she might suffer. He had not long left her till she called for him as if wanting something and like a Goose he went immediately, tho' I done all I could to make him pay her in her own coin. Since that time they live as you see them. *But* if you doubt of this also, you can easily make the experiment – chuse any one you please, and let her be ever so coy and shy, you will bring her as you want!!!"

Shortly after this I made some general enquiries of the man latterly in question, but he would not avow, tho' from his confusion and precipitancy with which he answered, I believe there is *something* in the business.

"It is with this medecine," continued the half breed, "that the young men so completely and universally succeed with all the women that please them."

[*Hunters Bewitched and Restored*]

With this also, principally, they succeed in bewitching any one they are averse to, and prevent them from killing such animals as they please. They draw the likeness of the animal or animals they do not chuse the others to kill, put of this medicine (tho' most commonly mixed with some others in this latter case) upon the hearts, and desire that they may become shy and fly off upon any the least appearance or approach of them. Or they will conjure, and desire some one of their *familiars*, one, or several, to *haunt such a one* in all his motions and scare and frighten off, and *render wise* any *such* and *such* animals; and let the distance be hundreds of miles off – their familiars that are spirits residing in the air, and transport themselves in an instant to any place they please and who see all that is going on *below*, keep *all* away accordingly. To evade this is a task that but few can succeed in. They must first Conjure to learn who it is that has bewitched them; then they inquire what is to be done: but here lies the difficulty – Sometimes they are told they *must* leave the appointed time run out: at others, such and such ceremonies, which is tantamount to the first answer; but at others again, it it easily dispelled – this depends entirely upon the precautions the *bewitcher* has taken, the Power, influence, or number of his Dreamed: as also on the other hand of the Dreamed, their power, influence &c, of the *bewitched*. But sometimes on a very slight or trivial cause depends the whole ——

I shall tell you another story. An old Canadian I have now with me has been in the habit of *living-free* [i.e., a "freeman," not in company employment] for many years back.* In the beginning of a winter he was tenting with some indians, and one of them, an impertinent, bombastic sort of Character, was boasting to him of the great power and effect of some medicines and a drum he had lately received from a Sauteux &c, &c.

"For some time [said the Canadian] I did not mind him, but finding he became at least troublesome, and insinuating as plainly as he durst that *he* was now invulnerable, or rather immortal and that *we* were helpless, a quarrel ensued till at last, 'I f--t upon your medecines and drum and the one also who gave them to you,' said I. We seperated in no good friendship. At night he made a feast and invited me amongst the rest with the design of poisoning me; but his friends remonstrated so effectually that he put this off and intended shooting me going out of the lodge; but this also the others would not allow: he was vexed – I kept my eye upon him, determined I should give the first blow on the least motion he might make. Finding himself prevented in these he said that I indeed should kill 2 moose, but that the rest of the year I should starve as a dog.

"I seperated next day with my wife and children – they were under great apprehensions, but I mocked all their conjurings. I very shortly killed 2 moose; but these indeed were the last. I walked and hunted every day – and seldom one day passed but I fired at the Buffaloe, moose, or some other animal, but never got anything, anything – I and my family were near dying with hunger. I tried every thing in my power, never giving myself the least trouble about the indian's menaces. At last the spring arrived – Ducks and Geese came; but no better success.

*"Freemen" or *gens libres* were those who had come to the Indian country in the employ of the North West Company (or some other Canadian concern) and later began to live independently in the northwest, subsisting by supplying or rendering other services to the fur trade and by living on country resources, usually in proximity to Indian friends and relatives. In 1823-24, five freemen were listed in the Ile à la Crosse district records as having transactions with the Hudson's Bay Company (HBCA B.89/a/7, p. 62); all bore French names, reflecting the fact that this was an old Canadian pattern and that the Canadians had dominated the area's trade before 1821 when the Montreal Nor'Westers and the Hudson's Bay Company merged. Doubtless there were numbers of others who were not named in this list.

"At last one day prowling in my Canoe I met 2 other *free-men*, who, after mutual enquiries &c, told me the same thing had happened him and that an indian told him to file off a small piece of the *muzzle* of his Gun and wash it well with water in which *sweet-flag* [prob. *Acorus calamus*, an arum] had been boiled, and killed after that as before. I laughed at the idea, but reflecting that it was an innocent experiment and could not offend the almighty, I tried, and the first animals I saw I immediately killed. This Sir," continued he, "I assure you is a positive fact!!!"

I find that the indians have recourse to this method also. But you must observe: as is the disease, so is the remedy.

[*An Iroquois Hunter Bewitched*]

Another story just now occurs to me which I shall relate, not so much to multiply these pretended proofs as to shew that our Iroquois,* Algon-quins &c, &c, are not such complete converts to the Christian faith as most people may complacently imagine, but rather have a mongrel religion like those whom the King of Babylon sent to inhabit Samaria when he carried Reuben and Ephraim captives (In the Bible). This winter an Iro-quois told me that one winter he was out a Beaver hunting with many of his friends. The oldest man of their party proposed one day that a certain number of them should go out a hunting Moose or Buffaloe, and the others Beaver. This one says, "I returned at night after a good success – the old man nothing – he became envious – a quarrel ensued, and after this many others. One day I fired at a moose as he was running past me, he fell – I went to him and just as I was for beginning to skin, he rose up, but with my axe I bro't him down – it was very far from home – I merely opened him and returned light, trusting to the others of our party; for I had no desire of partaking of the dry provisions the old fellow had, of his own. Immediately on entering the lodge we had another severe quarrel, and he told me I should not any more exult in my prowess as he should take care

*Iroquois from eastern Canada first appeared in the western fur trade in 1794. Hired by the Montreal concerns mainly as voyageurs and fur hunters, their numbers on the employ-ment lists reached a peak between 1800 and 1804 during the XY/North West Company rivalry. Many of them later became freemen and stayed in the northwest, particularly in Alberta (Nicks 1980).

I should not kill any more animals for some time. As we were coming to *knife work*, I ordered my wife to bundle up all our things and my lodge, and pitch off – it was then late, and I had not yet eaten. As none of my friends knew that I had killed, I did not chuse to tell them, but merely said as I was going off, 'Let those who are fond of me, or who chuse, follow me'; but none came, and I encamped upon my moose.

"Every day I went a hunting – scarcely a week passed but I fired 20, 30 and sometimes upwards of 50 Shot, upon Buffaloe or Moose, but could never kill – I would *miss*, or the *ball twisting in the hair would fall by the animal* without doing further injury. I starved for a long time – and became so weak that I could hardly walk.

"At last my wife (a woman of this country), one day that I had been out as usual, had prepared some good strong lye, and on my return washed my Gun with it; filled it, and stopping both the orifices put it over the smoke where it remained all night. She also took a number of the balls and boiled them likewise in the lye, telling me she had seen her uncle do so many years before, when he too had been bewitched. I thought at all events it could do no harm; and besides I could have done anything, I was so hungry. The next day I went out again – found another flock or herd of near 20 Buffaloe. I drew nigh and took all my usual precautions – I fired, one dropped; fired again – another dropped. I killed 14 out of that herd: and ever after missed not once!"

I asked him how the old fellow had done [the spell]? – he said, "I suppose it was as they frequently do – i.e., bury a piece of my meat in the Ground and pray the Devil to prevent my killing: for the Iroquois, when they take it in their head, are very wicked and do not want [lack] power!"

A few days ago a half-breed, abandoned with the indians, came in; and amongst his other *wantages* asked me for a small piece of (red) *sealing* wax, "because my brother cannot draw blood from the animals he fires at: by heating his Gun and applying this wax the blood will flow profusely from the wounds." He expressed himself afraid that his brother might have been bewitched and by retarding this operation he might enter *dans sa mal chance*!

These few *examples* will suffice to shew that they have different methods of *bewitching* and also different ways of clearing themselves. And the faith and dread they have of this is scarcely credible, and the consequences are often too uncommonly distressing.

[*Stories of Nay-han-nee-mis*]

I shall now give you of the Story of The Hairy Breasts. Near the days of *Noah*, nations were few and small. Weesuckajock (Noah, I shall call him for abbreviation sake) had a son as I told you before whose name was Nay-hân-nee-mis. Being strait'ned for provisions he went out to angle with some of the Hairy-Breasts. They came to a Lake, pierced several holes, but the North (or North wind as you chuse) being envious of Nay-hanemis, froze the water down to the very ground; so that in the deepest parts they found but Earth and after much digging at last reached the bottom; but behold that also was frozen! and who knows to what depth in the Earth?

[1. The Contest with the North Wind]

Finding this to be the case, Nays. addressed his friends thus – "I see this is the doings of the North Wind" (now by rights the North Wind ought to have been his maternal [great] Grd Father – but what cannot envy do?) "he is anxious of us, and wants to make us die of hunger – but he shall not! – I have to propose to you to cut off my head – rip up my body, beginning at the throat – You must not hurt or break any single one of my bones; but carefully take off all the flesh, dry it, and make Pounded meat of it. Of this you must sprinkle a little in every one of the holes: you must also *chop* up my Heart into very small pieces, and throw a few of these pieces also into each hole: then put in your lines, and you'll take as many fish as you please, But my bones you must put in a heap, carefully by themselves. Mind! upon your faithful observance of all these commands depends our mutual safety. The North thinks himself sole master, and would wish to crush us because we begin to have a little knowledge: but he shall know me!"

They done accordingly, and accordingly also they took abundance of fish. North perceived this: he came to see, and finding himself thus frustrated inquired how it came about? They told: He challanged Nays. who by this time had revived; and besides a beautiful large feather he had sticking in his cap or head, which none durst wear but such as have given incontestible proofs of their manhood, bravery, &c; he likewise had a smoking bag, of the skin of a badger. Nayhanimis accepted the challenge. "It seems Nayhanimis you are a great man, a man of extraordinary power and abilities! – let us have a trial, and see which of us has the most; for I also have some knowledge."

Nayhanimis answered, "No! I have but little power, but that little I employ as much as I can to the General benefit of my fellows: let us see what you can do, which if I cannot, then you will certainly be superior to me."

Here they performed one or two wonderful feats but in which Nayhanimis had the advantage most confessedly. The North pierced his body through, and done another extraordinary thing I cannot well recollect, but the other done more and recovered not only more suddenly but more perfectly.

At last the North put a bet and said, "Let us see for this last act; I will cut off my head and if I cannot replace and recover perfectly, the same as I am at present, then my *house* and all I have shall be yours: but if I succeed, and you cannot, then all your *possessions* shall be mine."

Nayhanimis consented; for he was secretly desirous of humiliating the self-sufficient spirit of North. They tried – North failed, but Nayhanimis completely succeeded: He deliberately severed his head from his body, put it down on the Ground beside him, very composedly, and then replaced it, when it became as tho' nothing had happened. But this was owing to the power and virtue of his *Plume*, which, however, the others knew nothing off [of]. It appears that the North also recovered but by the assistance of his friends, of whom he had a numerous train. North was faithful to his promise – Gave him his house which was beautiful and spacious, but mostly underground, or at least in the side of a mountain. All his [North's] friends turned out, put in Nayhanimis and gave him the full possession. But he was no sooner in than they secured all the outlets: doors, windows, &c, and set it on fire to destroy one whom they found so much more powerful than themselves!

Nays. finding this to be the case was not in the least dismayed, but took his smoking bag and thus addressed it: "Now *thou* Badger, our mutual safety depends upon thy obedience and expedition. Thou art made to pass *thro'* the Earth as *quick* as *upon* it: those fools think to destroy us, but thou must shew that we are superior to them." During the conflagration they were enjoying the scene and exulting in the idea of having at last succeeded in destroying so formidable an adversary: but what was their consternation when they saw him come to them without even one hair of his head singed! They were *appalled* with astonishment and had not the power of utterance. At last recovering a little, they endeavoured to pass it off as a joke and turn it to his own advantage, by silencing at one blow the envy and malice of his *all* enemies, pretending to be a staunch friend of his. But he was not thus to be duped; yet he shewed a superiority of sentiment, and generosity equal to his Powers and abilities by giving them (tho' contemptuous if you please) pardon. So much for this *Part*.

[2. The Hairy Breasts]

Thus did matters pass on for yet a few years. The indians began to *multiply* and inhabit the world: but the Hairy-breasts, a jealous, envious, and at best, foolish people, could not well behold *their* prosperity: they made *war* upon them (the indians) by stealth and destroyed numbers. Their affairs bore a most dismal aspect – no less than the total extinction of the whole race. At last Nayhanimis pitched off with his wife, *her father*, and another one – there were four of them. He found a Beaver lodge – here some of the Hairy-Breasts came up with him. Compliments at first, afterwards sneers, taunts and revilings; but so ambiguously that no hold could be taken.

"How numerous: how many are there of ye?" enquired the Hairy B.

"We are twenty of us," replied Nayhanimis.

"And so are we," rejoined the others.

Now, they here entered into an arrangement that whoever found *Beaver* for the future it should be his own; but to avoid any wrangles, he who *found* the Beaver should plant a stick or branch upon the lodge, as a mark. On their return home each recounted to his family what he had met with in the course of the day.

"Now," said *Nayhanimis*, addressing his family, "we must take 20 Beavers, one for each man of them (meaning the hairy-breasts) and make a feast. If it turns out that we be able to eat these 20 Beaver, and they not, then we shall be superior to them and have the upper hand." The Beaver were cooked accordingly: he took his *rattler* which he shook to the tunes of his Songs – performed the usual ceremonies, and they eat the whole 20 Beaver with ease. Then addressing his family thus, [he] said, "These Hairy-Breasts are great boasters, but cowards – they are a people of no account – tomorrow will decide all."

The Hairy Breasts on their return did the same as Nayhanimis and cooked also 20 B[eaver] thinking that his band did really consist of that number. They eat: but every one was already full and yet more than 3/4 of the feast remained.

"Give me my rattler" (said one of the oldest) "that I sing &c; it may happen that we find grace." He sang and shook his rattler, but it would not sound. After frequent repeated trials to no effect he became vexed and threw it out of doors among the Dogs.

"This dog of a rattler will not sound in spite of all my endeavours: but hold! hear how it rattles now that it is out – go for it one of ye, perhaps it was owing to some fault in me."

They bro't it to him: but still as before. He threw it out again in a rage; it was no sooner out than it sounded well as before. It was bro't in again: but as before again. Then he threw it out for good, vexed and disappointed to the utmost degree. But his friends were not pleased; they considered this a portentous omen and his behaviour foolish, and by no means calculated to reconcile their *Deities* to them. He comforted them by telling them the numbers of "the adverse party must be few, otherwise we had surely been able to *eat* the whole of this feast: they are few and we *shall* subdue them."

The next day they all pitched off. Nayhanimis came first to a Beaver lodge and marked it – came to another and marked that one also. But making a circuit, in which he hung up his Bow, quiver &c, &c, in a tree, at his own height, [he] came around to the same lodges and found that the Hairy-B. had put marks of their own and thrown his away – exasperated he threw theirs away and replaced his, and made another circuit, when he found the H.B. had replaced their own again: he also remarked that the H.B. had hung up their Bows &c, &c, *in the tops of very hi[gh] trees*, trusting to their numbers.

At last they met – greeted each other at first, then sneers, quarrels, a challenge and then the battle: they were to fight *man to man* – Nayhanimis killed 19 right out, but the 20th had near killed him: however this was but an accident usual in battles – he soon killed him also. The women were coming up when raising his voice to a pitch to be distinctly heard by all, [he] said, "Such of ye *indian* women as have been taken from your homes, had your husbands killed &c, such of ye indian women as are willing to return to your nation, take all axes and other arms out of the hands of those H.B. women; seperate yourselves from them; attack and destroy them *all*: leave not one alive to carry the news to the others."

They seperated accordingly and killed every soul. Then he took them to his tent and finding by their answers to his queries that there were still another band not far off consisting of 40 young and 2 old men of the H.B., he ordered a quantity of poles or pickets to be cut very long and made a kind of Fort of them round his own tent: gave orders to them to gather a vast quantity of snow round all the sides of it, to come over the points, so that neither the pickets nor the tent might be seen, and that his rising might have the appearance of a natural hill, something in short in the form of a pit. He immediately made a number of lances and spears and walked off in quest of his enemies.

He soon reached their camp – drew near and found that there were but 2 old men; all the others were out a hunting. Here he listened to their conversation and was burning with indignation at the stories these two old men told each other of the cruelties they had done to the *Indians* – they were chuckling at this when he sprung into the tent, took each by the head and thrust their faces in the fire, and sprang out again to listen.

One of them returning to his senses, for they had both fainted during the ceremony, exclaimed thus, "my old freind! What is the matter with me? I lost my senses quite suddenly and now that I am come to, I feel my face quite sore and cannot see."

"It is the same with me," replied the other one.

"Then it must be some evil spirit that has pounced upon us," resumed the first.

At last Nayhanimis addressed them thus. "I shall tell ye old men a story too. There were two old men formerly seated in their tent, relating to each other the exploits of their younger days and the cruelties they committed upon the *Indians* – Nayhanimis was near – he pounced upon them and thrust both their heads together into the fire. When your children and young men be returned from their hunting tell them this Story; in the mean time I shall return home and make ready for them – my name is *Nayhanimis* and I reside at *such a place*" (i.e., I am *called* (or named) Nayhanimis &c).

The old men as may be imagined, were Thunder Struck with this and durst not say a word more. But in the Evening the young men came home – they were astonished to see their fathers in such a plight.

"Children! behold your fathers!" said they – "Had any *miscreant* durst act in such a manner to *our* fathers, their villany should certainly not have passed off thus: but *we are now old men and of no more account*!!!"

This last apostrophe above all the rest roused them to vengeance: they merely scraped the snow off their feet and legs and went immediately in quest of him, vowing vengeance all the way of a most cruel and *exemplary* nature. Nayhanimis was on his guard: every soul able to weild a weapon had one in his hand, besides an infinite number of spears and sharp stakes stuck in the Ground. The H.B. came, but not perceiving the trap on account of the snow that was bro't over ends of the stockades they all fell in one upon the other and impaled themselves in their fall on these sticks &c. All of them but 2 or 3 met with instantaneous death – the few that were not injured were put to an excruciating, but immediate death to satisfy the *manes* [Lat., spirits of the dead] of the departed *indians*; and he proceeded immediately to the Camp; killed the remaining 2 old men, scoffing and taunting them at the same time. Immediately after this he ordered such of the *indian* women as had had their husbands killed, or were taken, by the H.B. to seperate from the other women and inflict the same punishment upon them and their children as had been done to their friends.

"Thus were the Hairy Breasts entirely extirpated, merely by their own folly and wickedness. Had they lived peaceably, and allowed the *indians* to partake of the blessings of this world without envy, as well as themselves, and to which they had an undoubted right, they might still have been in existence. However there are still 2 nations of them, one of which is on *Your* lands, the others, I believe, beyond the Seas: but they are an insignificant and most despicable people. They pretend to antiquity and would fain extort respect from the *moderns* (i.e., themselves, or the indians, principally) but their very countenance, appearance, every thing about them denotes folly and seems more to demand contempt then call for respect. I saw one many years back, who was bro't by the Traders from somewheres on your lands: his face was venerable, but still there was a meanness in the *whole* of him that I could not account for: I respected him, and wanted to treat him accordingly – this was from the Stories I had heard related of them; but the Traders laughed at *us* and asked me if I was inclined to respect folly, insignificance, and nothing!!!"

[*Man in his Natural State*]
I have been a long time in writing these Pages and have been frequently disturbed – I have been often obliged to put by my paper after seating myself 5 or 6 times to write only one word: from such long and frequent interruptions *much* method and correctness cannot be expected – I therefore send them to you in the form of *Notes*. My motives for thus employing my time and paper were first to amuse and instruct myself, but

principally for your own amusement and such few friends as you may think *worthy* of the communication. *Lend them not* [out] *of the house*, nor let too many see them; for I have some notion please God I live to digest them into form and regularity and have them published, besides a vast many others I purpose with God's help collecting: but this is merely between ourselves and immediately after perusal blot out all *this* Paragraph. Journals, voyages &c, &c, of these people have been frequently published; but I have met with none that gives so circumstantial a detail of their private life (if I may so say) as is necessary to give that insight to their ideas and notions (and this latter term too, I think, critically speaking cannot be applicable to them) that is required and so much wanted to form a proper estimate of man in his *natural* state. We all see them, hear them and relate of them; but where is there one who can give the *Why's* and *wherefore's* that these people do so, and so? I beg you will *blot* this last paragraph entirely out, at least the first part; and do not be premature in your condemnation or judgement of me, for I trust my motives are entirely destitute of vanity and only the desire of truth urges me, or at least true and just information &c, &c.

G.N.
April 16th, 1823

[Skepticism, Belief, and Innovation]
Such are the notions and ideas of these people. They acknowledge a Superior Power, not Wee-suck-a-jock, as I was erroneously informed, "but the same *one* you adore in the Christmas holidays." This one they have a great respect and veneration for but seldom it is (as far as I can learn) that they sacrifice or pray to him, i.e., make speeches, which tho' extempore *I* consider as much prayers as tho' they are composed after the most deliberate and mature reflection; and many parts of them so simple, plain, natural, and withal so sublime that I frequently felt great pleasure in attending to them. But these sentiments are so few comparitively speaking, and the absurdities so great and frequent that few men can hear them without lamenting their ignorance. They have often seemed to me as desirous in a hi[gh] degree of becoming acquainted with the true *mode* of worshipping, from the frequent changes, even during my time, they have made in their *worshippings*. As a proof of this is the avidity with which they

seize any new system introduced from their *Southern* neighbors: the short time they hold it; and how completely it is abandoned, if not entirely forgotten for another, equally if not more absurd than the former. To introduce a new system among them it is only necessary to report an extravagant tale of some wonderful character – the cures by *this* means that have been performed and such like miraculous and fantastic nonsense. But in their fundamental points I perceive no visible alteration.

The principal of these is what they call the Mee-tay-wee [Cree and Ojibwa *mitēwi-* 'Midewiwin', an esoteric religious order]. A ceremony I shall compare to Free-masonry; but the initiations are public – every one that chuses comes to see them and many are invited. Here, in the course of initiation are ceremonies or deviltries performed that no man of his own mere dexterity or Power *can* do.

The next principal one is conjuring. This is a principle I beleive as natural to man as the air he breathes (tho' not *so* necessary). Every one wishes to peep into futurity and there are few but who would not inquire into causes could they do it, or were it not forbidden them. These two of course are consequences or consequents of their mythology. There are many in the civilized or Christian world who absolutely and positively deny this power of theirs as being absolutely impossible and at best but absurd and idle stories. Many of the things related of these Conjurings I acknowledge to be so; but at the same time I am as positive and as firmly persuaded of the truth of the assertion "that they have dealings with some super-natural spirit," as I am convinced that I live and breathe in air; unless, indeed, we chuse to acknowledge and believe a certain sect of Philosophers (of the last century I believe) who *wish* to tell us that we *only imagine ourselves alive.* And I am by no means inclined to acknowledge myself as superstitious: I am convinced of this from reason, argument, comparison; in short from *analysis.* Let any one man, unless he be a headstrong brute who is *determined* before hand not to be convinced, analyse their *discourses* &c, &c, and I am confident he will beleive as much as many, or have great doubts at least. To absolutely deny this, we must first deny that there is a Devil, and afterwards deny his pernicious power and if we deny these points, we must descend to a third, more fit for an atheistical wretch and a beast than a Christian, or even rational creature. I have heard some sensible and well inform'd Gentlemen deny it on the plea of their *ignorance*; but this again is a *basis* and a very solid one.

These people are still in a complete state of nature: their ideas of the true God are far from clear or correct: they acknowledge him indeed as the Supreme and absolute Master of all, but more or rather as a passive *Deity* than as he really is: but their notions of their other Deities come far more near the truth. Their wants indeed are also few, but they are arbitrary and cannot be dispensed with, at least for any time; it is therefore very natural that they should employ their whole thoughts and most of their time in procuring means to warding off or averting their dangers. And I do not know of any method more adapted to this than the one they pursue, i.e. – Fasting and Sleeping to dream; and they do dream too; and many of these dreams are so complicated, or compounded of so many different things that it is absolutely beyond the power of *their* invention to fabricate them. Surely a man may beleive his senses. A man tied, wound up in a blanket, or Skin equally soft: here he is held by one, two, or 3 men – he slips out of the blanket and presents himself before you free, leaving the cords &c *untied* in the blanket: you hear him Speak, and perhaps 20 other voices besides, all at the same: again he is bound as a criminal, rather indeed as a Pig, crumpled into a heap and thrust in to his *hut*; at the very instant of his entrance the hut shakes as if ten thousand devils were for pulling it to pieces: you enter this, find the man absent, hear a fluttering about your ears, or see a vast number of small lights resting on the hoops that hold the poles together: immediately after you are out you hear the man speak within again; you look again and feel for him, but hear him talking at a distance, what can this be but supernatural agency? I have never seen feats of *this* kind, but others I have, not so *strong*, but equally convincing.

[*Conjuring for a North West Company Gentleman*]
I have been informed that a young half-breed, abandoned with the *indians* almost from his childhood, a few years back entered one of these conjuring *huts* at the solicitation of one of the N.W. Gentlemen to see what retarded the people so long. Previous to his entering a great deal of conversation on the subject had been: matters were settled between them and the conjuror. Some time after his entrance he began to cry (not weep) as a person uneasy; at first the voice was within, but it appeared as rising in the air, and at last was lost.

"Well!" said one of the indians addressing one of the half-breeds, living with the white. "Well! Enter now, and see if he be there: thou art always doubting and denying what we say of these things: enter then and see, if he be there, then indeed are our assertions false."

He raised the bottom of the *casement* and entered, but as he was not below, he rose on his feet and felt for him, but [the conjuror was] not to be found. However he was *paid* for his curiosity: there was a dreadful fluttering within, but especially about his head, his hair flying about in his face as if in a tempest and frequent appearances of small lights before his eyes which ever way he turned: he bawled out and asked those without what was the matter with him: he became afraid and walk'd out as quick as he could. Very shortly after they heard the same cries of pain, faintly, at first, but the voice soon entered. The *Conjuror* said he was carried to where the people were; "they are all asleep at such a place and tomorrow will be here" &c. He said there were 4 (spirits) of them that carried him off: each held him by the *little finger* and *little toe*!

[*The Lost Traveller and the Wolf Spirit*]

I shall here relate a couple more of these stories. An indian told me that several years back he left his lodge on the borders of a large Lake to go to the house [fur trade post] for some necessaries he wanted. He took a traverse for some islands – the weather was dull but mild: a storm very soon set in but he persevered: thinking the wind had changed, he also changed his course. He became very much fatigued and laid down on the ice to rest himself and wait for day light, for *the* night had overtaken him. He was not long down before reflecting on his situation he became extremely uneasy and was afraid of freezing. At last he heard a curious noise near him that he could not account for: at first his fears increased greatly dreading it was some malignant spirit; but having no alternative he resigned himself to his fate, "and I became as composed as tho' I were safe; and I was too: for an animal, much resembling a Wolf and black, came up and covered me; I was very cold, shivering in every limb, but I soon became quite warm: he rose from off me and went on as if inviting me to follow – his eyes appeared like 2 candles. I followed – he led me to an island where I made a fire and warmed and dried myself; and as soon as I was rigged I followed him, for he went off and looked at me so earnestly I took it for an order: he led me straight to the water hole: there happened to be people at the time there going for water – they saw *these* lights and asked me what occasioned them, or who it was that came with me – I told them it was a compassionate spirit that retrieved me from a dreadful death."

[*Pursuit by a Pah-kack*]

2nd! A young man lately told me the following: "I was returning home with my uncle when come to *that* point we heard something crying behind us, he! he! ha! ha! and whistling alternately. My uncle told me it was a Pah-Kack (Skeleton) and wanted to destroy us. It came up with us very soon and kept constantly buzzing and whistling in our ears so that indeed we were quite bewildered at last: it was at night and dark, but we kept strait on as we thought; we were mistaken, for after walking a long time, we at last came to the water hole again from where we had set off. We were both much afraid; but finding this path we minded it no more tho' it pursued us making more and more noise the nearer we got *home*."

Many of these stories bear a great resemblance to those extravagant tales of la Bête a la Grande Queue, Loup Garoup [werewolf], Chasse Galerie, and many others natural to superstitious people; it requires therefore a great deal of caution and attention to get at the true ones.* I have here *inserted* more than I originally intended, but they will serve to give you an idea of the notions of these people; and except a few, I have selected those that appeared most rational: *however, they will all come in time.*

[*The Windigo*]

There is a kind of disease (or distemper rather, and of the *mind* I am fully persuaded) peculiar to the Crees and Sauteux's, and of which they have the greatest dread and horor; and certainly not without the very great[est] cause, the consequences 49 times out of 50 being death unfortunately to many besides the *subjects* or objects, themselves. They term *this* Win-di-go (according to the french pronunciation, which is more correct than the English, in this word) – the proper signification of which, to me at least,

---

*This is an interesting point; Nelson seemingly recognized that the extended presence of Canadian traders in the Indian country (and his own partial use of "halfbreed" informants?) could complicate his sorting out of Indian and European folk traditions. On Chasse Galerie, see *The Canadian Encyclopedia*, vol. 1, p. 320 (Edmonton: Hurtig, 1985), entry by Nancy Schmitz.

and no one I think can doubt it, is *Giant*, of the anthropophagi *Genus*, sect, tribe, or kind &c. The stories related of these are as extravagant and fantastic as those we read in our old romances *in the days of Chivalry*; differing in no one circumstance hardly but the means used in their destruction, which of course is often done by the intervention or assistance of their Guardian Genii. However, there are some few more rational than those of *ours* and tho' still beyond all bounds of credibility, are as devoutly believed by these poor creatures as the Gospel is by the most orthodox among us. I do not remember any of these sufficiently correctly to give you a few of the stories, one excepted.

Suffice it to say that they are of uncommon size – Goliath is an unborn infant to them; and to add to their *dread*, they are represented as possessing much of the Power of Magicians. Their head reaching to the tops of the highest *Poplars* (about 70, or 80, feet) they are of proportionate *size*, of course they must be very heavy: their gait tho' grand and majestic, at every step the Earth shakes. They frequently pursue their Prey (*indians* of course) invisibly, yet they cannot so completely divest themselves of all the incommodities of nature as to prevent their approach being known. A secret and unaccountable horor pervades the whole system of one, several, or the whole band, of those of whom he is in pursuit: Phenomena in the heavens, earth &c, &c.

[*Baiting a Windigo*]

In the days of Noah (or near them, at least) there were a large party of *indians* collected together for mutual safety: many camps had been already destroyed by him, and the indians were in great danger [of] being entirely exterminated. At last they bethought themselves of a plan. "It is needless to go to war upon him – what can we do to him with our arms! Let us make an immense Large trap (of wood) and draw lots which of us shall serve as a bait: it is a dangerous essay indeed, but will any generous one amongst us refuse sacrificing his life for the safety of so many?" They made this trap on the opposite side of a small opening in the woods, so that he might see the person seated from afar: it was between large trees which were made to serve as *Posts*. It was finished.

An old woman stepped up and said, "My Grand children! I am now old and of no more account among ye: we are all in danger of being devoured by this insatiable and terrible beast, why should I then regret sacrificing a life that at best I can now enjoy but only for a short time, seeing it will in the end be productive of so much good? *I will go and be bait.*"

The others were extremely touched at her generosity, but they had no alternative, and circumstances admitted of no delay. The old lady seated herself very composedly in the trap and awaited his arrival: the others fled off of course. It was time too, for he soon *hove* in sight! Stalking along in all the stile and terror of Imperial Gra[n]deur, his head equal with the tops of the highest trees, and the ground shaking at every step, tho' froze, it being then depth of winter, and his countenance denoting an assemblage of pity, contempt, rage and voraciousness. All this did not dismay the old Lady: she remained quiet: he perceived her.

"What! What, old woman, art thou doing there?" But changing his tone, which he did several times, thus continued: "Thou art of my natural enemies and I shall presently Grind thee."

"Ah! my Grand Child! I am an old woman, abandoned and deserted by those whom I have suckled and bro't up: they are fled off in dread of thee, and being old and helpless they thrust me in this tuft of trees so as to be the less embarrassed: come now and assist me out and in acknowledgement I shall inform thee of their precautions, otherwise thou'lt lose thy life by their deceptions."

He was in no dread of the *indians*, so far as regarded their *own* Power, but he thought a little salutary advice would not be amiss, intending after this to *Grind* the old *thing* as he had promised himself. He drew up: "what a devil of a place they have put thee indeed – did they think to conceal thee from me?"

He stooped to enter, when she found he had entered far enough she touched a stick and down came all the weights and cross bar upon his back. Tho' he was uncommonly strong the weight, and suddenness of the blow was such that he gave way and was jam[m]ed between the two beams or bars – here he struggled denouncing vengeance and eternal destruction to the whole of the *human* race. The great bellowing he made was a signal to the men who were in ambush not far off: they came running up and soon dispatched him with a multitude of blows from axes and Chissels &c, &c. Thus were they for *one time* releived: the women and children returned to the camp and enjoyed themselves as usual without further apprehensions.

[*Sources and Forms of Windigo*]

These Giants as far as I can learn reside somewhere about the *North Pole*; and even at this day frequently pay their unwelcome visits, but which, however, are attended with a complete fright only. It seems also that they delegate their Power to the indians occasionally; and *this* occasions that cannibalism which is Produced, or proceeds rather from a sort of distemper much resembling *maniaism*.

There are 3 sorts or Kinds that I know of, and I beleive there are no more. The first I have already related as above, and the 2 I am going to give you are sometimes *compounded* together and sometimes *independent*; but they are both equally true and melancholy and distressing in whatever light we may view them: However, I shall not pretend by any means to palm *all* that is said about them upon you as true – of this you'll by and bye be able to judge as well as myself and not doubt.

The first of these are such as are driven to this dreadful extremity by starvation. In all *woody* countries where the inhabitants lead a wandering, roving life, and whose subsistence depend upon the Game they procure, they must of necessity be frequently pinched, and sometimes bro't very low. All *People* cannot bear this privation alike and tho' there is perhaps not a people in this world who take this so patiently as these people do, yet there are not wanting instances where even with them that *nature* gives-way and they vanish as a *dying* candle; but others cannot stand it out so long: they must have something to eat, be it what it may: sometimes, tho' with the most extreme reluctance at first, they feed upon the flesh of such as *have died*. Any kind of animal substance at such times, must come very grateful to the Stomack; and hence it is I believe that those who have once preyed upon their fellows, ever after feel a great desire for the same nourishment, and are not so scrupulous about the means of procuring it.

I have seen several that had been reduced [to] this disturbing alternative, and tho' many years after, there appeared to me a wildness in their eyes, a confusion in their countenances much resembling that of reprieved murderers.....Now if we consider how very precarious their mode of subsistance is, how devoted they are to superstition and prejudice, we, i.e., such of *us* as know more about them, we, I say, may wonder how they stand out so well: very many instances I have known seem to be far beyond the power of human nature to stand. Yet notwithstanding this dreadful privation lasts not for a few days, but even to weeks and months, during all which time the men are out from star-light to star-light and have ~~seldom~~ never anything more to *eat* than some bits of leather, moss, bark and such like, it is very rare they will kill a *fellow* to live upon him. This is not universal, there are unfortunately still too many exceptions; but these again would seem as denunciations from their Gods – they appear so to me – I can scarcely doubt it! and the indians themselves seem to them the same tho' in another way.

At this place where I am now writing (Lac La Ronge, English River) but a few years back several instances occurred. An old Canadian is said to have lost one of his Sons thus, tho' an excellent hunter: The old man sometimes speakes to me of that son: and the second died on his way to the house, and not far off. The same year an indian killed all his family but 2 daughters whom he compelled to partake with him, and for the rest of the route he.....

I shall here give you a few stories of the kind. "*That* same year" (I do not know precisely when but only a few years back) "a woman alone arrived at the house. Her appearance was haggard, wild, and distressed: However she was taken into *the* house – questions put as usual, but the answers, vague, indefinite and contradictory: they handed her something to eat – she acted as if eating indeed, but let the whole fall in the *inside* of her gown: this rose [roused] suspicion. But what added to this was the extraordinary stench she emitted from the heat of the chimney; and shortly after her entrance, a part of a human shoulder the Dogs bro't in from upon her road. She went off – being directed upon a road leading to a camp not far off. As soon as she made her appearance the indians immediately conceived what was to matter; but thro' charity as well as for safety and to find the truth they gave her to eat, principally marrow-fat." Now these people pretend that cannibals cannot bear this fat or grease, or course it was a kind of *ordeal*.

"Every thing she did and said, notwithstanding her great caution, betrayed her. She took up some of the children of her acquaintances to kiss as is customary but would have given it a bite had they not taken it from her. They watched her narrowly. All the men slept in one hut with her: she pretended to be asleep till she imagined the others were, then rose very cautiously and was beginning to prepare herself for *action* – one of the men perceived this – rose upon her with an axe; even tho' the blow was violent and upon the head she would have killed him had not the others interfered: her wretched fate was soon decided."

There is such a singular, strange, incomprehensible contradictoriness in almost all these cases, and many I have heard, that I do most verily believe they are denunciations, witch or wizardisms: in any other manner they are not rationally to be accounted for, unless we suppose all those who feed on human flesh to be thus possest – then it is natural to man in those cases; but why then not the same with us as with these people?

[*Windigo Dreams*]

The 3d Kind, or delegated, which by what follows, I believe may be allowed to be the term, are those who dream of the North, or the Ice, or both. Every one knows where the North resides, but only few know the abode of Ice, or the Ice. This they pretend is the Parent of Ice, is in the bowels of the Earth, at a great depth and never thaws – all ice originates from this. These 2 they are much afraid of, because they are both highly malignant spirits: there is no joking or jesting with them. Those who at *any* future period are to become cannibals thus dream of them.

After the certain things usual in all dreams, "I was invited by the North to partake of a feast of ducks, the most beautiful I had ever seen and well cooked – the dish was before me, I set *too*: a stranger by me touched me with his elbow and said, 'Eat not thou of that; look into thy dish'; behold that which I had taken for the wing of a duck was the arm of a child!

" 'He! what a narrow escape!' said I.

"Then he took me into another room and gave me most excellent meat, the most delicious in appearance I had ever seen. I would not eat – I discovered it was the flesh of *indians* thus served up to me! He took me into a 3d room and gave me Tongues: these I also perceived were the Tongues of *indians*.

" 'Why refusest thou what I offer thee? is it not good?'

" 'I feel no inclination to eat,' I replied.

"Then he took me in a fourth room where fine beautiful *hearts* were served up, and I was desired to eat, but I perceived that it was still the same. I therefore refused.

" 'Then,' said he, 'it is well done – thou hast done well.'

"Heh! Had I unfortunately eaten of this then had I become a cannibal in addition to all my other misfortunes!"

Those who eat at these feasts are frequently, but not universally, told thus: "This is a sign to Thee that thou shalt one day become a cannibal and feed on the flesh of thy fellows – when thou shalt see children play with, and eat, ice (or snow) *in* thy Tent say, 'my time is near'; for then thou shalt soon eat *indian* (human) flesh."

They have such a dread and horor of this that it is constantly in their minds. "You white people! who live at your ease, get your living out of your Nets or from your indians, and besides are not otherwise troubled as we, make light of these Things: I do not make much account of them either, but I tell you that he who thus once dreams of either of these Dys [Deities?] are for ever after continually troubled with them. We do every thing in our Power to drive him away from us, but still he hovers about us and we cannot avoid him. You are very fortunate – you live as you please, never care for him nor does he molest you."

Such I am told are the sentiments of these people in General. I look upon this as a sort of mania, or fever, a distemper of the brain. Their eyes (for I have seen [people who are] thus perplex'd) are wild and uncommonly clear – they seem as if they glistened. It seems to me to lodge in the Head. They are generally rational except at short, sudden intervals when the paroxysms cease [seize] them: their motions then are various and diametrically contrary at one time to what they are the next – Sullen, thoughtful, wild look and perfectly mute: staring, in sudden convulsions, wild incoherent and extravagant language.

[*Windigo Possession, Lake Winnipeg*]

There was one a few years back [ca. 1812–13] infected with this not far from where I was at the time: the accounts given of him, tho' I shall not vouch for their truth are thus. One night towards the latter end of December he began staring at his daughter with an extraordinary intenseness: "My daughter! I am fond of thee! I love thee extremely."

"I know thou dost," replied the woman abashed, for she was then very young.

"Yes! I love thee – I think I could eat a piece of thee, I love thee so much."

The Girl exclaimed at his rashness – there were but 3 of them, the father, daughter and her husband. When it was dark he put himself stark-naked and uttering a strong tremulous noise, and his teeth chattering in his head as if thro' cold, rose up and walked out of the Tent and laid himself curled as a dog in a heap upon the wood that his daughter had that day bro't to the door. Here he remained all night in spite of what they could do. A little before day he returned. Thus did he every night for about a month and every time slept out naked; nor would he eat, excepting at times a little raw flesh. In the day time he was more composed, but his face &c, bore the appearance of one possessed of the Devil. He recovered and became as usual, composed, and good natured – I knew them all well, but had no dealings with them from the year before (1812).

[*A Windigo Execution*]

A young Indian a few years back had *one* of the above dreams. He became very uneasy and thoughtful finding it recur so very frequently: and he would have willing[ly] undergone any torments, any death rather than become an anthropophagi: he also frequently desired his friends upon any, the least appearance of these symptoms in him to kill him. "For if you do not kill me till I have eaten of *human* flesh, you'll perhaps not be able to do it afterwards: but my Children! oh! my children! How grieved am I to leave ye! But it must be so – I have no alternative. Spare me not, my friends, I conjure you!"

He had been a good hunter and a peaceable *indian*, and of course much loved by his friends: this business depressed them a great deal. At last the time approaching fast his brother one day remained behind with him to watch him, whilst the others pitched off: about the time this one thought the others had finished the encampment he proposed their setting off to join them. But before long he left his brother behind and laid an ambush for him not far from the Tent. This was a preconceived scheme; the other men of course were not far off. The sick one drew near, in a very slow and thoughtful manner: however when he came near to where his brother was hid, he stopped, looked up and called out, "Thou thinkest thyself well hid from me my brother; but I see thee: it is well thou undertakest, it had been better for thee however hadst thou began sooner. Remember what I told you all – it is my *heart*; my *heart*, that is *terrible*, and however you may injure my body if you do not completely annihilate my *heart* nothing is done."

The brother was sure that he was not discovered, this *knowledge* being the information of some of the spirits: he therefore did not answer. Some of the other men had gone to meet him and endeavoured to amuse him that the brother might give the first blow: accordingly he shot, straight for the heart – he dropped, but rose immediately, and continued towards the camp that was within sight laughing at their undertaking. "The Ball went through and through, but not a drop of blood was seen – *his heart was already formed into Ice.*" Here they seized and bound him and with ice chissels and axes set to work to dispatch him. According to his desire they had collected a large pile of dry wood, and laid him upon it. The body was soon consumed, but the heart remained perfect and entire: it rolled several times off the Pile – they replaced it as often: fear ceased [seized] them – then with their (Ice) chissels they cut and hacked it into small bits, but yet with difficulty was it consumed!!!

[*Windigo Cures and Precautions*]

They fancy that the blood which circulates thro' the heart first forms into water, then coagulates or congeals, and shortly after becomes into solid and imperforable or impenetrable ice. The only antidote or remedy for this, is to give them large draughts of high-wines; double distilled spirits, or the spirits of wine, if any can be had the better: this taken in large draughts and frequently, and *kept* beside a large fire, flows to the heart and thaws the ice: if a profuse sweat ensues it is a happy omen. An indian with me this winter gave out his apprehensions that he was thus tormented – I communicated it to 2 others who happened to come in about that time.

"Why do you not give him large draughts of your strongest spirits to drink and keep him in the room beside a large fire."

I replied that I was afraid it would burn him.

"Oh! no – if he is a real Windigo it will only do him good by driving out the ice; but if he *lies* to you indeed, then it certainly will injure him, but it will be good for him, and teach him for the future not to impose upon people to frighten them!"

However, they are in general kind and extremely indulgent to those thus infected: they seem to consider it as an infliction [affliction?] and are desirous of doing all they can to assist. There are however many exceptions: but these again depend upon the circumstances &c attending them. One of my best hunters here is thus tormented, or at least thus torments himself; and very often desires his friends in compassion to put a period to existence the first symptoms he may shew of cannibalism. A young

Girl lately married, and scarcely worth a *Filip*, so small and diminutive, was this winter seized with this phrenzy – the consequence was that the men durst not leave the tent for any length of time, being obliged to assist the women in holding and preventing her from biting or eating any of the children, and perhaps herself. They bethought of a sacrifice, i.e., cropping her hair Short – she recovered and is now well. She says, "I do not recollect any single one circumstance of all that it told me – I thought I was always on the tops of the Trees."

There is another one of my indians thus affected too. The indians say it is a punishment (from some of their *familiars* of course) for so lightly esteeming their ceremonies: nay indeed and ridiculing them often. This fall he began: there were but 2 men of them together (with each his family) – things bore a most dismal aspect; at last the wife of the other, who by-the-bye is said to [be] a little affected that way too, told him one day that he sprang forward to seize one of *his own* children, to "Keep quiet, for thou dog if a Gun hath no effect on thee, my axe shall – I shall chop thee up into slices: thou hadst then better be quiet." This kept him indeed quiet for some time: how they are now I cannot say, not having heard of them from the beginning of Dec[embe]r (now April 20th).

They appear most inclined to prey *first* upon their own family: and they also think that fire arms are absolutely unable to injure them – "a ball cannot injure *Ice*: to destroy *Ice*, it must be *chopped up*: and the *heart then is all Ice*." They sometimes, indeed frequently, recover with the warm weather, "for the sun then *animates* all nature"!!! There are many other instances of a like kind in their tendency or consequences, but different in their proceedings that I cannot bring to mind at present: I mention several of these to shew you the different manner they are infected – in the mean time I shall relate to you others not less entertaining.

[*Malignant Spirits*]

There are several Spirits of whom these people are much afraid, but four principally, they being the most malignant and little accepting of *excuses* however great and urgent they may be for the non performance of *their* sacrifices. These are the *North, Ice, Skeletons*, and the *Crazy Woman*, or foolish, mad, jealous woman.

"Not very many years ago an indian had entered his conjuring *hut*. She came among the rest; but being displeased with the conjuror on account of some sacrifice to other spirits, she seized and carried him off! Skeleton perceived it, and being [fond] of the conjuror pursued Jealousy: finding herself nearly overtaken, she prefer[r]ed her own safety to vengeance and let the *indian* fall *in some place* at a vast distance from where he had been taken. Skeleton took him up and bro't him back to the great satisfaction of all parties!" She frequently comes with the *others* when *they* conjure, but on her appearance she is desired to be quiet, "*Pay-ah-tick*" [Cree *pēyahtik*], i.e., gently, quietly, peaceably &c.

Master Skeleton also is as much dreaded as Folly, if not more, because he shews himself at any time he pleases, it not being necessary to conjure to call him to.

There *is* an indian who before he married, had his *Dress Shoes* made by this Lady (Folly, or Jealousy) – she was of course extremely fond of him – "The shoes were beautifully garnished, far superior to anything of the kind done by *our* women!" There are not wanting Ladies living with the white who confer a full share of their *favors* on some of the indians; and from one of these I fancy it is he got these shoes; but to hide the business imputed them to Folly, which served him a double end. If I can see that Chap I shall be very particular in my enquiries at him – I know him well. This brings to my mind the *White Stag* or Hind, Sertorius had in his exile and during his wars with his country as mentioned by Plutarch [a white fawn, said to communicate to him the advice of the goddess Diana].

[*Affinities and Origins*]

Indeed – to be candid, *I* find a very great affinity between the ideas and notions of these people and those of the Greeks and Romans &c, &c, and by these much, far much better than by the incongruous hypothesis of the learned might be traced the *origin* of these people; and I am far from taking the task to be difficult: would *we* only divest ourselves of *our own* prejudices and take the proper plan, this great *Enigma*, if I may so explain myself, would not be perfectly cleared I allow, but a rational clew afforded to the unravelling of it. I have read many of these hypotheses but they are so filled with inconsistencies that I could scarcely believe man could employ so much time in them.....I could say something else instead of the conclusion of this last sentence. A Gentleman, and an Englishman too, but I forget his name, would wish to *insinuate* that these people are from a different origin with ourselves, i.e., Adam; and to prove his hypothesis he begins by anatomising hogs! (see the Encyclopaedia, not by Rees, but *Fitz-Patrick* I believe).* This puts me in mind of some of the *Newtonian Systems*, i.e., there is no such thing in nature as *Cold* – we must say *an absence of Heart*! [heat]. Why cannot we as well say there is no such thing as *darkness*, but merely an absence *of light*, or reverse either, and either will be as reasonable – most strange reasoning is this indeed!

[*Deviance, Confession, and Expiation*]

Confession. These People have a notion that *confession* saves them from many accidents and also preserves the lives of the Sick, or rather restores them to their wonted health &c. I have not learned the origin of this; when, why, or wherefore, but it seems to be very remote, to have sprang with their mythology. I shall it make a point to enquire very particularly into this: and for this, as well as other things, at different quarters, to find and detect errors &c. But all, however, that I have written in these pages, tho' there may be some difference in the recital and perhaps a *few* strag[g]-ling circumstances, are, I have great reason to think, fundamentally the same throughout among these people.....

When any one of them is particularly affected with diseases out of the common course of nature *here*, or, tho' the disease may be precisely the same as all others, yet from certain circumstances individually, or a combination of them, they say he is Oh-gee-nay [ohcinēw] in Cree, or On-gee-nay [ončinē], in Sauteux (the On- pronounced as in french and *not* English), by which it would seem as if they meant he was afflicted or chastised for his own sins, or those of some of his or her near relatives, i.e., father, mother &c, if children: if grown up and married persons, for their own. Whether they only imagine this, or are informed of it by conjuring, *private* information from their *Familiars*, or from the Symptoms of the Sick person &c, &c, I cannot say, but the thus afflicted person must confess his Sins publickly.

Now in these confessions as in all their other discourses or conversations

---

*Fitzpatrick's encyclopedia has not been identified, but that of Rees was quite possibly in the Nelson family home in Sorel or in a fur trade post library. In 1778–88, in London, Abraham Rees published an enlarged, revised edition of Ephraim Chambers's 1728 *Cyclopaedia* (Lyons 1878, 196).

(*initiating* and *giving of medicines, excepted*) they use no circumlocution, no secret or enigmatical word or term, to screen themselves; but all is delivered in plain terms and before every one that chuses to hear. These confessions are terrible things; and they seem far more sincere and complete than those of many catholics. They have wonderful retentive memories and no scene, no crime from their earliest years unto that day do they hide. But Great God! what abominations! – one would scarcely imagine the human mind capable of inventing such infamously diabolical actions as *some* do commit: murder, incest, and other things if possible an hundred fold more debasing the human soul. Whether they repent of these things neither can I say, but it would appear as if they were the acts of a contrite and most humbly penitent Soul. I have never had an opportunity of hearing these from *their own mouths*, but *other* indians have told me of them, and tho' before their families *sometimes*, have never omitted one single circumstance from the suggestion of the idea down to the very last *conclusion*.

When I heard of these things at first I *would not* believe them; but hearing them come so circumstantially *I trembled for the Land I sojourned in* "lest it should vomit me out as the land of Caanan did its inhabitants" or be swallowed up in its destruction as Sodom and Gomorrah! It is true they are not *all* so; no, I am told there are but few, and in charity I hope it is; otherwise what will be my fate seeing I am in a certain degree partaker with them! Surely the inhabitants of such a land, at *best*, cannot look for more than mere *present enjoyment*. When I reflect seriously on *all* these things as I sometimes do, revolving them in every different manner in my mind it is beyond the power of words to express my feelings. Poor unfortunate blind Creatures! That it is from *Blindness* they commit these things, I am fully persuaded, because I am equally confident that they do not attach that same degree of criminality to them we, *from the revealing of the Scriptures to us*, do: some, they consider in the light of trifles; some natural, some weaknesses: but all tend to the gratification of most Bestial appetites, whatever may have been the original cause, *curiosity*, or otherwise.

However, I received a piece of information in one of these, and *it* was circumstantially detailed, that has cleared a point to me I could never solve; and tho' I enquired of both Wool and Bob [brothers Wolfred and Robert Nelson], they were not wiser than myself. Indeed, without the *trial* or experiment, it seems impossible to say certainly where the cause lies: now I know it, if ever an opportunity offers, or that it pleases God I again revisit my own lands I shall be able to speak to a certainty. As I cannot write Latin, I shall say no more of *it* at present.

A few years back an indian at the next Post above *this* died: he had been a long time sick, and from this conceived himself *ongenay* and accordingly prepared for his Confession. Having received the details at 2 and 3d hand I shall endeavour to give *part* of them to you as near *their* Stile as I can; but really I find myself *very inadequate* to the task: there is a certain *Poetic* Sublimity in their language on such *like* occasions as will not easily meet with credit from those (the better informed) of the civilized world unacquainted with these people. Even amongst ourselves there are but few; for few can judge of the beauties of a language and most of these few have too hi[gh] a notion of their own mighty superiority to stoop to *regular* conversation with them.

But to return: after having revealed all, or most part of his Sins to the company in general he thus addressed his family in particular – "you see my Children my distressed state: I cannot move nor stir without assistance, and feel strengthened in my lungs (breast, heart) merely as it were by Permission of my Dreamed" (some particular one he meant) "to divulge my offences to the Gods (or God) publicly, before you all, to deter you from the same vices (wickednesses). I was once a young man also, the same as you are now, healthy and vigorous; nothing appeared difficult nor dangerous to me – I lived as became a man, and prospered accordingly; but I thought that this proceeded from my own Power only: had I so continued, all had been well! But no, I *unfortunately* heard speak of Such indians" (meaning *this* place [Lac la Ronge], *as my informants tell me*), "how powerful they were in their medicines, the extraordinary feats they performed. I envied them, and thought that I required but *that* knowledge more to render me perfect (immortal) and happy: I undertook a voyage to that place: I found that the bare truth had been scarcely told me – I burned with anxiety to becoming as knowing as themselves and I was gratified. Had I rested here, all had yet been well; but in learning their medecines I also learned of them those vices, those sins, that by *their practice* have reduced me to this wretched situation.

"My sons! Take example from your father! Be good, charitable, and peaceable indians as I was at the first set off of my life, and employ the same means, indulge use the same anxiety to *avoid*, that I did to *procure*, that information that hath reduced me so far below the level even of a dog. Never forget this, never indulge even the least desire of such acquisitions; for if you once begin you will be deluded by their flattery to that destruction I have found. But ye are young men! And unless you find grace you also will be deluded and lost as I am!"

I have heard a good deal said of *this* indian's confession and exhortations to his Sons – they were not lost. He himself lived but a short time and seemed much comforted by *it*.

There is a tribe of *Athabasca* that go by the name of *Beaver Indians*. From the tenets of their religion *I am told* that when laying under any malediction, bewitchisms, &c, or conceive themselves so; they make a vow that the first animal they shall kill they will *do So* – they do not fail, but immediately proceed in quest of another which by this diabolical action they think they will soon find and kill. They do not *touch* the animal afterwards as those Beasts among the Crees and Sauteux do, but leave it lay as a sacrifice: they consider it as a duty imposed upon them; but the others do it from mere beastiality. "Such a one did so, bro't home part of the meat, and we all of us eat it – Oh! the Dog!" said an indian not long ago to me.

Lest I may not soon have another opportunity of writing on these Subjects to *you* I shall add a few more *fragments*. An indian here, passing for a great Doctor, was applied to (and still is) by many to attend upon them. "Several of these he retrieved from death: One of his dreamed (I believe the North) was not pleased and told the Doctor 'never to administer his medecines to those he had doomed to death!' The Dr replied it was hard and uncharitable seeing he could prolong their days a little. 'Well! for every one that thou dost thus deprive me of I shall take one of thy children': and the Dr lost 8 or 9 (I cannot now remember well); but he is now grown more cautious." But this Dr is himself a beast. "Being unable to stand from sickness he told 2 of his wives, 'Take ye me one under each arm to my sweat [sweet]-heart – I feel myself dying and don't chuse *thus* to go': and he actually did." Remember, I *am told this*; but I have reasons to believe it. He is an incestuous beast; otherwise I find him a good indian and what is most strange, sensible beyond many of his equals.

I have got a caracature here of the Devil carrying off a Taylor. I asked one of my indians if any of their familiars resembled him and how they were – the reply was, "Yes, he resides in the North (at the Pole I suppose) and has a vast number of young men: the indians report of some finding their tracks that are very numerous and exactly resemble the tracks of the Grey Deer (carriboeuf): but neither him nor his young men are very wicked. North, Ice, Skeleton, and Folly are the most wicked and ill inclined of all those we dream of, or [who] enter the conjuring box!"

[*Feasts*]

Of their Feasts, I cannot say more than any common observer – I have been invited and Partaken of many of them, but I never thought of enquiring into their origin, the causes &c, of them. But from the little I could learn or rather understand from the speeches made at *all* of them, and what I have learnt in regard to other things, I think [I] may say without dreading contradiction, that as there are songs, ceremonies &c appropriate to every one of their Gods or Familiars or Devils, there [are] also *feasts* made for each according to the whim, dream, or some other circumstance of the one who makes them. We denominate these Feasts, and from their own Term it would seem they so mean; but I consider this again as a premature interpretation which I have not leisure to explain: I consider them rather as *sacrifices* – indeed they may perhaps rather be esteemed as partaking of both. I have somewhere above said that they are *obliged* to make an annual sacrifice to some of their Gods as the non-performance passes off not with impunity – those therefore are obligatory, or compulsory sacrifices; but besides these they also have Free-will sacrifices.

These Feasts or sacrifices are not *universally* of *Flesh*: they have them of Flesh, Grease, dried berries, rum, &c, &c, and few of these Feasts are made without *the one who makes it* offers a certain (very small, only a few mouthsful) to *him* whom it is in honor of, or intended for, which he most commonly puts into the fire, *in*, or on, the Ground. Some of them are very grand and ceremoni[o]us: the *tit*bits of the animal only, as the head, heart, and liver, tongue, and paws, when of a Bear: It is only the Great men that are allowed to eat of these: others again, besides the above, the brisket, rump and ribbs; and very seldom a woman is allowed to partake of them, particularly if it is *un festin a tout manger*, i.e., to eat the whole; tho' there may be sufficient for 2 or 3 times the number of Guests, all must be eaten before day; though in certain cases the Feaster is obliged, and commonly does take part back, providing a knife, a bit of tobacco, or something else attend with the dish.

In these great Feasts the feaster makes one or several Speeches before *we* begin to eat, and one again after all is done, and sometimes sings, beats the drum and speeches during the whole time of the feast, never partaking of a morsel himself. At Some of them there is dancing to be performed: I happened to be called to one of these many years ago – it was the principal parts of a bear; and the Paunch had been filled with the liver, heart and fat and blood, minced, and much resembling that dish the Scotch term *haggish*: we were all very hungry and though we gormandized (it cannot be called *eating*) there yet remained full 2/3ds. The Feaster was uneasy and said he would have been proud had we eaten all, for in that case his Dreamed would have been propitious: we were obliged to dance also; but when I could stan[d] no more I gave him my knife and a bit of Tobacco and walked off leaving him to settle with his God as well as he could; but indeed I was not very scrupulous then, otherwise I had most certainly avoided many of them, tho' it is oftentimes dangerous if there be not method or qualification in the refusal.

Their feasts of rum are often to some one of the 4 wicked ones, praying them to be propitious and not allow themselves to be influenced by the wicked sollicitations of wicked envious indians. Many years ago I happened to be out a hunting a few miles from the house and came unexpectedly upon the lodge of a few indians I had that day given rum to. I heard one of them harangue, and drew up cautiously to listen. He entreated the rain, snow and frost to have pity upon their young ones (that they might kill) &c.

I communicated this a few years after to a couple of Gentleman – one of them longer in the country than myself denied it – and enquired of his wife who had lived a long time with the indians – she corroborated his denial – I perceived the cause, and told him that it was because *they* do not chuse that we become too well informed of all their ceremonies: it was to no effect, and I had almost a mind to credit the woman too myself, but by *insinuation* I find I am perfectly right.

Thus it happens in almost every thing else: a thing that does not meet with our approbation, or be a little beyond the Sphere of our limited information we immediately deny or condemn: whereas by taking *proper* measures to inquire or inform ourselves, not only those things themselves but others far more interesting, and sometimes too of the greatest moment, whether to ourselves or others, are rendered probable, reasonable, certain.

Hence it is also that many upon receiving a piece of information there rest themselves as upon a Rock of certainty. Now either of these I consider equally blameable as they lead to distrust, doubt, and sometimes to a complete refutation or assertion of facts that very oftentimes cast a stain or stigma sometimes upon a whole people and without any other foundation than as might be said that all Powerful *Veto*.

They have feasts for the dead, most commonly berries – or in countries where it is made, [maple] Sugar: generally yearly a bark box of perhaps 2 or 3 Gallons is placed *in* the grave, upon it, or well hid in some private nook, if they are afraid, or do not chuse, it be taken. I ought rather to have said these are sacrifices; but independant of these they have Feasts also, and feasts of Baptism. Feasts in short for almost every occasion. Besides these they have *smoking* feasts: these are to deliberate. I shall, should it please God I live, make it a point to enquire particularly into the origin of all of these.

[*Conjuring at Lac la Ronge, June 1823*]

June 5th. These 3 last days have been busy and turbulent ones for me – it is now considerably past midnight (and of course the 6th of June) but my indians are drinking and as I cannot think of going to bed till they do I shall employ my few remaining *leisure* moments (till next year, please god I live so long) in giving you an account of a conjuring bout I with some difficulty got an indian to make last night (June *4th*). In the evening the hut was prepared at some distance from the houses on account of the Stink as *the Spirits* cannot, or will not endure any pollution – the hut consisted of 10 Poles about 7 feet out of Ground, well stuck in and somewhat better than 3 feet diameter – the Poles were secured with 2 hoops: they were covered with 2 Parchment skins (of Moose) well bound with many rounds of strong leather line: the *top was covered* with a dressed skin and secured also, to prevent its being carried off (by the wind).

About 10 p.m. (still broad day light with us) we drew up with the conjuror, smoked and chatted some time. After this he took his drum (much resembling a tambourine) and with a stick gently struck it all the time he made a speech: I was almost touching him (all seated) but from the noise of the drum and his low voice, for the man has a dreadful complaint in his lungs, I could only gather, "take pity upon me; take pity upon me; hear and come; let me not speak in vain, nor become abashed – *show me* charity" &c, &c – it was a moderate and decent prayer. After this *they* (for there were several men) began to sing, using the drum and rattler – they sang among others the moose, horse, Bear, and Dog Songs; about a dozen in number.

When he prepared by taking off his clothes, all to his cloute, and asked who should tie him, I replied that I would, but was afraid of hurting him: another conjuror did beginning with his fingers between the 2 joints nearest the hand as nearly as I can describe it thus giving a double turn to the line between each finger, and the line was new mackerel [cf. Fr. *macle*], small, which I happened to have in my pocket by accident. I drew up to *inspect* and observing the fingers to swell upon his complaining of the tightness I felt a good deal for him. After this his blanket was wrapped around him and tied in such a manner, lengthways, crossways and every way, and a good knot *I* tied at each meeting of the cords; for I assisted in *this*, that I could have laid wager that it was beyond the Power of Spirits themselves, thus tied, to eradicate [extricate] themselves; and his hands were *under* his hams – as he could no more move than fly, of *himself*, the other conjuror and I put him to the door, but behold! it was with difficulty we could just get his head in, the entry being too narrow by about 10, or 12 ins. screwing and jam[m]ing considered.

"It will do, it will do," said the conjuror – "cover me now" – his back was covered with a blanket and we all retreated to our seats, myself about 4 feet distant. The others took the drum and began to sing. I could not help but laughing in myself and pitying the boldness of their vanity, but I had soon occasion to think otherwise and had I not predetermined that reason should conduct me throughout the whole of this, I cannot say how far in the *other* extreme *I* might have gone.

But to return: the conjuror desired the others to sing, they began a short song, I beleive it was that of the *Stone*, and the man entered in an instant! I was struck dumb with astonishment; for he appeared to me to *slide* in by something that was neither invisible nor discernible – I heard some thing that for the life of me I cannot account for, and that's all: from the time we covered him (25 past 10 p.m.) to the time we had done hunting for the twine that tied his fingers, not quite 5 minutes elapsed, and not 1 1/2 minutes before his blanket and the cords were thrown out to us! – not one of them, apparently (i.e., one knot) *untied*! My astonishment and apprehensions of his being entirely carried off from us were such, that I was nearly springing up to haul him out, for fear of his being for ever lost. The others continued singing a few other songs and I had the utmost anxiety in hearing [him] repeatedly call out as if in the greatest apprehensions himself, "enough! enough! Enough of ye I say"; and frequently for the space of some minutes repeating the same, and now and then calling out, "do not *Thou* enter."

The *Stone* was the first one known to us, by his song; for every one almost that entered sang *his* song, to which those (the indians) on the outside would keep chorus. A vast number entered, I verily beleive upward of an hundred; for upwards of that number of times the frame shook back-and-forwards and very smartly as if to fall; and among the first were some truly terrible characters. I have almost entirely converted myself from these foolish ideas of Ghost and hobgoblins, but I assure you in truth that I more than once felt very uneasy.

The Ice entered – he made a noise extremely resembling that made by a person shivering with cold, loud, and hoarse and *liquid*. The Devil *himself* also entered in *propria persona*, in a very authoritative and commanding manner: I assure you there was no laughing nor giggling outside, all the time he sang and spoke.

The Turtle spoke as an old Jocular man. "I hate the french; for in their travels when they find me, they kill me and eat me: I shall answer none of their questions," but this was a joke; for he laughed.

"Speak out, Turtle, speak out, louder, that we hear thee," said those without.

"I would too," replied he, "but my voice is so strong I must contract it thus, otherwise ye could not endure the sound of it. Stop!" continued he, "I must imitate the drunk," which he did to the great diversion of us all and concluded with snoring, the natural end of all drunken feasts, and then became quiet, on which another voice (which I also perfectly heard and understood as well [as] the Turtle herself [*sic*]) cried out – "see! see! if she does not look like a frog stretched out," and this raised a proper laugh both in and out.

The Dog entered, and spoke perfectly plain and distinct, and with a more elegant and harmoni[o]us voice [than] I ever heard in my life. Bears, of 3 or 4 different sorts, the horse, moose, Skeletons, spirits of departed and *still living friends* entered; but none but the latter and above mentioned were to be understood by any but the conjuror himself.

On the entering of one, "that is my (*adopted*) Son," said an Indian seated by me and called out his name to which he readily answered besides questions: this young man and a girl, both living, spoke very plain (you must observe that it is not their bodies, but their Souls or Spirits that enter) – Children almost at the instant of birth, Dwarfs, Giants; but this latter did make a noise indeed.

We all laughed very heartily when the horse entered; for it appears he passed too near the Turtle who called out as the horse was flying about (in the inside) singing and rattling his rattler, "I wish you would take care of yourself and *not tread on one*," in allusion to his diminutive size in comparison with that of the horse.

It is somewhat surprising that every one that entered, whether he spoke plain, or was interpreted – their First words were, "your lands are distressed – keep not on the Gr[an]d River" – sickness, sickness; "but from amongst *ye here* I shall select only a few aged ones," said one of the latter, but in a *voice* no one but the conjuror could understand.

.As he went out, however, the Conjuror paid him a most bawdy compliment – we all laughed and asked what was the matter. "Pah! nothing, I am only afraid of him," said the Conj.

One of them that entered, apparently the Devil himself for he spoke and acted *en veritable maitre*, startled us all a great deal and enquired authoritatively and angrily, "what want ye of me? – Speak?" Upon several hurried enquiries put to him he said that some things I saw and heard in my house this winter, were by Mr. [Benjamin] Frobisher, who expired so dreadfully in 1819 [from exposure, after escaping from Hudson's Bay Company hands during bitter HBC/North West Company rivalry] – "he is a Skeleton (Pah-kack); and it is he who built *this* house – he comes to see"!!!

Tho' I did certainly both hear and see, several times this winter, and once in particular, about 2 a.m., yet I do not feel much inclined to add faith to this assertion of Davy's [the Devil] – I must have something more substantial. But I am much inclined to doubt master Davy's assertions and consider *this* and several others of his sayings at former Periods in the same light as those he delivered at many of Grecian temples; for I have every substantial reason to consider him as the same identical Gentleman: however, a short time hence will decide.

The Turtle said we should have a good deal of rain; but not a *very great deal*, and a very hi[gh] wind, and as soon as the Sun should appear, "at its setting an indian" (naming him by a very extraordinary and bawdy feature in his person) "should arrive and bring us meat; *but this you will eat of course, and I shall go without.*" ("Beware of yourselves – Tomorrow night you shall drink and be drunk: drink and leave the house as soon as you can; *for there are from that wind*" (by which he designated the *South*) "*who if they drink with ye, ye shall become pitiful,*" alluding to two blackguard half breed brothers, who proud of the bravery of their deceased father are ever and anon insulting and domineering over the other indians: it is worthy of remark that an aged man in the course of this last winter was advertised of the Same, and repeatedly pressed not to drink at the house on their account.)

This is now the 6th (June) the Sun appears, but the wind is very hi[gh]: and we have frequent showers of rain and Snow.

About midnight the Conjuror addressed me and asked if I wished to see any of *them* (the Spirits). I accepted the offer and thrust my head underneath, and being upon my back I looked up and near the top observed a light as of a Star in a Cloudy night about 1 1/2 in. long and 1 broad; tho' dim, yet perfectly distinct. Tho' *they all* appear as lights, some larger and others smaller, this one was denominated the Fisher Star [Cree *ocēkatak*], the name by which they designate the Plough. I beleive *we* call it, or Great Bear, from the supposed resemblance it bears to that animal, the fisher [Cree *ocīkacahk*, Ojibwa *ocīkanank* or *cīk* 'fisher star, ursa major'].

When I was entering, several of the Indians on the outside called out to the Spirits, "Gently! gently! It is our Chief who wishes to see ye: do him no evil" &c. I had my apprehensions.

A little after one p.m. [a.m.] one of my men looked in, with several indians, and saw several small lights about as large as the Thumb nail. A few minutes before 2 p.m. [a.m.] being day light, they gave another shaking to the frame and made their exit.

The above is an account of only a small part, for I am too much pressed for time – I cannot therefore enter into particulars, nor a larger detail; nor give you my opinion further than a few words. I am fully convinced, as much so as that I am in existance, that Spirits of some kind did really and virtually enter, some truly terrific, but others again quite of a different character. I cannot enter into a detail by comparisons from ancient and more modern history, but I found the consonance, analogy, resemblance, affinity, or whatever it may be termed so great, so conspicuous that I verily beleive I shall never forget the impressions of that evening; but above all things that sticks most forcibly in my mind is the unbounded Gratitude we owe, and ought to shew, every instant of our existance to that almighty Power that deigned to sacrifice his only Son for us for our Salvation! Oh my God! let me never forget this! and teach me to thank thee not only with my life but with every action of my life! x x x x &c, &c.

Here I must close and in a few minutes Seal up this for your perusal, sincerely wishing I may find an opportunity, safe, of conveying it to you. How earnestly I wish Rob[er]t had been present and understand the language – this would convi[n]ce the most skeptic.

To Mr Wm. Nelson, Wm. Henry [Sorel]
G. Nelson
Note: Read these Pages among yourselves, and lend them not out of the house ——

DRAMATIS PERSONAE

The following "cast of characters" identifies most of the spirit beings whom Nelson discussed and compares his information with what is known about them from other written sources and Northern Algonquian communities. This section is intended as a glossary to which readers may refer as they progress through the Nelson text itself. Detailed discussions of these beings as they figure in the broader contexts of Cree and Northern Ojibwa mythology, dreams, conjuring, and medicine are found in Part III, "Northern Algonquian Religious and Mythic Themes and Personages," which follows this section.

"Key-shay-mani-to" [Cree *Kisemanitōw*; Ojibwa *Kisēmanitō*]
Literally 'great spirit,' *Kisemanitōw* is the superior being of subarctic Algonquian cosmology, benevolently inclined towards humans and usually identified as the ultimate creator of the world and of living beings. Cooper (1934) argued that the creator deity concept among Cree, Naskapi, and Montagnais antedated European contact. Vecsey (1983) discusses the concept among Ojibwa groups. Nelson initially confused *Kisemanitōw* with the trickster *Wīsahkēcāhk*, and consequently probably erred in stating that it appeared in the shaking lodge. Several sources, however, demonstrate that *Kihcimanitōw* was not of the passive, uninvolved type but rather actively influenced human affairs (Cooper 1934, 39–40; Thompson 1962, 80, 101). The epithet 'master of life' was shared by Ojibwa and Cree (Cooper 1934, 37n; Kinietz 1965, 289). Contemporary Manitoba Cree identify *Kisemanitōw* with the Christian deity, and missionaries have long used the name in this

sense (Brightman 1977–79).* It remains unclear whether the superior being concept antedates European influence. Early documentary sources suggest that it does, but its range of distribution could also reflect mediated Christian influences from other Indian groups. Possibly some Ojibwa and Cree communities possessed the concept aboriginally while others did not. The early history of the name *Kisemanitōw* is also uncertain; some sources identify the name only as *Manitōw* (cf. Long 1986, 174–75).

"Kee-jick-oh-kay" [Cree *Kĭsikohkēw*; Ojibwa *Kĭsikokkē*]
In Nelson's manuscript *Kee-jick-oh-kay* refers to the primary evil deity *Macimanitōw* (Cree), a being conceptually opposed and subordinate in power to both *Kisemanitōw* and the trickster *Wĭsahkēcāhk*. Nelson translated the name as "he who made the Sky or Skies or resides in the Sky" and observed that only some Indians used it. Although Cooper (1934, 39,67) doubted the aboriginality of the evil deity, references to such a being in Cree religion occurred as early as the late 1600s (Tyrrell 1931, 226, 382). Lahontan (1905, 2:446) recorded a cognate to *Macimanitōw* among the Ottawa in the same period, although he considered it a generic term rather than a proper name for a single being. Contemporary Manitoba Cree use the form both generically and as a proper name for the Christian Devil (Brightman 1977–79). The appearance of the evil deity in the shaking lodge performances observed by Nelson was attested also by Bacqueville de la Pothèrie in the 1600s (1931, 228–29) and Drage in the mid-1700s (1968, 1:235). Contrary to Cooper's (1934, 67) conclusions, *Macimanitōw* was probably not identified as the patron of conjurors but rather was one of many spirits understood to enter the shaking lodge.

"Wee-suck-a-jock" [Cree *Wĭsahkēcāhk*]
Nelson made numerous references to the trickster–transformer character of the Crees west of James Bay and of many or most subarctic Ojibwa, *Wĭsahkēcāhk*. Like Coyote, Raven, and other comparable characters in the oral literatures of North American Indian groups, *Wĭsahkēcāhk* combines attributes of great magical power, pathetic helplessness, wisdom, stupidity, altruism, and moral chaos. Contemporary Manitoba Crees regard him with mingled respect, contempt, and affection.

"Michi-Pichoux" [Cree *Misipisiw*; Ojibwa *Misśipisī* 'great lynx']
Nelson translated *Michi-Pichoux* as 'Water Lynx,' 'Tyger,' 'water-Cat,' and 'water-dog,' prefiguring difficulties experienced by many others in rendering the name and the concept

*References to Brightman 1977–79 pertain to Robert Brightman's fieldnotes from his work among the Rock Cree or Rocky Cree (cf. Rossignol 1939, Smith 1975) of northern Manitoba. These people use the terms *asinīskāwiðiniwak* 'people of the rocky area' and *kiwĭtinawiðiniwak* 'people of the north' as ethnic self-designations and distinguish themselves from the groups known in the literature as Swampy Cree, Plains Cree, and the Woods Cree of northern Saskatchewan and Alberta. As defined locally, the designation Rock Cree includes the communities of Brochet, Nelson House, Pukatawagan, and South Indian Lake, Manitoba. They share the /ð/ dialect spoken by Nelson's Cree associates, and some Manitoba Rock Cree trace their ancestry back to Lac la Ronge and Ile à la Crosse, Saskatchewan.

intelligible in English. Seventeenth-century sources on Ojibwa and Ottawa religion mentioned cognate words referring to a spirit associated with lakes and rivers who was offered
prayers and sacrifices for good fishing and safe water travel (Perrot 1911, 1:45–62
["Michipissy"]; Rasles 1900, 159–61 [Michibichi]; LeMercier 1899, 289 [Missibizi];
Allouez 1899, 155 [Missibizi]). The most detailed account was provided by Pachot in the
early 1700s (Kinietz 1965, 286). He described "Bichi Bichy" as the god of waters or the
master of spirits of lakes and as possessing the form of a sea tiger with fins. *Misipisiw*
and its cognates translate literally as 'great lynx' or 'big lynx' although the connection
with terrestrial lynxes is obscure. More recent references attest the continuity of the aquatic
habitat and also emphasize associations with danger and evil not evident in the earlier
sources. The term is both a generic word for a class of malignant aquatic feline beings,
and the proper name for the ruler of the species; both exert control over riverine and lake
environments, especially dangerous rapids.

In Nelson's version of the flood myth, the *Misipisiwak* (plural) figure as the transformer's
antagonists and the murderers of his brother, a role they share in many other Cree and
Ojibwa versions (cf. Bloomfield 1930, 14–20 [Cree]; Ahenakew 1929, 309–27 [Cree];
Radin and Reagan 1928, 63–67, 67–70 [Ojibwa]; Blackbird 1887, 72–8 [Ojibwa]). The
malignant character of the Great Lynx(es) is exemplified also in myths describing child
abduction (Jones 1917–19, 2:258–61; Skinner 1928, 169–70), and in apparent association
with the evil deity *Macimanitŏw* (Kohl 1860, 422–25; Rogers 1962, D6). Along with other
malignant beings associated with water, the Great Lynxes are often conceived of as the
antagonists of thunder spirits and as equivalents to succubi and incubi who seduce human
partners with disastrous consequences (Landes 1968, 31–32; Howard 1977, 113–14; Dusen-
bury 1962, 109–10). A Great Lynx appears also as a patron of the Ojibwa Midewiwin
or grand medicine society (Landes 1968, 102, 108; Hoffman 1891, 169) and occupies
a comparable role in the ceremony of the non-Algonquian Omaha (Fortune 1932, 85).
Gatschet (1899, 257–58) discussed similar beings among Peoria and Shawnee, and Dewdney
(1975, 123–30) has examined Great Lynxes in relation to the Midewiwin lodge and to
their associations with water, snakes, and danger. As among Dewdney's instructors, some
Manitoba Cree continue to fear a Great Lynx and are reluctant to discuss it, associating
it with drowning and unexplained deaths in the bush (Brightman 1977–79).

"Sea Serpent" [Cree *misikinīpik*; Ojibwa *missikinēpik* 'great snake']
Nelson mentioned the "sea serpent" only as one of the spirit beings summoned into the
shaking lodge by conjurors, but it possesses associations comparable to those of the Great
Lynxes and figures prominently in Algonquian ritual and mythology. Like the Great Lynxes,
Serpents are associated with subterranean or underwater spaces usually considered inimical
to human beings. Included among the spirit patrons of the Ojibwa Midewiwin lodge, they
are conceived of as eternally at war with the Thunder beings of the upper air (Chamberlain 1890, 51–52; Jenness 1935, 35–36, 39; Landes 1968, 102). In many versions of the
Cree and Ojibwa transformer myth, the Serpents figure as associates of the Lynxes (Bloomfield 1930, 14–20 [Cree]; Jenness 1935, 69–70 [Ojibwa]) or substitute for them as the
hero's antagonists (Schoolcraft 1839, 134–71 [Ojibwa]; Paget 1909, 177–84 [Cree]). Among

Plains Ojibwa, the Lynxes are specifically identified as the "masters of all underwater creatures and also of snakes." Both Lynxes and Serpents are often said to possess horns (cf. Dewdney 1975, 124–25; Morriseau 1965, 27; Howard 1977, 113–14; Bloomfield 1934, 159; Skinner 1938, 161–62). The concept of spiritually powerful serpents, often possessing one or more horns and viewed as enemies of thunder, is widespread in American Indian religions in the eastern United States (Gatschet 1899; Beauchamp 1888).

"O-may-me-thay-day-ace-cae-wuck" [Cree *omēmīhðētēhēsiwak* 'hairy-heart beings']
In Nelson's manuscript, the "Hairy Breasts" or "Ancients" appear as a primitive although marginally human race of beings who contest with *Nēhanīmis* and other humans for occupancy of the earth. Displaced or destroyed in a decisive final battle, they were thought to have passed out of existence in the Cree country, although Nelson's informant believed that two bands of them still persisted, one in the land from which the traders came (eastern Canada?) and the other overseas. In shaking lodge performances observed by Nelson, they bragged of their ancient lineage and their hunting prowess without the use of guns. Taken together, these associations suggest that Crees incorporated folk historical knowledge of past conflicts and of precontact stages of their own society into their image of a culturally primitive race that preceded human beings in the world. Their hairiness also implies associations with Euro-Canadians. Rock Cree today describe the same beings, but refer to them as *kayāsiðiniwak*, 'ancient people,' or in English as "cavemen." The word *mīmīhðītūhīsiwak*, a cognate to Nelson's form, refers to a distinct early race of cannibal beings comparable to human-appearing windigo monsters (Brightman 1977–79). As malignant cannibals, the Hairy-Heart beings were the enemies of the transformer *Wīsahkēcāhk* in a Plains Cree myth which resembles the story told to Nelson to some degree (Ahenakew 1929, 339–42).

"Mermaid" and *"Sea Man"*
Nelson mentioned these beings only as spirits summoned into the shaking lodge performances that he witnessed. Probably the "Sea Man" was cognate with the underwater spirits known to the Attawapiskat Swamp Cree (Honigmann 1956, 67–68) and the Montagnais-Naskapi (Speck 1935, 68–69). The "merman" described by Morriseau for Nipigon Ojibwa (1965, 22–23) appears to belong to a distinct class of miniature beings called by Crees *mīmīkwīsiwak* who occupy aquatic or riverbank habitats (Brightman 1977–79). The Swamp Cree "underwater man" was feared, consistent with the conventional associations of underwater or underground beings with evil and danger. As noted in relation to the Great Lynxes, water spirits in general appear to have been seen as exerting a sexual and romantic influence over humans (Landes 1968, 31). It is interesting that Nelson mentioned both male and female forms of these beings; they are probably connected with the seductive male and female manifestations of the being "Mendo" (East Cree *Manitū*) which, according to Fort George Cree of Quebec, lures young men and women into the water or causes them to drown (Bauer 1971, 15–20).

"Mee-key-nock" [Cree *Miskināhk*, 'turtle'; Ojibwa *Mikkinākk*, 'turtle' or 'snapping turtle']
Cree *miskināhk* and its cognates refer generically to turtle and also to an individual spirit

being often translated as "Great Turtle" who functioned as messenger or interpreter during the performance of the shaking lodge among most Cree and Ojibwa groups. Among some Southwestern Ojibwa, *mikkinākk* refers specifically to the snapping turtle (Nichols and Nyholm 1979:232), suggesting an identification of the spirit with that species. Nelson's description of *Mikkinākk* agreed with others attesting his amiability, humor, veracity, and popularity with audiences: the Great Turtle requests tobacco, chats and exchanges ribaldries, complains humorously about the French who include him in their diet, and performs an evidently hilarious impersonation of a drunken Indian (cf. Hallowell 1942, 23, 44–50). A spirit identified as a turtle appears as one of the many Midewiwin patrons and is probably identifiable as *Mikkinākk*, given the joint competences of some individuals as conjurors and Mide priests (Hoffman 1891, 158, 182, 185, 251–52).

"Bull or Buffaloe" [Cree *Mostos*; Ojibwa *Maskotēpisikki*]
At conjuring events observed by Nelson, the Buffalo appeared as a stern and formidable alien spirit who resented disparaging remarks from the audience and, in the conjuring narrative with which the manuscript begins, possessed sufficient power to forestall a monster threatening the Cree petitioner. The Buffalo shared with some other animal spirits the characteristic of communicating in a language intelligible only to the conjuror, possibly reflecting its associations with a different environment, the prairie-parklands to the south of Lac La Ronge. Among Cree and Ojibwa groups who took up residence on the plains during the eighteenth century, the Buffalo emerged as a spirit strongly associated with shamanism (cf. Howard 1977, 118).

"Pah-kack" *(Skeleton)* [Cree *Pākahk, Pākahkos*]
Nelson recorded considerable detail on ambiguous beings which, although associated with death, starvation, illness, and other misfortune (Thompson 1962, 76; Landes 1968, 23; Morriseau 1965, 85–86; Schoolcraft 1839, 240–41), were understood to grant great hunting and curing power to those possessing them as guardian spirits (Bloomfield 1934, 204–11; Stevens 1971, 97–98). Although common to both Cree and Ojibwa, attributes of *pākahk* are variable through time and space. Shared elements are their ability to fly, their appetite for burned grease sacrifices which they appropriate through the smoke, their skeletal or emaciated appearance, their origin as human victims of starvation or disease, and the signalling of their presence by weird laughter, moans, or rattling bones. Their irascible behavior towards humans and even towards their own visionaries is noted also in other accounts (Ahenakew 1973, 99–100). Some Plains Crees conceptualized them as small creatures (Dion 1979, 56), but elsewhere they were apparently of human size. Nelson's mention of a "chief" of the skeletons indicates that *pākahk* functioned both as a generic term for this class of beings and as a proper name for their leader. Among Plains Cree and Plains Ojibwa, *pākahk* is identified as the originator and patron of the Give Away Dance or Trade Dance (Cree *mahtāhitōwin*) sponsored in its honor (Dion 1979, 56; Ahenakew 1973, 99–100; Bloomfield 1934, 208). Some of these groups have redefined *pākahk* as a benign minor deity with Santa Claus-like attributes (Howard 1977, 117–18, 169–73). Bloomfield's three *pākahk* texts (1934, 204–53) provide insight into the concept from a Cree point of

view; and interesting wooden carvings of the being illustrate Johnson's discussion of the Give Away Dance (1974, 66–67).

"North Wind"/"North" [Cree *Kīwētin*; Ojibwa *Kīwētin*]
The varied aspects of the North Wind in Nelson's manuscript exemplify both the dynamic character of subarctic Algonquian religious thought and the disparate sources from which Nelson drew. North Wind appears in the *Wīsahkēcāhk* myth as the transformer's benign grandfather, but figures elsewhere in the manuscript as the malicious opponent of Wīsahkēcāhk's son *Nēhanīmis*, and also as a malignant spirit associated with misfortune, freezing, and windigo cannibalism. The association of North Wind with the transformer clearly represents a Cree reinterpretation of Ojibwa narratives, although in the latter the winds figure most typically either as the impregnators of the transformer's mother (Schoolcraft 1839, 134 et seq.; Josselin de Jong 1913, 5–6; Jones 1917–19, 36; Landes 1968, 24–25) or as his brothers (Schoolcraft 1939, 134ff.; Speck 1915, 28–32; Hewitt 1925:116–17; Radin and Reagan 1928, 70–76). The tendency to conceptualize the four wind spirits as brothers with distinct behavioral attributes is widely distributed in the Algonquian subarctic and northeast (e.g., Tanner 1979, 95; Schoolcraft 1860, 337–38; Brightman 1977–79; Brown 1977).

"Thunder" [Cree *Piðēsiw*; Ojibwa *Pinēssi* 'thunderer'/'thunderbird']
Nelson briefly mentioned Thunder as a visitor to the conjuring lodge and as a spirit guardian who appeared in the form of a beautiful peacock. The majesty and power ascribed to thunderbirds are hinted at by the conjurors' stipulation that they remain outside the lodge in order to avoid breaking it apart. Although sometimes dangerous or malignant (Stevens 1971, 93), thunder spirits typically were benign and powerful spirit guardians associated with success in war and medicine (Landes 1968, 25, 47–49; Jenness 1935, 34–38; Morriseau 1965, 4–14; Dusenberry 1962, 79; Howard 1977, 112–13). Some groups, for example the Lake Nipigon Ojibwa (Morriseau 1965, 4–14), recognized different classes of thunder beings. When used as a proper name, *Piðīsiw* and its cognates refer to a primary or "chief" thunderbird to which the others were theoretically subordinate. The cosmic antagonism between Thunderbirds and the Great Lynxes and Serpents was noted above.

"Crazy Woman"/"Foolish, Mad, Jealous Woman"/"Folly"/"Jealousy"
Nelson's observations on "Crazy Woman" suggest a dangerous succubus-like creature sexually and romantically drawn to human males; this pattern appears also with beings associated with the water. The "Foolish Woman" described by Landes (1968, 22) among southwestern Ojibwa may be a related character, although the latter is a personification of irresponsible elder siblings.

"Nay-han-nee-mis" [Cree *Nēhanīmis*]
In Nelson's manuscript, the human or anthropomorphic hero *Nēhanīmis* appeared as the son of *Wīsahkēcāhk* the transformer, and as the protagonist of two myths detailing conflicts with the North Wind and with the Ancients or Hairy Breasts. Nelson furnishes the

only Cree source identifying this character with the transformer. Curtis (1928, 18:129–31) collected a Plains Cree myth evidently related to Nelson's in which the hero "Neyanimis" wins a magical contest with a giant and then creates from its body the four wind spirits.

"Mee-shaw-bose"/"Mi-shaw-bose" [Cree *Misapos*; Ojibwa *Missapos*]
In Nelson's version of the transformer myth, *Misapos* is *Wisahkēcāhk's* younger brother who meets his death at the hands of the Great Lynxes and thereby precipitates the events leading to the deluge. The rabbit name and (presumably) characteristics are borrowings from the Ojibwa transformer cycle.

"Sun" [Cree *Pīsim*; Ojibwa *Kīsiss*]
Often confused with the creator deity by early observers (e.g., Bacqueville de la Pothèrie 1931, 227–28), the Sun was one of the major spirits in subarctic Algonquian cosmology, although it was conceptualized in many different ways. In some versions of the Ojibwa transformer cycle, the Sun appears as the father of Nēnapos (Speck 1915, 28) or as his brother (Jones 1917–19, 1:3–6). Nelson placed on record the only known identification of the Sun with the Euro-Canadian traders: the spirit speaks English, wears English clothing, and possesses the power to repair firearms.

"Moon" [Cree *Tipiskāwipīsim*; Ojibwa *Tipikk-kīsiss*]
Like the Sun, the Moon spirit in Nelson's text was identified with Euro-Canadians through use of the English language. In another context, the Moon appeared as the originator of the first female in the post-deluge creation or recreation of human beings. Data on Algonquian conceptions of the Moon are scarce, although like Thunder, the Sun, the stars and other beings of the upper air, it was defined as a powerful spirit (Thompson 1962, 76) by Crees. A myth representing the sun and moon as brother and sister exists among Swamp Cree (Clay 1938, 24).

"Esculapius"
Nelson used the Latin name of the classical father of medicine to refer to the spirit owner or controller of medicinal plants and minerals in whose mountain of caves and rivers visionaries were instructed in medical knowledge and techniques [see also Morriseau 1965, 112]. The theological elaboration surrounding this personage perhaps indicates connections to the esoteric Midewiwin cosmology of the Ojibwa.

"Sickness"/"Plague"
Nelson believed that he encountered one of the four spirits associated with epidemic diseases in a visionary dream early in 1823. One of his Lac la Ronge Cree acquaintances, who had one of them as a spirit guardian, was warned by it that "Sickness" would follow the major fur trade routes in 1819 and inflict, albeit unwillingly, illness and death on a predetermined number of victims. Measles and whooping cough in fact caused much distress in the western interior in 1819–20 (Ray 1974, 107). The personification of disease is a melancholy testimony to the recurrent epidemics, notably measles and smallpox, to

which the boreal forest Crees and Ojibwas were subject (cf. Thompson 1962, 92–93).

"Strong Neck"/"Hercules"
Apparently a spirit personifying physical strength, Strong Neck is another being who is not attested outside Nelson's manuscript. In conjuring performances, he was represented as the one spirit who could not become invisible; consequently those present were required to cover their heads when he approached. Like the Buffalo and others of the more powerful spirits, Strong Neck reacted dangerously to skepticism and ridicule.

"Pike"/"Jackfish" [Cree Nacwāpew or Iðinitōkinōsēw; Ojibwa Kinōsē]
Like the Great Turtle, the Pike appeared in Lac la Ronge conjuring performances as an amiable and humorous spirit who exchanged jokes with the audience; it was also distinguished from the others by speaking French. In the shaking lodge of the Berens River Saulteaux, the "Little Jack Fish" provoked amusement by its imperfect recitation of English words called out to it from the audience (Hallowell 1942, 845).

"Loon" [Cree Mwākwa; Ojibwa Mānk]
Another humorous visitor to the shaking lodge, the Loon would call out "Nee-weah-wee-wey," a cry which, according to Nelson, was thought to resemble Cree and Ojibwa verbs meaning, "I want to marry!"

"Wolverine" [Cree Omiðāhcīs; Ojibwa Kwinkwa'ākē]
Although the wolverine was and is despised by hunters as a skilled plunderer of traps and trapped animals, the spirit Wolverine of the shaking lodge was also a comic presence, distinguished by its offensive smell.

"Flying Squirrel" [Cree Caswēkanikwacās; Ojibwa Sakaskāntawē]
The Flying Squirrel appears as another animal visitor in the shaking lodge, distinguished, however, by the fact that its utterances must be construed in reverse to be properly interpreted. This speaking style provides an interesting parallel to the discourse of the Oglala Sioux Heyoka or "Contrary" society and other similar Plains associations. Rock Cree today associate the flying squirrel with bad hunting and trapping prospects, perhaps because of the lack of a commercial market for the fur (Brightman 1977–79).

"Bear" [Cree Maskwa; Ojibwa Makkwa]
Nelson noted that bears "of 3 or 4 different sorts" entered the conjuring lodge, but provided no further information. The Algonquian evaluation of the bear as the most intelligent, hominoid, and spiritually powerful of terrestrial animals is well-known and has been discussed comparatively by Hallowell (1926; cf. Speck 1935, 92–110; Skinner 1911, 68–76). Rock Crees sometimes refer to bears as āpihtawiðiniw or 'half-human' and regard them as sources of power for hunting, trapping, and curing.

"Dog" [Cree *Atim*; Ojibwa *Animoss*]
The Dog, when it visited the conjuring lodge, was distinguished by an "elegant and har-moni[o]us voice" that perhaps reflected its integration into human society. Apparently neutralized in this context was the antagonism between dogs and game animals exemplified by such rules as disposing of animal bones so dogs cannot gnaw them (Brightman 1977-79).

"Snow" [Cree *Kōna*; Ojibwa *Kōn*]
Nelson stated only that the Snow being was white in appearance and visited the conjuring lodge. In contrast to their views of other beings linked with winter and cold (North Wind, Ice), Rock Crees do not associate the Snow being with danger or *wīhtikōw*.

"Kingfisher" [Cree *Okiskimanisiw*; Ojibwa *Okiskimanissī*]
The Kingfisher occurs in many Cree and Ojibwa versions of the transformer-trickster cycle as the bird who reveals to *Wīsahkēcāhk* (or Nenaposh) the location and fate of his brother. Often the transformer rewards the Kingfisher with attractive plumage (e.g., Stevens 1985, 20); in other versions the bird is punished for its predatory intentions toward the brother's remains.

"Horse" [Cree *Mistatim* 'great dog'; Ojibwa *Pēpēsikōkansī*]
The horse was another visitor to the conjuring lodge, but Nelson did not describe its attributes. To Crees at Lac la Ronge, the horse, like the buffalo, would have appeared as a somewhat alien species associated with the parklands and Plains Cree groups to the south, and with the fur posts (Nelson had one or more horses at Lac la Ronge).

"Ice" [Cree *Maskwamiy*; Ojibwa *Mikkwam*]
At Lac la Ronge in 1823 and also among present-day Rock Crees of the Churchill River, Ice is a malignant being linked with *wīhtikōw* disorder. Nelson described this being as "the Parent of Ice" and as "in the bowels of the Earth, at a great depth and never thaws [permafrost]." Some Rock Crees localize Ice in Granville Lake and give similar descriptions of its characteristics (Brightman 1977-79).

"Stone" [Cree *Asinīy*; Ojibwa *Assin*]
A song belonging to "The Stone" was sung at the beginning of the shaking lodge ceremony that Nelson witnessed in June 1823. The context suggests that this being was recognized as a potential visitor to the shaking lodge; other sources suggest that individual stones might (or might not) turn out to be animate and responsive (Hallowell 1976: 362-64). Rock Crees recognize particular stones or rocky sites as possessing a spiritual component; one rocky ledge on the Laurie River, for example, was the *pawākan* or dream guardian of a woman and aided her in an encounter with a *wīhtikōw* monster (Brightman 1977-79).

III

Overleaf: GiNc–4, Stanley Rapids Face iii

NORTHERN ALGONQUIAN RELIGIOUS AND MYTHIC THEMES AND PERSONAGES: CONTEXTS AND COMPARISONS

Nelson wrote the Lac la Ronge text for a narrow familial circle rather than for a general audience, and he lacked a comprehensive knowledge of Algonquian peoples and religion. As a consequence, even though his account exhibits a breadth and accuracy unparalleled in other pre-twentieth century writings on Cree and Northern Ojibwa religious practice and belief, some of his Lac la Ronge materials are rather inaccessible and obscure to non-specialists and non-Algonquians, and must be placed in a broader comparative context to be fully appreciated.

Nelson's manuscript makes no mention of animal ceremonialism including doctrines of animal reincarnation or regeneration and rituals regulating the hunting and eating of animals and the disposal of their remains. Such ceremonialism was described for Manitoba and Saskatchewan Cree by David Thompson in the late eighteenth and early nineteenth century (Thompson 1962, 23, 26, 75, 81, 88). Nelson's omission of this topic may reflect a local de-emphasis on this aspect of Cree religion at the time of his observations, or a lack of interest in the subject on the part of his local informants, several of whom were métis Cree who doubtless filtered information through their own knowledge and interests.

Also curious is the lack of attention to the Ojibwa *Mitēwīwin*, or Grand Medicine Society, a religious association concerned with healing. Nelson was familiar with the Midewiwin from his years in the Jack Head area of Lake Winnipeg. Although Nelson was seemingly an appreciative student on Midewiwin theology (Brown 1984), he made only passing reference to it in the Lac la Ronge manuscript. The explanation is probably that Lac la Ronge offered no reinforcement to his earlier interest since the Midewiwin was not present there, although modified cognate organizations and rituals did develop among some Cree groups (Hallowell 1936). Much more at center stage for Nelson in 1823 was the conjuring complex which was highly visible and flourishing among both the Cree and métis Cree of Lac la Ronge.

Several pervasive themes of Northern Algonquian thought are traceable in Nelson's materials. For Northern Algonquians, mythic beings are not confined to another or an ancient world, and their revelations are not a closed book. Such beings appear in dreams and visions and in the divination rituals of the conjuring or shaking lodge, and they may predictably take on a variety of human, animal, and other forms in real-life encounters. Since they participate in the social and mental life of ordinary human beings, they may be thought of as persons and classificatory relatives. Cree and Ojibwa often describe these personages as "our grandfathers," and in recitals of myths such characters may address human beings as "grandchild" or "younger sibling."

The fact that such beings may manifest themselves in what Europeans would describe as the natural world lends a quality of indeterminacy and potentiality to everyday life; seemingly ordinary events and encounters may turn out to be quite otherwise. Familiar entities, animate or inanimate (stones, for example) may prove to have surprising properties. It is unwise to make up one's mind too soon about any object of perception; it may have hidden attributes and could later reveal itself to be quite different. Patience and the suspension of a too-ready belief or decision about what one is perceiving are appropriate tactics in these situations of "percept ambiguity" as Mary Black-Rogers has termed them (1977a).

The importance of these beings carries over into Northern Algonquian theories of causation, which tend to be highly personalized. The origins of countless attributes of the Ojibwa–Cree cultural and natural universe are traced back, in a rich oral tradition, to the actions, wisdom, mistakes, or conflicts of the trickster–transformer figure known commonly to the Cree as Wīsahkēcāhk (Nelson's Weesuckajock) and to the Ojibwa/ Saulteaux as Nenaposh or Misaabooz. In ordinary life, too, the causes of events such as accidents, illness, hunting successes and failures, and the like, are personalized, being linked to the actions of one's spirit guardian, the intervention of other human beings through sorcery or "medicine," the pleasure or displeasure of animal spirits at their treatment by hunters, and so on.

A corollary of the personalization of the universe is that human and animal worlds may be seen as reflections of one another, and as being, in fact, ancestrally related. A story about the origin of the beaver, recorded by George Nelson from the Saulteaux of Dauphin River west of Lake Winnipeg in his letter-journal of April 1811, makes this point very clearly. It also encapsulates the other themes just noted – the potentialities for interaction between human and other-than-human beings, and the sometimes slow process by which such encounters reveal their true character and consequences.

"The Origins of the Beaver"

The origin of the beaver according to the indian accounts (stories rather) is no less curious than foolish or superstitious; – particularly as it has some kind of affinity with what the Canadians say of it, that is, "Le Castor auterfois etoit un monde" [probable translation: "Formerly the Beavers were a (human) society"]. The indians say they were a family. Now, as I have not paper enough to give you a more ample account of the indian way of living than I have already stated, and as I have too much to let by unemployed at all risks of displeasure I shall attempt giving you a short account of what the indians say of the origin of the beaver particularly.

It happened formerly in the first days of the world, that there were several indian families living in a camp together, one of their band (with his wife & two children) having some particular errand that he was absolutely obliged to execute, and as these people seldom travel at any distance without their family following, this fellow took his with him; and having a small river to cross, tho' very narrow he was afraid of its effects or powers; for he knew according to tradition that as Menabojou [Ojibwa *Mēnapocŏ:* Saulteaux name for *Nēnaposʹ*, the trickster-transformer] or their Creator had yet left several things undone; and which he could not do or accomplish without sacrificing some of "his children," he resolved to leave this to certain rivers or creeks, whose waters were empregnated by him with such fascinating powers as he knew would accomplish his designs without his passing for a bad *liver* (un mauvais vivant). The indian, I say, fearing the powers of these waters and not being able conveniently to go by any other road, resolved to pass this way, but to avoid the river by passing beyond its source. He therefore set off, but as he arrived at the river much sooner than expected, he continued travelling several days, but the river continued as before, and thinking the most dangerous part already passed, and by the perpetual solicitations of his wife who by this time was very tired and unwilling to proceed much further prevailed upon her husband to cross opposite to where they were. The *woe-to-man!* proposed crossing first, the river being very narrow and a few small sticks laid across and their appearing to be solid enough, she attempted, having one of her children upon her back and the other in her *arms!*, but in proportion as she advanced, the sticks Grew weaker, when down she went with her children!! Her husband raving

mad, and distracted for the loss of his children was searching in every direction crying
and calling, "Oh my wife, Oh my Children, let me see you appear only once more that
I may rightly know what has become of you &c." All this was useless – no one appear'd;
– now as he had waited here a day or two and seeing no appearance of anything, he returned
to the lodges. Here he made a dream: he thought that his woman &c. were a certain place
in the river, when he returned, as he approached the river he thought to have heard a
noise in the water, but on his arrival on the beach he found all very quiet, but he thought
to see something, that looked as if somebody had been at work, & concluded it could
be no one but his woman and children; – he therefore hid himself and about sunset he
perceived her and the Children; and altho' greatly altered, he thought it was absolutely
them. He called out to her, when down she went; this hurt him very much. But as it is
quite useless to repeat all their ceremonies let it suffice to say that the woman prevailed
upon her husband to come to the edge of the water, when he was suddenly drawn in; and
all were immediately changed to what they are at this day.

   This is the reason say the indians, why the beaver has so much "sense"; and how could
it be otherwise say they, were they not indians. The indians, when they find any thing
that is well done, or any thing (animal I mean) that is any way more sagacious, or ingenuent
etc. than is customary they will say it has as much sense as an indian – *He anishenabe
bego-hen* just as or like an indian.* They honor us too sometimes with this compliment.
But as they have no word or words in their language to signify a human-being; and frequently make use of the word indian as such I think that they mean a human being instead
of indian – tho' some say not, and as some of them are better acquainted with the language
than myself I shall not say any more on the subject [Nelson 1811, 26 April].

   Nelson's beaver origin myth is of particular interest in exemplifying
aspects of boreal Algonquian religious thought relating to humans and
animals. Algonquian beliefs concerning the resemblances and differences
between humans and animals have often been oversimplified and over-
formalized under the general rubric of "anthropomorphism." Northern
Algonquians, however, make a basic distinction between human–animal
relations in the earlier mythological period and in the contemporary world
(cf. Tanner 1979, 136–37). And going beyond this distinction, it is clear
that Algonquian thinkers have explored for each period both the continui-
ties and discontinuities between humans and animals.
   Some Manitoba Crees state that humans and animals have always been

---

*It is probable that, as in the speech of contemporary Ojibwas, Nelson's Saulteaux com-
panions used the noun *aniṡṡināpē* to refer to 'human being', in contrast to other living
entities, and also to 'Indian' or 'Ojibwa Indian', in contrast to other social groupings.
This multiple referential function is common in folk classification systems; e.g. the English
word 'animal' in different contexts subsumes and contrasts with 'human.'

different categories of being, but that animals possess human-like appearances, language, dwellings, manufactures, and social life which are concealed from humans or not available to their conventional waking perceptions (Brightman 1977–79). Myths set during an earlier condition of the world often represent animals as possessing human characteristics and as interacting with human or proto-human characters, although they may simultaneously possess the behavioral and physical attributes of their species. Nelson's myth is consistent with others both in explaining the origins of particular animal species and in specifying a *human* or, in any event, hominoid ancestry (cf. Speck 1935, 49; Bloomfield 1930, 82, 120, 295; Skinner 1911, 95, 107–8; Ahenakew 1929, 323). Alternatively, Algonquian mythology and theology may simply presuppose the existence of animals with various human characteristics. Today, Manitoba Crees say that the creator being *Kihcimanitōw* made animals or that the different species came into the Churchill River country from the four cardinal points. Other myths explain animals as the transformations or descendants of monsters or a single proto-animal (Ahenakew 1929, 320, 342; Skinner 1916, 344; Brown 1977, 44). It is significant that Nelson's myth specifically identifies the beaver as having a *human* origin, since Manitoba Crees, as noted above, emphasize concealed similarities between humans and beavers. Similarly, Crees sometimes conjecture that bears, which are also seen as more hominoid than other animals, were once human.

Other Algonquian myths make clear the original separation between human and animal, or make such a separation the point of departure for stories of transitions between the two categories. For example, David Thompson was told in 1797 by Crees or Ojibwas in the Swan River country of Manitoba that "the Beavers had been an ancient people, and then in the remote past lived on the dry land; they were always Beavers, not Men, they were wise and powerful, and neither Man, nor any animal made war on them" (1962, 155). Thompson's informants went on to describe how the beavers came to take up their aquatic habitat and manufactures, a rare example of an account describing a "historical" transition between the hominoid animals of the mythological era and the less overtly human-like animals of the present. It is interesting, from this point of view, that the motifs of the proscribed watercourse, the broken bridge, the association of water with the transformation, and the eventual aquatic reunion of the family in beaver form all occur in the somewhat different context of animal marriage myths recorded from Crees and Montagnais in Quebec (Bell 1897; Steager 1976; Savard 1979; Tanner 1973; Bauer 1971). In these stories, the wife is represented initially as a beaver and her fall into the waters effects a temporary or permanent separation from the human husband. In some versions, the transformation of the human husband into a beaver is made the basis for an explanation of the beavers' knowledge of lodge and dam building, or in other words, for the beavers' most human attribute. These accounts base human–beaver resemblances essentially on diffusion (the human beaver instructs his beaver wife's relatives in architecture) whereas Nelson's Ojibwa version explains them in terms of the human or proto-human ancestry of all beavers.

COSMOGONIC MYTHS AND
BEINGS FROM LAC LA RONGE

Nelson's manuscript contains two lengthy myths from Cree informants at Lac la Ronge. The first describes the birth and exploits of the subarctic Algonquian trickster–transformer "Wee-suck-a-jock" or *Wīsahkēcāhk* and exhibits certain Ojibwa influences unparalleled in other Cree versions. The second myth relates the successive conflicts of the transformer's son "Nay-han-nee-mis" or *Nēhanīmis* with North Wind and a primitive race called the "O-may-me-thay-day-ace-cae-wuck" [Cree *omēmīhðētēhēsiwak*], which Nelson translated as the "ancients" or "Hairy Breasts."*

The myths Nelson recorded are "cosmogonic"; that is, they relate events in an earlier condition of the earth to characteristics of the contemporary social and biophysical environments. Native North American cosmogonies are basically of two types: accounts of the initial creation of the world, usually by a benign and subsequently inactive deity; and accounts of secondary renovation and innovation by the transformer (Schmidt 1933, 66). Some accounts of primary creation, representing perhaps the esoteric synthesis of religious specialists (cf. Boas [1914] 1940, 312), have been

---

*Nelson's is one of a very few versions of this myth known to the editors; the others (unpublished) are recorded in 1986 field notes of Robert Brightman in northern Manitoba, and in A. Irving Hallowell's research notes from Berens River, Manitoba (Ms. Coll. #26, American Philosophical Society, Philadelphia).

recorded from Cree and Ojibwa sources (Landes 1968, 89–113; Dusenberry 1962, 65–66). However, most Algonquian and indeed North American cosmogonic myths, like those recorded by Nelson, presuppose an already extant world (although one distinct from the present) within which the transformer interacts with animal and human characters.

Rock Cree (like other Northern Algonquians) distinguish two separate categories of oral narrative which they call *ācaðōhkīwin* and *ācimōwin*. Nelson's stories pertained to the *ācaðōhkīwin* category; that is, they were set in the remote past, the narrators lacked direct knowledge of the characters, and cosmological contrasts with the present world were clearly drawn. Cree say that such stories pertain to an ancient period when humans and animals could converse and when animals shared social and cultural characteristics with humans (cf. Boas [1914] 1940, 455). Stories of the *ācimōwin* category, in contrast, occur in the contemporary condition of the world and their characters include human beings of whom the narrators have direct or indirect personal knowledge. Events classified as "supernatural" by non-Algonquians figure prominently in stories of both categories (cf. Hallowell 1955, 231–33; Hallowell [1960] 1976, 364–65; Preston 1975, 288–93).

The Trickster–Transformer, Wīsahkēcāhk

Nelson's first myth describes the birth and subsequent exploits of Wīsahkēcāhk, the central character of Cree and Saulteaux oral literature. Contemporary Manitoba Cree state that Wīsahkēcāhk was either a spirit or an extremely powerful human being, and many of them understand the stories about him as factual accounts of events that occurred in an earlier stage of the world when there were only a few human beings on earth (Brightman 1977–79). The behavior of Wīsahkēcāhk juxtaposes benign, malicious or stupid, and creative attributes, sometimes separately labeled as those of "culture hero," "trickster," and "transformer." This multiplicity of attributes is typical of trickster–transformer characters in other Subarctic and Eastern Woodlands Algonquian groups. The name 'Wīsahkēcāhk' is not, as has sometimes been supposed (Speck 1915, 1), a variant of the Cree *wiskacānis*, the gray jay (*Perisoreus canadensis*) or "whiskey jack." Nor is it a derivative of the root *wīsak-* 'bitter'. The name *Wīsahkēcāhk* goes back to the Proto-Algonquian parent language (Goddard 1974:107) and was unanalyzable even three thousand years ago. Names cognate to

Wīsahkēcāhk refer to comparable beings in the mythology of some Algonquin bands (Speck 1915; Davidson 1928, 275; Aubin 1982, 49–50) and such midwestern Woodlands Algonquian groups as the Potawatomi, Sauk, Fox, and Kickapoo. The earliest eighteenth-century European references to Wīsahkēcāhk among the Cree conflated his identity with that of the creator deity Kihcimanitōw (Isham 1949, 5; Graham 1969, 160). Nelson also initially made this error ("Supreme Being"), but characteristically inquired further and corrected it ("Skepticism, Belief and Innovation").

Contemporary Cree attitudes toward Wīsahkēcāhk link amusement and derision with respect and affection. When discussing Wīsahkēcāhk, Manitoba Crees remarked that he is always hungry and sexually adventurous (cf. the Sandy Lake Ojibwa epithet, "sex maniac of the north," Stevens 1971, 11), that he was capable of changing his form and of conversing with animals and other non-humans, that he addressed everyone as *nisīmī*, "my younger sibling," and that he altered the biophysical environment to render it habitable by humans. Johnny Bighetty of Granville Lake, Manitoba, remarked in 1977, "Wīsahkēcāhk was the first one up here in the North. He fixed things up for the old Indians and taught them how to live here in the Churchill River country" (Brightman 1977–79).

Some contemporary Crees, unlike those whom Nelson met, regard Wīsahkēcāhk simply as a legendary hero and reject both his role as mythical creator or transformer and his contemporary significance as a spiritual entity. The Lac la Ronge Crees of 1823 differed widely from some present-day Crees in their interpretation of him. For the Crees of the 1820s, Wīsahkēcāhk was an active spiritual presence who interacted with the operator and audience at shaking lodge performances; he also appeared in the 1930s performance that Stan Cuthand describes in this volume. Such interaction is explicitly rejected by some Crees today who state that Wīsahkēcāhk does not appear in dreams, visions, or the shaking lodge.

Nelson's Wīsahkēcāhk myth differs from other Cree versions as a result of borrowing of plot elements from the comparable cycle of the Southwestern and Southeastern Ojibwa trickster–transformer *Nēnapoš*, whose name is given here in the Walpole Island (Ontario) Ojibwa dialect described by Bloomfield (1957, 220). The earliest seventeenth and eighteenth century references to the trickster–transformer of the Ojibwa-speaking people did not use the name Nēnapoš or its cognates, but rather variants of the Ojibwa noun *miššapoš* 'big rabbit' that were first glossed by Europeans as "Great Hare" in the 1600s (Perrot 1911, 1:31; Allouez 1899, 201 ["Michabous"]; Raudot in Kinietz 1965, 371–72 ["Michapoux"]; Rasles 1900, 155 ["Michabou"]. Nēnapoš and its variants together with forms of miššapoš clearly refer to the same mythological personage; Nēnapoš has definite rabbit associations and some Southwestern Ojibwa identify him in English as "great rabbit" or "white hare" (Coleman et al. 1962, 56; Landes 1968, 22). The Ojibwa borrowings in Nelson's version of the Wīsahkēcāhk cycle are paralleled by those in another Cree cosmogonic myth told at York Factory in 1823 (Brown 1977). These influences raise questions regarding both the distribution and the differentiation of Wīsahkēcāhk and Nenaposh/Nēnapoš as characters in the literatures of subarctic and Eastern Woodlands Algonquians.

Broadly speaking, Wīsahkēcāhk is the primary trickster–transformer character among all Cree-speaking peoples west of Quebec and Nenaposh is the corresponding character among most Southeastern and Southwestern Ojibwa. The situation among the northernmost of the latter groups and among the Northern Ojibwa and Lake Winnipeg Saulteaux is more complicated. Some bands such as the Timagami band in Ontario retain the name Nenaposh together with plots and motifs that are identifiably Ojibwa rather than Cree (Speck 1915). Other Subarctic Ojibwa groups refer to the trickster–transformer character with cognates of Wīsahkēcāhk (Skinner 1911, 173; Stevens 1971). The Lake Winnipeg Saulteaux of Berens River in Manitoba appear to have recognized Wīsahkēcāhk as the principal transformer character, but also retained distinct stories about *Nēnapos* that are of obvious Ojibwa derivation (Hallowell 1976, 365, 367–68; Young 1903). Southwestern Ojibwa in Ontario show similarly mingled traditions. Some bands retain the name Nēnapoš (Laidlaw 1927, 52; Radin and Reagan 1928, 62) while others use cognates of Wīsahkēcāhk (Masson 1889–90, 2:353–54; Cooper 1936, 12; Laidlaw 1927, 51; Radin and Reagan 1928, 63–67). In all probability, myths dealing with both characters were told in the same communities, but it is unclear whether identical stories were told of both characters or whether the characters were themselves conventionally identified as the same.

Since many plot elements are shared between Cree and Ojibwa transformer cycles (cf. Dixon 1909; Fisher 1946), early European observers recognized the correspondences and identified Wīsahkēcāhk and Nēnapoš as two names of the same character. In 1809, for example, Alexander Henry the Younger observed, "Their [Fort Vermilion Cree] ideas of creation are nearly the same [as Ojibwa], and they have the same wonderful stories concerning Nainauboushaw, whom they call Wee-suc-ha-jouck" (Coues 1897, 2:512). Some Algonquians themselves clearly regarded the two names as synonymous, as indicated by two Plains Ojibwa (Howard 1977, 111) and Plains Cree (Ahenakew 1929, 333) narratives. If Allouez was correct, this identification dates from relatively early in the contact period; he wrote that the Ottawas in 1670 were using the names interchangeably, describing the Mackinac area as "the native Country of one of their Gods, named Michabous – that is to say, 'the great Hare,' Ouisaketchak, who is the one that created the earth" (Allouez 1899 [1669], 201). Alternatively, Allouez may have confused two beings whom the Ottawas regarded as distinct. As in Nelson's version, the two may occur as distinct characters in the same myth, an arrangement that occurs also in a Southwestern Ojibwa variant from Ontario (Radin and Reagan 1928, 63–67).

Reconstruction of earlier distributions and affiliations of the Cree and Ojibwa transformer cycles requires further knowledge of the precontact and early contact locations and movements of these Algonquian communities. If Ojibwa or proto-Ojibwa–Cree populations were resident in the boreal forest before European contact (Greenberg and Morrison 1982), the occurrence of Wīsahkēcāhk as the Lake Winnipeg Ojibwa transformer, or the coexistence of Nēnapoš and Wīsahkēcāhk as identical or distinct characters in the literature of the same Ojibwa–Saulteaux bands, is probably of considerable antiquity. Alternatively, if Ojibwa-speaking populations first took up permanent residence in the subarctic in the 1730s (Bishop 1974, 221–31), some may subsequently have fused with or been influenced by Cree and consequently replaced or augmented Nēnapoš with Wīsahkēcāhk.

Nelson's Version of the Wīsahkēcāhk Cycle

The unique characteristics of Nelson's version of the Wīsahkēcāhk cycle stand out if it is placed in the context of other Cree versions. The following comparative analysis and tabulation delineate the contrasting Cree and Ojibwa varieties of the cycle and identify both the shared and variable plots and motifs within the Cree "type." Since no one version is "correct," authoritative, or complete, the variants complement and amplify

each other. Characteristics of one version often aid and enrich the interpretation of the motifs and plot elements of others.

Figure 1 compares Nelson's version of the transformer cycle with corresponding passages from other Rock Cree, Swamp Cree, Woods Cree,
and Plains Cree versions. Despite derivation from a shared Algonquian
literary background and continued minglings of plot and motif between
Cree- and Ojibwa-speaking communities, the Wīsahkēcāhk and Nēnapoš
characters and their cycles remain distinguishable. Nelson recorded the
only known Cree occurrence of the Ojibwa "virgin birth" motif as an
account of the transformer's origin. Additionally, in Nelson's version,
Wīsahkēcāhk's wolf brother from the conventional Cree cycle is replaced
by a character called Mišapoš. This also reflects Ojibwa influence, specifically the incorporation of a character [inspired by *Nēnaboš*] in a
secondary role. The representation of the two transformers as brothers,
an interesting cosmological synthesis, occurs also in a Southwestern Ojibwa
variant from Ontario (Radin and Reagan 1928, 63–67). The circumstances
of the multiple birth and of the mother's sometimes temporary death are
also Ojibwa in derivation. For the rest, Nelson's account is characteristically
Cree in plot and motif. Lacking in Nelson's and other Cree versions are
such characteristic Ojibwa elements as the transformer's multiple brothers,
his fratricidal or patricidal campaign against the slayers of his mother
(Schoolcraft 1860; Blackbird 1887; Josselin de Jong 1913; Coleman et
al. 1962; Barnouw 1977), his designation of one slain brother as lord of
the afterworld (Coleman et al. 1962; Barnouw 1977; Jones 1917–19;
Schoolcraft 1839), the gift of the Grand Medicine Lodge or Midewiwin
society to the hero in recompense for his brother's death (Hindley 1885;
Jenness 1935; Kinietz 1947; Barnouw 1977), or the occurrence of a preliminary flood which recedes after the water beings are wounded (Jones
1917–19; Radin and Reagan 1928; Jenness 1935).

Compared to other Cree versions, Nelson's text is distinguished primarily
by its Ojibwa borrowings in its account of the transformer's origin. Those
Cree versions that identify Wīsahkēcāhk's parentage name him as the son
of the unfortunate principals of the rolling head story (Ahenakew 1929;
Blomfield 1930; Maclean 1897; Russell 1898; Vandersteene 1969) or of
stars into which they were transformed (Dusenberry 1962). Nelson's version omits the events leading to the pursuit of the transformer by his
mother's animated severed head; it omits also the typical Cree elements

Figure 1
The Cree Wīsahkēcāhk Cycle: The Flood Myth

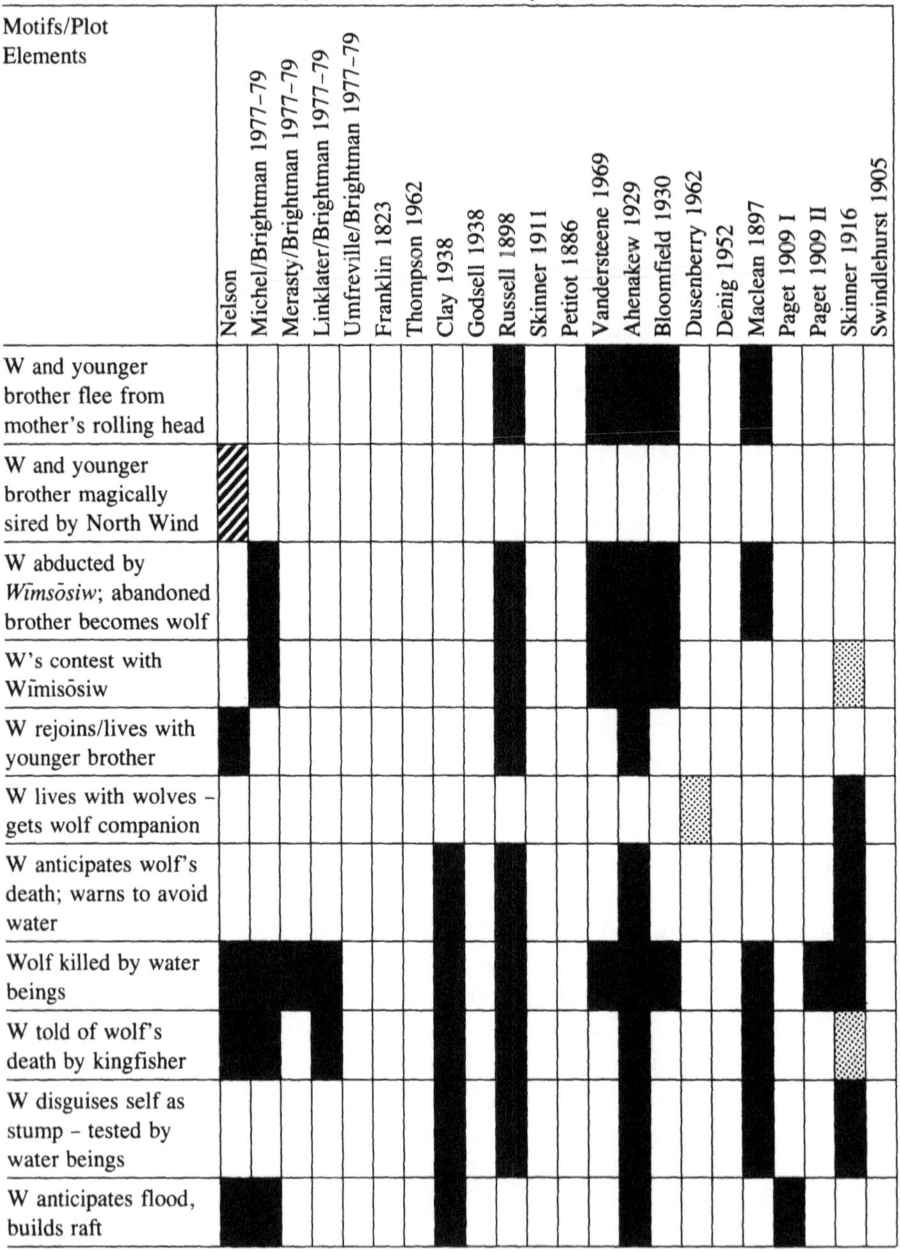

Motifs/Plot Elements	Nelson	Michel/Brightman 1977–79	Merasty/Brightman 1977–79	Linklater/Brightman 1977–79	Umfreville/Brightman 1977–79	Franklin 1823	Thompson 1962	Clay 1938	Godsell 1938	Russell 1898	Skinner 1911	Petitot 1886	Vandersteene 1969	Ahenakew 1929	Bloomfield 1930	Dusenberry 1962	Denig 1952	Maclean 1897	Paget 1909 I	Paget 1909 II	Skinner 1916	Swindlehurst 1905
W and younger brother flee from mother's rolling head										■			■	■				■				
W and younger brother magically sired by North Wind	▨																					
W abducted by *Wīmsōsiw*; abandoned brother becomes wolf		■											■	■	■			■				
W's contest with *Wīmisōsiw*		■											■	■							░	
W rejoins/lives with younger brother	■													■								
W lives with wolves – gets wolf companion																░					■	
W anticipates wolf's death; warns to avoid water									■	■			■	■				■				
Wolf killed by water beings	■								■	■			■	■			■				■	
W told of wolf's death by kingfisher	■								■	■			■	■							░	
W disguises self as stump – tested by water beings		■							■	■			■	■							■	
W anticipates flood, builds raft	■								■	■			■	■				■			■	

continued

Motifs/Plot Elements	Nelson	Michel/Brightman 1977–79	Merasty/Brightman 1977–79	Linklater/Brightman 1977–79	Umfreville/Brightman 1977–79	Franklin 1923	Thompson 1962	Clay 1938	Godsell 1938	Russell 1898	Skinner 1911	Petitot 1886	Vandersteene 1969	Ahenakew 1929	Bloomfield 1930	Dusenberry 1962	Denig 1952	Maclean 1897	Paget 1909 I	Paget 1909 II	Skinner 1916	Swindlehurst 1905
W kills chief of water beings at beach	■	■	■					■		■										▨		
W wounds chief of water beings; later kills after killing/impersonating frog doctor										░			■	■	■			■				
W retrieves wolf brother's hide from doorway		■		■						■				■				■			■	
W reanimates hide				■						■				■				■				
Revenge of water beings results in flood	■	■		■						■				■				■			■	
Kihcimanitōw unleashes flood to punish humans and animals								■					■			■						
W builds/embarks on raft as flood waters rise	■						■	■	■	■	■			■	■	■	■	■			■	■
W forgets moss/earth to recreate world	■									■				■			■					
W climbs tree to escape flood	■		■																			
W takes animals on raft/canoe	■							■		■	■		■		■		■	■				

continued

Motifs/Plot Elements	Nelson	Michel/Brightman 1977–79	Merasty/Brightman 1977–79	Linklater/Brightman 1977–79	Umfreville/Brightman 1977–79	Franklin 1923	Thompson 1962	Clay 1938	Godsell 1938	Russell 1898	Skinner 1911	Petitot 1886	Vandersteene 1969	Ahenakew 1929	Bloomfield 1930	Dusenberry 1962	Denig 1952	Maclean 1897	Paget 1909 I	Paget 1909 II	Skinner 1916	Swindlehurst 1905
W attacked by water beings while afloat	□	□	□	□	□	□	□	□	□	■	■	□	□	■	■	□	□	□	□	□	□	□
Earth Diver – muskrat successful	■	■	■	■	■	□	■	■	■	■	◪	■	■	■	■	■	■	■	■	■	■	□
W remakes world from mud or moss brought by Earth Diver	■	■	■	■	■	□	■	■	■	■	■	■	■	■	■	■	■	■	■	■	■	◪
Testing of earth's size	■	□	□	■	■	■	■	■	□	■	□	■	□	■	□	■	■	■	■	■	■	■
W creates human beings from earth/clay	■	□	□	■	■	■	■	■	■	■	■	■	■	■	■	■	■	■	■	■	■	■
Kihcimanitōw creates or recreates human beings from earth/clay	□	□	□	□	▦	□	■	□	□	□	▦	□	□	□	□	◪	◪	□	□	□	□	□

Note:
- ■ Indicates that the motif is present.
- □ Indicates that the motif is absent.
- ▦ Indicates that the motif is present but occurs detached from the narrative of Wisahkecahk's conflict with the water beings and his renovation of the world after the flood.
- ◪ Indicates that the motif diverges from the conventional pattern established by comparison.

The Cree divisions and bands from which the versions were recorded are indicated below:

Rock Cree (including all /ð/-dialect groups)
  Nelson (Lac la Ronge, Saskatchewan)
  Michel/Brightman 1977–79 (Brochet, Manitoba)

continued

Merasty/Brightman 1977–79 (Brochet, Manitoba)
Umfreville/Brightman 1977–79 (Brochet, Manitoba)
Linklater/Brightman 1977–79 (Pukatawagan, Manitoba)
Franklin 1823 (Cumberland House, Saskatchewan)
Thompson 1962 (Churchill and Nelson River drainages, northwestern Manitoba)

Swampy Cree
Clay 1938 (Fisher River, Manitoba)
Godsell 1938 (? North-central Manitoba)
Russell 1898 (Grand Rapids, Manitoba)
Skinner 1911 (Fort Albany, Ontario)

Woods Cree
Petitot 1886 (Cold Lake, Alberta)
Vandersteene 1969 (Wabasca, Alberta)

Plains Cree
Ahenakew 1929 (Thunderchild, Saskatchewan)
Bloomfield 1930 (Sweet Grass, Saskatchewan)
Dusenberry 1962 (Rocky Boy, Montana)
Denig 1952 (?)
Maclean 1896 (? - Saskatchewan River)
Paget 1909 (Qu'appelle, Saskatchewan)
Skinner 1916 (Crooked Lake, Cowessess, Sakimay, Saskatchewan)

Unidentified
Swindlehurst 1905 ("James Bay")

See Map 1, page 6.

of Wīsahkēcāhk's combat with his sorcerer father-in-law *Wīmisōsiw* and the transformation of his abandoned younger brother into a wolf or wolf-life creature. The presence of a wolf at the scene of the brother's death in Nelson's version is interpretable as a retention from the typical Cree versions. An anomalous Plains Cree variant (Skinner 1916) represents Wīsahkēcāhk as having been a wolverine prior to assuming a more human identity.

Nelson's version is typical in identifying the transformer's antagonists as the *Misipisiwak,* 'great lynxes' or 'water panthers,' a race of aquatic beings who figure prominently in Algonquian theology and mythology.

Nelson's narrator omitted the common Ojibwa motif of the hero's transformation into a stump to deceive the water beings and also the passage, common in Ojibwa versions, in which the hero disguises himself as a female toad-shaman and delivers the *coup de grâce* to the chief of the water beings wounded in their first encounter. Also ommitted is the hero's retrieval of the hide of his slain brother from the lodge of the lynxes and, in some versions, the latter's magical re-animation. However, Nelson recounted an episode noted in only three other versions: Wīsahkēcāhk's trickster-like conquest of the giant aquatic beings dispatched to kill him and his companions while they are afloat after the flood.

As indicated in Figure 1, the elements of the earth-diver, world-renewal, and the testing of the earth's size are present in most Cree versions and remarkably uniform in their particulars. More variable is the identification of the transformer as the creator of human beings. Nelson's account of the creation of humans by Wīsahkēcāhk is one of four (cf. Bloomfield 1930; Vandersteene, 1969; Stevens 1971) that date this event as a post-deluge innovation. Since human or seemingly hominoid characters figure in mythic events prior to the flood, David Thompson's (1962, 78) early reference in the 1790s to "renovated Mankind" is perhaps more accurate than the idea of an unprecedented human creation. Wīsahkēcāhk may, therefore, have been conceived of as a secondary creator or recreator of humans. Other Cree myths of human origin do not specify when human beings were created in relation to a flood or other mythological events (Skinner 1911; Wales in Cooper 1933, 56; Rossignol 1938; Simms 1906; Brightman 1977-79); and they identify the creator deity rather than the transformer as the primal sculptor.

In Nelson's account, Wīsahkēcāhk hews a male human figure from stone, but then substitutes clay after reflecting that the new creature would be excessively insolent and imperishable; in Ojibwa versions, hardness and asocial characteristics are also conceptually merged in the person of Nēnapoš's flint brother. In a Lake Winnipeg Saulteaux version (Simms 1906), the original stone image is ruined by a jealous bear and clay is substituted. Wīsahkēcāhk then imparts life to the image by breathing on it, the same method used to resurrect the earth-divers and create the new earth after the flood. Nelson described the creation of a male and female pair (cf. Bloomfield 1930; Vandersteene 1969; Wales in Cooper 1933, 56), but departed from cognate myths in identifying the Moon as the creator of women and menstruation. Like other versions, Nelson's portrayed Indian and white creations as separate. It is interesting that in his text the motif of female creation from the male rib pertained only to whites, rather as though Cree were integrating biblical elements into their account of the Europeans' origins but not, as yet, their own; later versions relate the rib motif to Indians as well (Bloomfield 1930; Vandersteene 1969; Dusenberry 1962). Some versions of human creation account for blacks as well as for Indians and whites (Wales in Cooper 1933, 56; Skinner 1911; Stevens 1971; Brightman 1977–79), variations in skin color being related to differential baking or to the use of different colored clays. In these versions, the creator was displeased with the excessively dark and light coloring of the black and white prototypes and continued experimenting until the aesthetically satisfying pigmentation of the Indian was secured.

Two unparalleled Plains Cree variants of human creation state that humans derive from a two-dimensional outline drawing on the earth (Dusenberry 1962) or from multiple images animated by the heat of the sun (Denig 1952). Ojibwa accounts of human creation are also divided between post-deluge episodes in the transformer cycle (Perrot 1911, 1:31–36; P. Jones 1861; W. Jones 1917–19; Stevens 1971) and independent stories that ascribe the active role to the creator deity (Landes 1968; Barnouw 1977; Cooper 1936, 6, 21).

The symbolism and cultural logic organizing the characters and events in the Cree and Ojibwa transformer cycles exhibit themes and patterns found in large areas of Eastern and Subarctic North America and in New World mythology as a whole. Nelson's version follows others in representing cosmogonic events and processes as consequences of antagonism between beings representing opposed terrestrial and aquatic or subterranean spheres. The characteristics of these beings sometimes reflect factual environmental associations, as when the hominoid Wīsahkēcāhk and his rabbit-like brother exemplify terrestrial beings. In other instances, the myths creatively invert such facts as when the rulers of aquatic and subterranean domains are represented as lynxes, animals whose nocturnal habits may have associated them with darkness. It is consistent with this dialectic that the earth is remade through the efforts of amphibious mammals such as the beaver, otter, and muskrat whose habitat encompasses both land and water. Events in these myths could be seen to symbolize ambiguities and antagonisms perceived by Cree and Ojibwa in the human–animal or hunter–prey relationships. Nelson's is the only version in which Wīsahkēcāhk exhorts the surviving animals to behave morally and "not secret or hide themselves too much from my little brothers (the human beings which he was about to create) when they might want to eat &c &c" ("The Making of the Land"). One paradoxical aspect of the symbolism of Water Lynxes is perhaps their identification with the welfare of terrestrial as well as aquatic animal life and their antagonism to human predation. The wolf brother who precipitates the struggle is a hunter who meets his death while pursuing prey. Three Ojibwa versions (Jenness 1935; Barnouw 1977; Ellis in Chamberlain 1891) identify as the motive for the brother's death the angry reactions of the lynxes to his excessive predation and their fears that he would exterminate game animals if left unchecked (cf. Vecsey 1983, 94–98).

Not exemplified in Nelson's myth are the thunderbirds' respectively positive and negative relations with the terrestrial and aquatic-subterranean spheres. In myths detailing these relationships, the thunderers are conventionally represented as the allies and advocates of human beings while the giant lynxes, horned snakes, and other aquatic-subterranean creatures are portrayed as dangerous and malevolent (Skinner 1928, 169–70); W. Jones 1917–19, 258–61; Chamberlain 1890, 51–52; Bloomfield 1934, 159–65; Jenness 1935, 35; Dusenberry 1962, 109–10). These relations are modified in the theology of the Ojibwa Midewiwin, whose esoteric cosmology appropriates the giant lynxes and snakes as patrons of human beings (Jenness 1935, 39–40; Howard 1967, 113–14; Simms 1906, 334–35). In some popular myths, the giant horned snakes figure also as protectors of orphaned children (Bloomfield 1930, 15–16; Petitot 1886, 455; Brightman 1977–79; Stevens 1971, 114–15).

Nehanimis, North Wind, and the Hairy Breasts
Later in the manuscript, Nelson described the successive conflicts of Nēhanīmis, the son of Wīsahkēcāhk, with the North Wind and with the "Hairy Breasts," a race of primitive hominoids contending with humans for dominion on the earth. Evidently, no cognate stories have been

published although this text shares certain motifs with myths recorded by Curtis (1928, 18: 129–31) and Ahenakew (1929, 339–43).

Nelson's reference to a story in which Wīsahkēcāhk becomes a woman in order to wed his misogynous son suggests a unique conjunction of the themes of incest and female metamorphosis figuring in other Cree and Ojibwa trickster stories (cf. Josselin de Jong 1913, 20–23; Skinner 1916, 350–51; Coleman et al. 1962, 93–94; Speck 1915, 16). The identification of a named hero as the son of Wīsahkēcāhk appears to occur only in Nelson's account, and perhaps represents a synthesis unique to the Lac la Ronge area. The only other reference to a Cree hero named Nēhanīmis in existing sources is in Curtis's myth of "Niyanimis" collected from the Woods Cree of Alberta (1928, 18:129–31). This narrative parallels Nelson's account in describing the contest between Nēhanīmis and *Misāpēw*, a giant. A magically charged feather ornament figures in both stories as the source of the hero's victory, but the Curtis version adds the cosmogonic motif in which Nēhanīmis divides the defeated monster into four beings of diminished power who become the prototypes of the four winds.

Nelson's myth of the conflict of Nēhanīmis with the "Hairy Breasts" and his earlier observations on them suggest some comparisons regarding these symbolically complex beings. Nelson gives their Cree name as "O-may-me-thay-day-ace-cae-wuck," a form that he translates as "Hairy Breasts" or "Ancients." This term is cognate to contemporary Woods Cree *mīmīðīhtīhīsiwak*, which is analyzable as 'hairy-heart-beings' and refers to a race of cannibal monsters living in the remote past. Northern Manitoba Cree distinguish "hairy-heart-beings" from the *wīhtikōw* (windigo) by emphasizing their lack of human ancestry and the fact that they no longer exist (Brightman 1977–78). In a myth collected by Ahenakew (1929, 339–43), Wīsahkēcāhk cleverly defeats their cannibalistic designs.

The beings described by Nelson are not specifically identified as cannibals and share rather a constellation of attributes and associations with a category of persons now referred to by Manitoba Cree as the *kayās-iðiniwak*, 'old/ancient people' (Brightman 1977–79). The kayās-iðiniwak are represented as anthropomorphic in appearance, but as lacking the intelligence and technology of the Cree people who displaced them, in time beyond memory, along the Churchill River from Ile à la Crosse to Hudson Bay. Crees cognizant of Western archaeological knowledge readily equate the kayās-iðiniwak with the Old World Paleolithic humans, remarking that both were hairy, used stone implements, and dressed only in rags or loincloths. This cultural and intellectual primitivity is shared with the "Hairy Breasts" of Nelson's manuscript to the degree that the two terms may be regarded as synonymous. The emphasis on the rudimentary technology of these beings suggests that they may perpetuate or encode Cree traditions about conditions of life prior to the introduction of steel tools. In Nelson's manuscript, the Hairy Breasts attempt to exhort others to respect their seniority, a motif that may express ambiguous attitudes towards the aged in Cree society. This ambiguity was given a rather elegant expression by Nelson's Cree informant:

There are still 2 nations of them, one of which is on *Your* lands, the others, I believe, beyond the Seas: but they are an insignificant and most despicable people...I saw one many years back, who was bro't by the Traders from somewheres on your lands: his face was venerable, but still there was a meanness in the *whole* of him that I could not account for: I respected him, and wanted to treat him accordingly – this was from the stories I had heard related of them; but the traders laughed at *us* and asked me if I was inclined to respect folly, insignificance, and nothing!!!

One can only speculate about the identity of the person observed by the narrator, but the circumstance of a trading Indian tendering respect to a person symbolic of an earlier Indian society and thereby provoking the derision of the European agents of social transformation has complex and tragic connotations. An additional element of ambiguity in the image of the Hairy Breasts preserved by Nelson is their proclivity for capturing and enslaving human women; these passages in the Nēhanīmis myth suggest that Cree perceptions of their Athapaskan or Inuit enemies also figured in the image.

DREAM GUARDIANS AND THE VISION FAST

Nelson used the word "Dreamed" (with possessive adjective) as a noun to translate *pawākan*, the individual spirit guardian sought by Cree and Saulteaux during a solitary vision fast at or shortly after puberty. The concept of the pawākan and the associated ideas about dream communication and interpretation are the most central yet most abstruse aspects of

Northern Algonquian religious thought. The subjective encounters of Crees and Saulteaux with their guardians in dreams, visions, and waking states pose formidable difficulties for cross-cultural understanding, even supposing the willingness of individuals to communicate these often intensely private spiritual events to others. Nelson was able to describe the details of visionary experience and to explore the many-faceted relationship between human and pawākan well before missionaries and other Europeans influenced the indigenous Northern Algonquian religions.

The Cree noun pawākan and its Ojibwa cognate refer to any nonhuman animate agent who enters into an enduring relationship with a human being, bestowing information, technical and spiritual abilities, and sometimes physical aid. In return, the human being is required to respect the pawākan, carry out its wishes and instructions and offer to it gifts such as tobacco, food, and manufactured goods. Tobacco has particular importance both as an offering and as a signal of the desire to communicate. Many of the beings identified as pawākan by Crees are members of a taxonomic class called 'spirit' in English [Cree *ahcāk*]; these are often associated with biophysical phenomena such as the winds, the sun, the moon, and thunder, and with particular animal species. In other instances, the pawākan is the animating spiritual component or soul (also ahcāk in Cree) of an individual, animal, tree, tool, or other entity not itself classified as a spirit (Brightman 1977–79). The human–pawākan relationship, with its components of love, respect, obligation and danger, exemplifies the uncertainties and dynamics of interaction between humans and nonhuman beings more generally. The pawākan was distinguished from these other entities by the enduring character of its tie to a specific human dependent. As one Manitoba Cree expressed it: "You can have the pawākan for your whole life as long as you believe in it. The more a person uses it, the more it does" (Brightman 1977–79).

The Vision Fast
Nelson described both the circumstances of the initial vision fast and the content of the fasters' experiences ("Dreaming to Conjure and Predict"). Some of Nelson's observations need qualification. The vision fast was undertaken by most Cree or Saulteaux males and not exclusively by those who desired power to conjure with the shaking lodge. Likewise, the age

range of eighteen to twenty-five named by Nelson as the period within
which most initial fasts took place appears too late, although it is true
that men might undergo successive isolated fasts well into middle age
(Brightman 1977–79). To judge from other sources, the typical age of the
faster showed some regional variation, ranging from the age of ten (Honigmann 1956, 71 [Attawapiskat, Ontario]), through ages fourteen to sixteen (Boulanger 1971, 50 [Oxford House, Manitoba]; Rossignol 1939,
69 [Ile à la Crosse, Saskatchewan]). Girls sometimes underwent an isolated
fast as well. More typically, however, they acquired spirit guardians
during their first menstrual isolation or during dreams or trances not
purposely induced. Males also sometimes experienced uninduced visions,
and not all vision seekers were successful; failure usually prompted further
attempts.

Nelson indicated that ideally the faster was sexually inexperienced,
although for those fasting after puberty, this requirement probably referred
to a period of prescribed abstinence prior to the fast. It is unclear whether
sexual activity *per se* or contact with women generally (or both) was understood to interfere with a successful vision. The experience also typically
entailed the separation of the faster from human society, although brothers
or parallel cousins might fast together (Brightman 1977–79). In Nelson's
account, the faster selected a site for the vigil in the bush at some distance
from his family's camp. After preparing a bed of grass, the boy desposited
his clothes elsewhere and then returned to begin a program of fasting and
concentration to attain a visionary state in which communication with
the pawākan would occur. As Nelson stated, the preferred season for the
fast was spring, it being seen as a period of intensified spiritual activity
(Brightman 1977–79), although its advantages of temperature and free-
dom from insects were also important. Nelson claimed that total fasting
was required; other sources (Honigmann 1956, 71; Boulanger 1971, 50)
mention, however, that small quantities of water and preserved food could
be consumed.

The choice of the vision site was motivated by the nature of the spirit(s)
with whom the faster desired communication. Typically a senior relative
specified the time and location. Those seeking a pawākan associated with
the earth or water fasted on the ground while those seeking beings of the
air "fasted at some distance from the Ground." In many cases, tree platforms or scaffolds were utilized apparently as a matter of course (Skinner

1911, 61; Rossignol 1939, 69; Hallowell 1955, 403n; Semmens 1884, 109–10), the distance of the platform from the ground being thought proportional to the power of the spirit who would appear (Honigmann 1956, 71). Platforms in trees on the shores of rivers and lakes were favored because they juxtaposed the faster simultaneously with the earth, the sky, the water, and, through the roots, with subterranean and underwater domains. Such intersections were thought to be conducive to a successful experience (Brightman 1977–79). Nelson stated that fasters slept with their heads oriented toward particular cardinal points; this practice would be intended to induce communication with spirits associated with the four winds and directions.

Communication with the pawākan was said by Nelson to occur during dreams in sleep. The Cree verb *pawāmiw* ['he/she dreams'] however, while it includes the sense of English 'dream,' can refer also to mental activity during trance states and waking periods of intense exhilaration and concentration (Brightman 1977–79; Landes 1938, 9). Visions were not necessarily associated with sleep and with "dreaming" (in the English sense) although many and perhaps most of them occurred in sleep (Brightman 1977–79).

Anthropological or psychological explanations of North American Indian vision experiences and of comparable phenomena in other societies emphasize the effects of fasting, isolation, and expectation in inducing waking trance states or vivid dreaming. From this point of view, the faster's cultural preconceptions prefigure the content of the vision as spirit communication and enter into its retrospective interpretation and reconstruction. As Nelson wrote, "They know many of *these spirits* as soon as they see them (in their dreams) by the descriptions the other indians have given of them" ("The Spirits, their Shapes, and their Songs").

Nelson's remarkable description of the spirit guardian vision, perhaps a composite of what his informants told him, confirms and clarifies the sparse ethnographic sources (cf. Radin 1914b, 1936; Hallowell 1955, 178; Vecsey 1983, 127–31). In his "dream," the faster is approached by a human-looking figure who asks to be identified or recognized. When the faster admits his ignorance, the two travel to the spirit's domain or domicile and there the spirit changes form, appearing as an animal, tree, stone, or other familiar animate being. During this period, the faster is taught a song with which to summon the pawākan, is given information about his experiences and abilities in the future, and is perhaps instructed in particular spiritual or other skills. During visions, fasters may also be asked to perform certain actions that predestine events to occur many years later.

The complex symbolism of the vision experience gives some insight into the philosophical complexities and dualism of Algonquian religious thought. In the vision itself, as in waking life, Algonquians recognize the possibility of discontinuities between individual perception and the underlying and perhaps objectively more valid inner characteristics of objects and events (cf. Black 1977). Nelson stated that the pawākan might visit the vision-seeker as many as six times (possibly an arbitrary number), sometimes appearing as a human being before revealing its "proper form" with which the faster was familiar. Information on the powers and abilities to be conferred was similarly couched in symbolic disguise, and actions and objects recalled from the vision could be both more or less than they seemed. In one instance described by Nelson ("Windigo Dreams"), the faster was exhorted by North Wind to eat from platters filled with tempting foods. Through the intervention of another spirit, the dreamer realized that what he perceived as animal meat was really human flesh; he rejected the cannibalistic meal and thereby escaped becoming a windigo in later life. The philosophical dualism underlying Algonquian visions and dreams is exemplified in the anthropomorphic character of beings identified as trees, animals, or kinds of spirits; as "Dreamed," these entities wear clothes, speak, and physically resemble human beings. It is possible that dreams and visions were understood to offer privileged perceptual access to an underlying commonality between humans and nonhuman beings, allowing the dreamer to recognize that the contrasts between them, as seen in waking life, were from this theological point of view, epiphenomenal or illusory.

Following the vision, the faster dressed himself and returned to his family's camp where he smoked and ate in a composed fashion. The identity of the spirit guardian might be revealed to some senior relatives, but was not otherwise explicitly communicated (Brightman 1977–79). Nelson stated that the vision period might last for three, four, ten, or even thirty days, a range of variation attested in other references (Godsell 1938, 135 [one night]; Honigmann 1956, 71 [two-four weeks]; Semmens 1884, 109 [five-six days]; Skinner 1911, 61 [seven-ten days]; Boulanger 1971, 50 [one week]; Rossignol 1939, 69 [three-four days]; Mason 1967, 49 [one-twenty days]).

The Human-Pawākan Relationship

The dreamer emerged from the vision with obligations – some culturally stereotyped, some individual although culturally patterned – which he owed to his guardian(s). In general, at least portions of the information communicated in dreams and visions were kept secret. One of Nelson's informants, for example, would discourse only on topics "not forbidden by his Dreamed" ("Sickness in Spirit Form"). Similarly, a La Pointe Ojibwa revealed to Kohl (1860, 296–97) only certain aspects of his puberty vision. In cases where the identity of the pawākan was concealed, it was often possible for others to infer it from the behavior or possessions of the dreamer. Nelson, for example, observed that the songs taught to a man by his spirit guardian were recorded with mnemonic symbols on birch-bark scrolls (cf. Dewdney 1975) and the symbols were at least to some degree interpretable by others. Nelson noted that the dreamer might be instructed to sponsor a feast of an animal whose species and location were revealed in the vision. Offerings of food, tobacco, and goods such as clothing and knives were burned or deposited next to wooden statues (Cree *manitōkan* or *manitōhkan*) carved to represent the spirit (Brightman 1977–79; see also Stan Cuthand's description in this volume).

Nelson's discussion of sacrificial feasts show that the spirit guardian complex had its collective aspects although feasts were also sponsored to propitiate spirits other than the individual guardian. Nelson distinguished between calendrical feasts carried out annually and voluntary feasts sponsored by individuals to honor their spirit guardian(s), ancestors, the spirits of slain animals, and perhaps other beings. Dancing, drumming, and singing were intended to communicate with and show respect for the spirits. Feasts involved explicit acts of sharing: portions of each kind of food and beverage were burned or poured onto the ground. During collective feasts, it was understood that spirits extracted and consumed an immaterial aspect of the food (Landes 1968, 34; Brightman 1977–79). Nelson, for example, noted that a bladder of grease was offered to a wooden image of the skeleton spirit pāhkāhk before being shared among the guests ("Sacrifices and Feasts for Pah-kack"). This economically practical doctrine explains one aspect of the *festin à tout manger* or "eat-all" feast (cf. Graham 1969, 165–66; Franklin 1823, 122–23) whose ritual influence on successful hunting depended on total consumption of the prepared food. Every participant was also required to eat some of each type of food. At one such feast,

Nelson made use of the satiated guest's expedient (attested elsewhere) of offering gifts to the host in compensation for not eating his full share. These gifts were then presumably offered to the host's pawākan to assuage its displeasure over the improper conduct of the ritual: "though we gormandized (it cannot be called *eating*) there yet remained full 2/3ds. The Feaster was uneasy and said he would have been proud had we eaten all, for in that case his Dreamed would have been more propitious: we were obliged to dance also; but when I could stand no more I gave him my knife and a bit of tobacco and walked off leaving him to settle with his God as well as he could" ("Feasts"). The symbolism of the "eat-all" rule in these feasts is complex and merges concepts of offering, consubstantiation, and the creation of an artificial famine which will be followed by successful hunting and trapping (Brightman 1977–79).

In exchange for offerings and other expressions of respect, the pawākan was understood to render different varieties of assistance to its human dependent. The guardian spirit was a source of information regarding spatially or temporally remote events, especially those pertaining to the future. Predictions about health, life expectancy, and hunting prospects were communicated in dreams, often in a symbolic medium requiring interpretation. In at least some cases, experiences in dreams were thought to reflect the activities of the dreamer's soul which could be absent from the body for limited periods. In some instances, spirit guardians physically intervened in dangerous situations to protect human welfare ("Conjuring at Lac La Ronge, December 1819," "The Lost Traveller and the Wolf Spirit").

Nelson's observations help in understanding Cree and Saulteaux views of the relationship between the spirit guardian and the "power" exerted by humans in such practices as sorcery (spiritual practices harming others), curing, and hunting medicine:

Yes, most certainly; it is not the root alone [that effects sorcery], but with the assistance of that one of his Dreamed that is most powerful, and most fond of him ("Sorcery for Protection and Revenge").

Now he desired in the beginning [before using hunting medicine] that if his familiar would have compassion on him, he would render these three moose foolish: that they might not be possessed of their usual cunning &c ("Hunting Medicine").

These passages make clear that the effectiveness of magical techniques was thought to be dependent on the simultaneous collaboration and assistance of the pawākan. They are therefore relevant to a longstanding discussion regarding the "animistic" versus "animatistic" basis of Algonquian religion (Jones 1905; Radin 1914a,c), or the question of whether the individual spirit being or an impersonal spiritual power was the basic religious concept. Possibly some magical operations were thought also to proceed independently of the guardian's collaboration, and it may be that, as in Southwestern Ojibwa belief (Landes 1968, 52), some persons exerted such powers without simultaneous assistance from the spirits who had granted them.

Although the human–pawākan relationship was ideally one of love, respect, and assistance, uncertainty attached to this most central of spiritual relationships as it did to other areas of interaction between human beings and spirits. Some individuals experienced their guardians as unpredictable, demanding, and dangerous (cf. Bauer 1973, 10–15). As Nelson also emphasized, the spirits reacted angrily to skepticism about their powers or existence, a fact that helps to explain the reluctance of Algonquians to expose their religious concepts to Euro-Canadian disparagement ("Feasts," cf. Thompson 1962, 74-75). Spirits might also provide misinformation ("Dreaming to Conjure and Predict"), a possibility which sometimes led to the testing of the veracity of important dreams with the shaking lodge or through other means (Brightman 1977-79). Persons undergoing the vision fast felt a serious need to identify and reject ineffectual or malignant spirits that might come to them. In addition, the pawākan was easily offended by ritual omissions or neglect. As Nelson wrote: "Indeed, from what I can learn, there are but few of these familiars but do evil to their votaries if they . . . neglect performing the regular annual, or perhaps more distant periodical sacrifice; and this sacrifice, their familiar tells them what it is he expects" ("The Spirits' Gifts and Demands"). In an especially memorable example, Nelson detailed the persecutions of a Cree by his voracious and irascible spirit guardian, pākahk or Skeleton ("Encounters with Pah-kack").

Nelson viewed Northern Algonquian religion as an effective adaptation to the dangers posed by illness, accident, lack of information, and uncertain animal resources. As with conjuring and the shaking lodge, his reflections led him to credit his informants' explanations of the complex relations between knowledge, practical action, spirit guardians, and the literal or interpreted messages in dreams: "And I do not know any method more adapted to this [averting danger] than the one they pursue, i.e. Fasting and Sleeping to dream and they do dream too; and many of these dreams are so complicated, or compounded of so many different things that it is absolutely beyond the power of *their* invention to fabricate them" ("Skepticism, Belief, and Innovation").

THE SHAKING LODGE

Early European observers of boreal Algonquians described, some with contempt, and some with fascination, a divinatory practice used to discover or manipulate information and events in the future or at a distance.*
At nightfall, the diviner (or "conjuror" as Europeans often termed him) entered a small barrel-shaped lodge that concealed him from the audience assembled outside. Alternatively he was placed in the lodge bound hand and foot, and when he was seen to be freed, his release was attributed to the spirits. The diviner then sang and drummed or rattled in order to summon different spirits into the lodge. The shaking or waving of the

---

*The foundation text on conjuring and the shaking lodge is Hallowell's monograph *The Role of Conjuring in Saulteaux Society* (1942), which integrates field data from Manitoba with a nearly exhaustive compendium of comparative material. To Hallowell's annotated bibliography of early references can be added Robson ([1752] 1965); Kelsey ([1683/1722] 1929, 20–21); Drage ([1748–49] 1968, 1:235); and Graham ([1767/91] 1969, 162), who described the ritual among Cree along western Hudson Bay in the eighteenth century. Since the publication of Hallowell's monograph, the conjuring complex has been described among the Pīkangekum Saulteaux (Dunning 1959, 177–80), the Sand Lake Wisconsin Chippewa (Ritzenthaler 1953, 200–4), the Oxford House Swampy Cree (Mason 1967, 63), the Sandy Lake Cree (Stevens 1985), the Attawapiskat Swampy Cree (Honigmann 1956, 73–75), the Rupert House Cree (Preston 1975, 25–90), the Mistassini Cree (Rousseau and Rousseau 1947; Rousseau 1953; Burgesse 1944; Tanner 1979, 111–16), the Lac St. John Montagnais (Lips 1947, 476–82), the Natashquan Montagnais (Vincent 1973; 1977), and the Fort George Cree (Bauer 1971, 21–27). The accounts by Rousseau, Ritzenthaler, Dunning, and Preston are based on firsthand observation of the ritual. The shaking lodge has been discussed comparatively among Algonquians by Cooper (1944). Schaeffer (1969) and Flannery (1944) discussed Blackfoot and Gros Ventre conjuring, respectively. Ray (1941) examined cognate practices among Plateau groups still farther to the west.

structure from side to side signalled the arrival of these beings. During the performance, they spoke among themselves, with the diviner, and with the audience outside, responding to questions either in known languages or with speech that required translation. The continuous or intermittent agitation of the lodge has caused the practice to be called the "shaking lodge" or "shaking tent" as well as "jugglery" or "conjuring." *Kosāpahcikēwin* (Cree) or conjuring with the shaking lodge continues to be practiced in some subarctic communities. Nelson appreciated the central position of the conjuring complex in Saulteaux and Cree religion and his writing on the topic, based on his own interviews and firsthand observations, is the richest and most detailed of any pre-twentieth century source. Nelson's interest in conjuring exceeded the purely academic; he commissioned performances both in order to observe them and because he believed, with some equivocation, in their practical effectiveness.

Purposes of Conjuring

Nelson identified the universal wish to "dive into futurity" as motivating the Indians to become conjurors, but prophecy as such was only one of several objectives that might be combined in a single performance. A primary purpose of conjuring was to obtain information about persons or events distant in space or time or otherwise inaccessible to the diviners. This information most often pertained to the future but could concern the past or present. Typical questions addressed to the spirits in the lodge concerned the diagnosis and treatment of sickness, the location of game animals or lost articles, when game would next be killed, the welfare of absent relatives, and the whereabouts and arrival time of visitors. Nelson was one of a few Euro-Canadian fur traders who are known to have commissioned conjuring sessions in order to ascertain the whereabouts of delayed employees and missing supplies ("Conjuring for a North West Company Gentleman"; cf. Young 1893:226–27).

The use of conjuring as a medical technique involved questioning the spirits about the cause of the disorder and about appropriate treatment. Illness was often thought to result from sorcery or misdeeds committed earlier by the sufferer or by his or her relatives; spirits would be asked to identify the sorcerer or offense and they sometimes exhorted the sufferer or other implicated persons to confess publicly their misdeed as a preliminary to cure (cf. Hallowell 1942, 53–64; Dunning 1959, 180).

Although Nelson did not specifically discuss connections between conjuring and medical treatment, his manuscript begins with a narrative in which the shaking lodge assisted a troubled Cree Indian by revealing the causes of threatening events and outlining a positive course of action ("Conjuring at Lac la Ronge, December 1819"). Interpreting unaccustomed lights and sounds as signs of impending misfortune, the man commissioned a shaking lodge performance to discover their meaning and cause. He was told that the signs were harmless but later requested a second session; the spirits, angered that their first counsel was disregarded, proclaimed ominously that he would be indulged in his evident desire to be haunted and revealed that he was being stalked by the monstrous emissary of a sorcerer. At a third session, the spirits instructed the sufferer to use the sweat bath and prepare an offering while they themselves deflected the monster from its path. Upon observing weather changes that signalled the monster's defeat, the sufferer made the suggested offering, but, afflicted with persisting anxieties, again commissioned a conjuring session. At this fourth and final interview, the spirits reassured him that the threat was past and, clearly fatigued by his petitions, advised him that they would communicate any further danger that might arise.

From the perspective of the conjuror, the spirits' messages appear to have been organized in a deliberate attempt to allay his client's anxieties. After an unsuccessful attempt to explain the disconcerting events in "natural" terms, the spirits identified a specific locus for the client's fears which was then decisively eliminated. The client's repeated applications for information and reassurance demonstrated less than absolute faith in the veracity of the spirits' advice, a skepticism probably not unusual in other faiths as well. The narrative also makes clear that spirits summoned into the shaking lodge were understood not only to provide information but also to take practical action on behalf of their human dependents. The physical combat of the spirits with the approaching monster is paralleled by more mundane services, such as repairing a defective gun or retrieving lost possessions. The spirits in the lodge also often played an active role in dealing with witchcraft and sorcery.

The Practice of Conjuring

Nelson provided three detailed accounts of conjuring with the shaking lodge. The first was of the 1819 Lac la Ronge performances just described. The second discussion ("The Manner of Conjuring" and "The Spirits Enter") is a composite account of different performances that he witnessed or heard of among both Saulteaux and Cree. The concluding narrative ("Conjuring at Lac la Ronge, June 1823") described a Cree conjuring performance that Nelson himself had commissioned and observed some twenty-four hours earlier.

Nelson observed correctly that, although most Saulteaux and Cree men participated in public and private ritual, the ability to operate the shaking lodge was limited to specialists. Nelson's account of the vision fast at puberty ("Dreaming to Conjure and Predict") is misleading, however, in its suggestion that only aspiring conjurors underwent the fast; in fact, most males fasted at puberty in order to obtain one or more spirit guardians. Among the Saulteaux, the ability to conjure successfully derived from a specific vision or dream that was understood also to confer the spirits' permission to do so (cf. Hallowell 1942, 19, 23–24). In another context, Nelson stated that the ability to conjure derived from possessing a requisite *number* of spirit guardians and it is also probable that their identity was significant. There can be little doubt that most conjurors experienced dreams or visions that they understood as licensing and empowering them in this way. It is, however, likely that the specialists' understanding of conjuring differed in certain critical points from that of the audience (cf. Hallowell 1942, 23–24, 78–79); the manner in which conjurors integrated knowledge of their own ventriloquism and other techniques with the conventional assumptions of the audience remains an interesting problem. Unlike Midewiwin priests, Saulteaux and Cree conjurors were said not to form esoteric fraternities or associations. It was believed that they learned their skills independently of instruction by other specialists, but this remains open to question.

The structure used by the conjuror was usually erected by others during the daylight hours that preceded the performance. The lodges described by Nelson conformed in dimensions and manufacture to a type that is essentially uniform throughout the eastern subarctic. They were built by implanting between four and eight poles, each about eight feet long, vertically into the ground to a depth of two feet, enclosing an area approximately three feet in diameter. The poles were secured to each other horizontally by three or four encircling flexible hoops; and birchbark sheets, animal hides, or canvas were then secured over the frame with babiche or semi-tanned animal hide cords (cf. Hallowell 1942, 37–40). Some conjurors' powers required the construction of lodges of double thickness; essentially a smaller lodge was enclosed by a larger one and the two then bound together ("The Conjuror's Power"). Unlike some observers, Nelson did not mention the relative age of the poles or the tree species from which they were taken as factors influencing the clarity of the spirit voices or other aspects of the performance (cf. Lips 1947, 476; Preston 1975, 33, 40–41, on Quebec groups). However, he noted the importance attached to constructing the lodge at some remove from human habitations "on account of the Stink as the *Spirits* cannot, or will not endure any pollution" ("Conjuring at Lac la Ronge, June 1823"). Conceptions of the bush as "clean" and of settlements and camps as "dirty" persist among contemporary Manitoba Cree and other Northern Algonquians (cf. Tanner 1979, 166); it is said that spirit entities are repelled and offended by the sight and smell of human or dog excreta and other refuse. When, as in winter, the shaking lodge had to be erected within a dwelling, efforts were made to clean the vicinity (Hallowell 1942, 36).

Before the performance witnessed by Nelson in 1823, the audience assembled by the lodge at sunset and sang and drummed after listening to a preliminary invocation by the operator. As in other conjuring sessions that Nelson observed, the operator was a practitioner of the "Davenport trick" involving the ability to escape confinement by ropes or other bonds (Hallowell 1942, 70). After removing his clothing down to the breech cloth, he was tied by the wrists, bound in blankets or animal hides, and then placed inside the lodge. Shortly thereafter, the coverings and ropes, with knots still tied, were tossed out to the audience, it being understood that *Miskināhk* (the Turtle) or another being had entered the lodge and freed the operator. European observers were sometimes involved in this aspect of the performance; Nelson, for example, helped to tie up the operator. After the ropes were thrown out, the audience continued to sing the songs of individual spirits whose successive entries into the lodge were signalled by its movements, by the sound of the rattle, and by their singing voices.

Many of the spirits sang their own distinctive songs upon entering, and they could be heard talking among themselves as well as addressing the operator and the audience. In addition to the spirits, the souls of living but absent persons could be summoned into the lodge to "visit," as when the Indian seated next to Nelson conversed with his adopted son. The spirits delivered prophecies and advice; among the examples noted by Nelson were a warning to avoid the Churchill River because of epidemics and to avoid drinking at Lac la Ronge with two hostile halfbreeds. The spirits responded also to specific questions. In his composite account, Nelson described one question about the arrival of traders and another concerning the prospective lifespan of the questioner. In 1823, "Key-jick-o-kay" was asked about certain manifestations in Nelson's house the preceding winter.

From an Algonquian religious perspective, as Nelson and other sources attest, the spirits are invisible when they enter and leave the lodge but assume some kind of perceptible form inside. Their ability to discourse on remote events derives from their capacity for travelling immense distances by flying. In so doing, they occupy elevated spheres from which they can observe terrestrial events. In consequence, as Nelson reported, they represent themselves as omniscient:

"How durst thou doubt anything I say – knowest thou not how clearly and distinctly objects are discovered and seen in a plain, from an eminence; and my abode is in the regions above – I see every object as distinctly as you see at your feet, doubt then no more, and never hereafter call our Power to question."

"Aye!" replied some of the other spirits. "We not only see *all that you do, however secret and hid you think yourselves*, but we also hear every word you utter" ("The Spirits Enter").

Nelson was informed that the spirits were capable of physically removing the operator from the lodge; a skeptical halfbreed once entered a shaking lodge and found the conjuror missing ("Conjuring for a North West Company Gentleman"; cf. Hallowell 1942, 43). The lodge was also understood to channel remote sounds and voices. Nelson noted an instance when the conjuror's voice was audible despite his physical absence ("Skepticism, Belief, and Innovation"). In a performance described by George Bauer, the sounds of animals travelling through the bush emanated from inside (1971, 24). The association of the shaking lodge with long-distance communication and revelation of events remote in time or space is reflected in its equation by Manitoba Cree today with radios, television, telephones, and telescopes, and also by the formal relations between the nouns referring to "shaking lodge" and these classes of objects (cf. Bauer 1971, 22–23; Granzberg 1980).

The forms that spirit beings possess in the lodge are not necessarily consistent with those ascribed to them in other contexts. In general, it appears that their spiritual rather than physical component enters the lodge: "They [spirits] don't come in like the body, just like a spirit" (Preston 1975, 79). In the case of human beings, Nelson stated that only the soul entered ("Conjuring at Lac la Ronge, June 1823"). Among the Saulteaux and Cree known to Nelson, the spirits were perceptible as tiny luminous specks of light hovering near the top of the lodge (cf. Hallowell 1942, 51 fn; Mason 1967, 63). Other images include miniature hominoid figures (Jenness 1935, 66 [Parry Island, Ontario]), or birds (Bauer 1971, 23 [Fort George, Quebec]). A perhaps exceptional feature of conjuring noted by Nelson was the exhibition of one of the spirits to the audience; the operator held out the two-inch long figure of Mikināhk the Turtle, who astonished the audience with its beauty.

The Cree performances seen by Nelson concluded when Wīsahkēcāhk, the trickster–transformer, dismissed the other beings from the lodge, their departure being signalled by the sound of the rattle and the increased agitation of the structure ("The Spirits Enter"). Among the Saulteaux, this dominant role was assumed by a spirit "master of conjuring" (Hallowell 1942, 49). The 1823 performance witnessed by Nelson lasted about four hours, from 10:00 p.m. to 2:00 a.m., and was clearly scheduled to coincide with the brief period between sunset and sunrise during the boreal summer.

The Languages of Conjuring

Nelson's descriptions reveal the complexity of the shaking lodge as a three-way communication among spirits, audience, and conjuror. The audience understood the spirits to be physically present in the lodge and to speak independently of the operator; there was no understanding that the spirits "possessed" him and spoke through his voice. That the operator might himself produce the voices of the spirits is readily acknowledged, although Crees emphasize that only a charlatan would do this. In genuine performances, operator and spirits speak independently (Brightman 1977–79); this feature appears to be a basic characteristic of the Algonquian conjuring complex. Many of the beings of Cree and Saulteaux religion possessed individuating speech characteristics including distinctive grammatical and intonational styles. Adopting, for a moment, the Algonquian conjuror's perspective it is evident that successful conjuring required considerable linguistic versatility.

The conjuring performance involved communication among different spirits, between the spirits and the operator, between the audience and the operator, and between the spirits and the audience. In the first two of these types, members of the audience played primarily a passive role, although they responded with jokes to some verbal exchanges between spirits. Other instances of such interaction appear to have been regarded seriously, for example, the verbal conflict between the benign Wīsahkēcāhk and the evil *Kīsikōkē*, "Old Nick". The role of the conjuror was to facilitate communication between spirits and audience, sometimes by translating. At times he commanded, petitioned, and joked with the spirits; he also spoke with the human audience, identifying spirit voices and commenting on events that were transpiring in the lodge. Members of the audience might also address the spirits collectively or appeal to a specific individual; reciprocally, a spirit might address either an individual or the whole assemblage.

Nelson distinguished between spirits whose utterances were intelligible to the audience and those for whom the operator had to interpret; this distinction is relevant to other descriptions of the lodge ritual and probably is a widespread feature of Algonquian conjuring. On the basis of Nelson's and other data, it is possible to discriminate among degrees of intelligibility. Some spirits spoke in non-Algonquian languages known to some but not all of the observers: "When any one conjures if he is a renowned *Medicine* Man, *they* [spirits] all appear, and Speak to him mostly in his own language, some few excepted as the Pike (or Jack fish) who speaks french; the Sun and Moon, both speak English; the Bull or Buffaloe in an unknown or at least strange language; but all perfectly intelligible to the conjuror" ("Other Beings"). In Cree performances at Oxford House, Manitoba (Mason 1967, 64), the spirits used Cree, Saulteaux, and English; other Manitoba Cree state that spirits used Cree, French, Saulteaux and Chipewyan. Of the beings described by Nelson, Wīsahkēcāhk, Kīšikōkē, Miskināhk (Turtle), Flying Squirrel, Dog, and visiting human souls spoke Cree while the Sun and Moon spoke English and the Jackfish spoke French.

Even when the spirits spoke languages known to the audience, their use of archaic phrases and distorting intonational effects sometimes limited their intelligibility (Preston 1975, 73). Also, the voices might be too low to be heard easily or might be drowned out by the sounds of the rattle or of the lodge shaking. However, some spirits also spoke one or more languages that were completely unrecognizable to the listeners. Alexander Henry the Elder (1969, 161–62) stated of a conjuring performance in 1763 that "Articulate speech was also uttered, as if from human lips, but in a tongue unknown to any of the audience." Manitoba Cree stated to Brightman that there was more than one such language, that they were used exclusively by spirits and animals, and that they were comprehensible only to certain individuals such as conjurors. Nelson reported that the Buffalo, three varieties of Bear, the Horse, the Moose, pakāhk (Skeleton), and the souls of the human dead used such languages.

Nelson did not make clear whether the beings enumerated – Turtle, Flying Squirrel, Dog, Bear(s), Horse, Buffalo, Moose, Pike, Loon – were understood as spirit prototypes or rulers of their species or as exemplars of conventional animals. Since these characters appeared to possess individuating characteristics, however, most of them, like Miskināhk the Turtle, were probably well-defined spirit personages rather than typical examples of their species, although Manitoba Cree state that both the spirit rulers of animal species and individual animals from the bush might appear in the shaking lodge. Of the animal beings mentioned by Nelson, Mikināhk, Dog, and Flying Squirrel spoke in Cree while the others used an unknown language or languages. Other accounts of the shaking lodge (Preston 1975, 80–81; Bauer 1971, 24) state that animal voices spoke from the lodge, but it is unclear whether these used Cree or were interpreted by the operator. A Woods Cree from Alberta stated that both animal calls and human speech were audible in the tent, but it is not certain whether the same or different speakers were involved (Honigmann 1956, 74). Characteristic animal sounds such as the mating call of the moose or the heavy breathing of the bear were heard in the lodge by Rupert House Cree (Preston 1975, 74). In at least some cases, these beings combine characteristically animal and human modes of expression. According to Manitoba Cree, a bear or caribou brought into the lodge might begin by producing animal calls and gradually switch to progressively more intelligible Cree. This pattern of improving facility is paralleled by Nelson's statement that the "Sun" speaks very bad English at the offset, but by degrees becomes [begins] to speak it very easily and fluently" ("The Spirits Enter"). A similar account from the Cree of Oxford House, Manitoba, states that the

Crow prefaces its Cree utterances with a characteristic "Caw-caw" (Mason 1967, 63). Also heard in the shaking lodge were animal calls, for example that of the loon, that were perceived as resembling Cree or Saulteaux utterances.

Nelson makes clear that the conjuror interpreted unintelligible utterances for the audience; it is uncertain whether he reciprocally translated human messages into the language used by the spirits and animals. In a performance among the Woods Cree of Alberta, the conjuror's wife sat outside the lodge and functioned as translator, an interesting exception to the conventional exclusion of women from active roles in collective ritual (Honigmann 1956, 74). Among some Algonquian groups, a particular spirit replaced or supplemented the conjuror as interpreter between human beings and spirits. Among the Eastmain Cree of Quebec, this function together with that of messenger is filled by a being called *Mistāpēw* or 'Giant Man' who exercises general control over the shaking lodge ritual (Flannery 1939; Tanner 1979, 114). Alternatively, the noun *mistāpēw* is a generic term for spirit guardian, including that of the conjuror who may perform the role of interpreter and messenger (Rousseau 1953, 189; Preston 1975, 73). Among some Ojibwa groups, Mikkināhk or cognate characters interpreted and had other essential roles in conjuring (Schoolcraft 1860, 5:421; Flannery 1940, 16), and Nelson stated that Mikkināhk was usually the first to enter the lodge ("The Spirits Enter"). The complexities of translating in the shaking lodge are fully evident from a Menominee account (Skinner 1915, 194); the Turtle, who spoke only Ojibwa, served to interpret the spirits' utterances, which the conjuror then translated into Menominee for the audience.

In addition to their personal songs which carried identifying melodies and lyrics, the spirits were distinguished by a number of other linguistic attributes. Animals could be identified by their calls or by the way that their calls interfered with their pronunciation of human speech. In Manitoba Cree conjuring, for example, bears and lynxes speak Cree with attendant growling and hissing, respectively. Similar onomatopoeic effects evoked the identity or habitat of other beings. At Lac la Ronge, Ice communicated with noise like that of a person "shivering with cold, loud, hoarse, and *liquid*" ("Conjuring at Lac la Ronge, June 1823"). Similarly, water beings spoke with a gurgling pronunciation in performances at Oxford House (Mason 1967, 63). Miskināhk the Turtle spoke with the voice of an old man. The speech of the spirits, however, did not invariably entail distortion of conventional human discourse. The Dog, perhaps reflecting the integration of its species into human society, "spoke perfectly plain and distinct, and with a more elegant and harmonious voice than I ever heard in my life" ("Conjuring at Lac la Ronge, June 1823").

Different characters were distinguished by the semantic content of their utterances as well as by their speech styles. The messages of Miskināhk and Pike, for example, were distinguished by their humor. Wīsahkēcāhk and Kīsikōkē could be identified from their respectively benevolent and abusive conversation. If the Cree texts of the performances observed by Nelson were available, they would probably exhibit different speech styles, distinguished by degrees of formality, that were used by and in addressing different spirits. The greatest familiarity and informality existed between the audience and Miskināhk, who exchanged jokes in egalitarian fashion. At the other end of the range Kīsikōkē and "Strong Neck" appear to have required respectful or subordinate verbal behavior from others. Other beings such as the Buffalo probably fell in between these extremes.

Nelson's Explanations of Conjuring
Nelson's attitude to conjuring was doubly ambiguous. He combined a disparaging skepticism with an enthusiastic conviction of the reality of conjuring, and in various passages clearly addressed himself to dispelling the skepticism of others. There is evidence also that he was uncomfortable both with the reality of conjuring and with his own belief in it. Nelson succeeded only partially in placing the shaking lodge intelligibly within Christian cosmology, and his writings indicate that he regarded conjuring ambivalently, as both inconsistent with Christian theology and actuated by the latter's scriptural Devil.

Nelson was sometimes skeptical of secondhand accounts and he characteristically emphasized the need for discriminating between fact and elaboration. But on the basis of his own observations and his comparisons with the religions of antiquity, Nelson was prepared vehemently to argue that the conjuror does communicate with the supernatural, a conclusion, as he pointed out, that was arrived at not from superstition but rather from rational assessment of the facts:

There are many in the civilized or Christian world who absolutely and positively deny this power of theirs as being absolutely impossible and at best but absurd and idle stories. Many of the things related to these Conjurings I acknowledge to be so; but at the same time I am as positive and as firmly persuaded of the truth of the assertion "that they have dealings with some supernatural spirit," as I am convinced that I live and breath in air; unless, indeed, we chuse to acknowledge and believe a certain sect of Philosophers (of the last century I believe) who *wish* to tell us that we *only imagine ourselves alive*. And I am by no means inclined to acknowledge myself as superstitious: I am convinced of this from reason, argument, comparison; in short from *analysis*. Let any one man, unless he be a headstrong brute who is *determined* before hand not to be convinced, analyze their discourses &c, &c, and I am confident he will believe as much as many, or have great doubts at least. To absolutely deny this, we must first deny that there is a Devil, and afterwards deny his pernicious power and if we deny these points, we must descend to a third, more fit for an atheistical wretch and a beast than a Christian, or even rational creature ("Skepticism, Belief, and Innovation").

At the time he wrote this passage, Nelson had probably observed numerous conjuring performances, but in this context he gave less weight to his own observations than to his theological and ethnological conclusions.

Nelson's ethnology was rooted in correspondences that he recognized between Algonquian beliefs and practices and those of classical antiquity ("Affinities and Origins"). On one hand, he suggested that these resemblances could be used to reconstruct the origins of the Indians. On the other, he appeared to take the similarities between Algonquian and classical deities as evidence for their substantive reality: "I am fully convinced, as much so as that I am in existence, that Spirits of some kind did really and virtually enter, some truly terrific, but others again quite of a different character. I cannot enter into a detail by comparisons from ancient and more modern history, but I found the consonance, analogy, resemblance, affinity, or whatever it may be termed so great, so conspicuous that I verily believe I shall never forget the impressions of that evening" ("Conjuring at Lac la Ronge, June 1823"). Of these analogies, Nelson noted particularly those between "Strong Neck" and Hercules; the spirit master of medicines and Esculapius; and Windigo and the Anthropophagi.

Nelson not only saw a relation between Indian and Greek beliefs, he also thought that both could be understood in terms of the Christian tradition. For example, he believed that the Cree possessed some imperfect knowledge of the scriptural God and that therefore their belief in Kisēmanitōw was a distorted reflection of a transcendent spiritual reality: "These people are still in a complete state of nature: their ideas of the true God are far from clear or correct: they acknowledge him indeed as the Supreme and absolute Master of all, but more or rather as a passive *Deity* than as he really is; but their notions of their other deities come far more near the truth" ("Skepticism, Belief, and Innovation"). The last observation appears to associate most of the other spirits recognized by Crees and Saulteaux with the infernal legions. Nelson's explanation of conjuring in terms of the powers of the Devil represents an attempt to comprehend Algonquian religion within the framework of Christian orthodoxy. As he stated, a categorical skepticism towards conjuring entails an atheistical and heretical rejection of the Devil's existence; this argument had a long lineage among Europeans seeking to discredit those skeptical of witchcraft.

As early as 1637, some Europeans attributed the powers of Algonquian conjurors to the Devil (Le Jeune 1897, 12:17); this interpretation recurred as recently as 1965 (Richardson 1975, 89–90). Nelson appears to have equated the malign spirit Kīsikōkē with the scriptural Devil and he was prepared to speculate that the latter could manifest himself in various guises to peoples widely separated in time and space. Of Kīsikōkē, the Devil, Nelson wrote: "I am much inclined to doubt master Davy's assertions and consider *this* and several other of his sayings at former Periods in the same light as those he delivered at many of the Grecian temples; for I have every substantial reason to consider him as the same identical Gentleman; however, a short time hence will decide" ("Conjuring at Lac la Ronge, June 1823").

However, Nelson did not develop a consistent explanation of conjuring in terms of demonic agencies, partially, perhaps, because he was aware that the spirits included those who were benevolently inclined toward human beings. As he wrote, some of the spirits were "terrific," in the sense of terrible or frightful, while others were "quite of a different character." It would have been consistent for Nelson to equate such beings as Wīsahkēcāhk and Miskināhk with the angels of Christian orthodoxy. This equivalence has been proposed by Algonquians themselves who seek to coordinate indigenous and introduced religious systems.

THE WINDIGO COMPLEX

Nelson's discussion of the windigo or cannibal–monster complex among Saulteaux and Cree is the most lengthy and analytical of any pre-twentieth century source. Nelson combined a useful typology of the category with information on the causes, symptoms and cures for windigo behavior in human beings. His observations are relevant to the interpretation of windigo symbolism and to reconstructing historical transformations of the concept.

The word '*windigo*' (Cree *wīhtikōw*, Ojibwa *wīntikō*) refers to a spiritually powerful anthropomorphic monster that overcomes and feeds upon human beings. Although some windigos are seen as members of an autochthonous nonhuman race or class of harmful spirits, it is believed that many windigos were once human beings who were transformed into their monstrous condition by committing famine cannibalism, by dream predestination or spirit possession, or by death from freezing or starvation. It is thought that a person who "goes windigo" initially retains a conventional appearance, but ultimately loses human identity and cultural knowledge. The term windigo has referred also to practitioners of famine cannibalism without necessarily implying their transformation to a chronic monstrous condition. Contemporary Manitoba Crees use the term metaphorically to denote insane, aggressive, murderous, or gluttonous individuals.

The phrase "windigo psychosis" refers in a sizeable body of scholarly literature to a psychological disorder reported among pre-twentieth century boreal Algonquians in which the sufferer expressed the desire to eat human flesh or an anxiety that this compulsion would develop. Scholars have postulated that culturally transmitted beliefs in the reality of windigo transformation were primary components of these disorders, causing the sufferers to experience their symptoms as signs of an incipient monstrous condition. A number of theories explaining the disorder in terms of anxieties about hunger and famine cannibalism (Cooper 1933, 21; Landes 1938, 214) or the interplay of Algonquian personality with the belief system (Parker 1960; Hay 1971) have been proposed and debated (Marano 1982).

Human and Nonhuman Windigos in Historical Context

Nelson defined the windigo as a 'Giant of the anthropophagi Genus' ("The Windigo") and elaborated upon its attributes with a myth describing the conflict of a band of Indians with one such cannibal giant. This myth, which was known also to the Tête de Boule of Quebec (Davidson 1928, 267), is one of several characterizing windigos as a race of giants without human antecedents. Nelson and his informants distinguished these giants from transformed human beings, and this distinction between nonhuman and human windigos persists in some boreal Algonquian communities (Landes 1938, 213–14; Flannery et al. 1982, 57).

Conceptualization of the windigo as a giant is conventional among Ojibwa groups in Manitoba (Hallowell 1955, 256), Ontario (Jones 1917–19, 175–79), Saskatchewan and North Dakota (Howard 1977, 115), Michigan (Schoolcraft 1839, 105–18), and Wisconsin (Barnouw 1977, 120–31). The idea of the giant windigo is shared also by Crees around Hudson and James bays and the inland Cree, Naskapi, and Montagnais of Quebec and Labrador (Honigmann 1956, 68; Flannery et al. 1982, 58). Among some of these latter inland groups, the name *ahcān* labels a class of nonhuman cannibal giants distinct from the human windigo, whereas in others ahcān was a synonym for the latter (Speck 1935, 67–68). Rock Crees in northwestern Manitoba say that windigos are of ordinary human size (Smith 1976, 25–26) and this image is also general among the Plains and Strongwoods Cree groups (Vandersteene 1969, 53; Ahenakew 1973, 92). The Ojibwa of southwestern Ontario conceptualize the nonhuman windigo as a giant *skeleton* of ice, suggesting an assimilation of the windigo to the idea of the skeletal pākahk. Gigantism is more typically ascribed to nonhuman than to human windigos, although there are exceptions. Southwestern Ojibwa of Wisconsin describe human windigos that alternate between normal and giant conditions at will (Barnouw 1977, 120–31). The Ojibwa of Parry Island, Ontario, believed, at least in some instances, that the human windigo began to enlarge as his or her former identity deteriorated (Jenness 1935, 40–41), and this pertains also to the *atūs*, a being cognate to windigo among the Cree of Rupert House (Preston 1975, 109).

Nelson's manuscript contains the earliest known written use of the Ojibwa word *wīntikō* and may also contain the earliest evidence of the concept of windigo as a class or race of giant nonhuman monsters. The other earliest recorded forms of 'windigo' are transcriptions of Cree *wīhtikōw*, a term known from Crees trading at the coastal forts of the Hudson's Bay Company during the eighteenth century. An early record from Churchill in 1714 suggests that wīhtikōw referred to a class of "apparitions" (Smith 1976, 21), but other early references suggest that wīhtikōw was the proper name of a single evil deity conceptually opposed to the benign creator being Kīhcimanitōw in a dualistic cosmology (Isham 1949 [1743–49], 5, 65;

Drage 1968 [1748–49], 2:17; Graham 1969 [1767–91], 160; Ellis 1748, 193–94; Umfreville 1954 [1790], 21–22; Wales in Cooper 1934, 56). The attributes of Wīhtikōw as interpreted by these English sources are identical to those ascribed by others to the evil deity called *Macimanitōw* (Bacqueville de la Pothèrie 1931 [1753], 226; Thompson 1962 [1784–1812], 76); both, for example, were associated with disease and functioned as interlocutors in the shaking lodge. Taken together, these sources imply that during the eighteenth century Wīhtikōw was another name for Macimanitōw, or at least that Europeans understood the term as such.

David Thompson's narrative, written in the 1840s with reference to the years 1784 to 1812, is inconsistent on the subject. In discussing Cree beliefs, Thompson described "Weetego," "the evil Spirit that devours humankind," separately from Macimanitōw. In another context, however, he wrote, "Weetego is one of the names of the Evil Spirit" (Thompson 1962, 76, 103, 194). Nelson and other nineteenth-century sources clearly differentiated windigo from the evil deity (cf. Franklin 1823, 1:119); they also evidently lack any reference to windigo as a *single* individuated personage. The eighteenth-century sources, in contrast, suggest that the word wīhtikōw, like the English 'devil,' functioned both as a proper name for the evil deity and as a label for a class of harmful entities.

The fact that the earliest references to windigo mention neither cannibalism nor gigantism as attributes (Fogelson 1965, 77) reinforces the inference that the concept has changed historically. Besides its possible progressive differentiation from Macimanitōw, it is possible also that the attribute of cannibalism or the concept of windigo as a category or race of nonhuman entities developed after European contact. Alternatively, early Europeans may themselves have confused and conflated the identities of windigo and Macimanitōw as they did those of the creator deity Kihcimanitōw and the transformer deity Wīsahkēcāhk (Isham 1949, 5; Graham 1969, 160), thereby missing the evidence for the probable aboriginality of the multifaceted windigo complex described by Nelson and in other nineteenth and twentieth century sources.

Contemporary Rock Crees clearly distinguish Macimanitōw from the wīhtikōw and the identification of the latter as a single evil deity, if it ever existed, has not persisted into the present. The distribution of conventional windigo beliefs among contemporary Algonquians may provide clues to older or precontact variations; the idea of windigo as a "species" of non-human monsters, usually of giant size, is nowhere attested for Plains, Thickwoods, or Rock Cree groups and appears limited to Ojibwa and to Swamp Cree bands (Norman 1982, 179; Flannery et al. 1982, 57).

Nelson's manuscript is rich in information on *human* windigos, persons who were categorized as incipient or transformed cannibal monsters with a craving for human flesh and intensified spiritual control over human prey. Such persons were sometimes thought to be indistinguishable from other human beings (Speck 1935, 69; Landes 1938, 221–22), although the conventional image of the fully transformed human windigo includes such distinguishing features as emaciation, dirty and ungroomed hair, ragged clothing, loss of speech, and the eating of one's own lips and fingers. Charles Bishop (1975) has suggested that the belief in transformed human windigos developed among Algonquians after game shortages associated with the fur trade resulted in growing frequencies of starvation and famine cannibalism. Alternatively, some argue that these experiences were sufficiently prevalent in aboriginal times to have shaped an indigenous windigo complex including concepts of both nonhuman and human windigos (Waisberg 1975; Smith 1976).

The belief in transformed human windigos as well as actual instances of behavioral disorders influenced by windigo beliefs are attested early in the contact histories of boreal Algonquian groups. The two earliest reported cases of windigo disorder occurred among the Montagnais in the seventeenth century (Teicher 1960, 76–77, 103–104). A Hudson's Bay Company account from Churchill (Manitoba) in 1741 described a Cree hunter who killed and ate some of his family despite the availability of game animals in the vicinity (Smith 1976, 22). The belief that famine cannibals subsequently became obsessional cannibalistic murderers existed among Saskatchewan Crees in 1775 (Hearne 1911 [1795], 85–86) and Ontario Ojibwa in 1766 (Henry 1901 [1809], 199). The first explicit use of the Cree word for windigo to refer to such transformed humans dates from 1772 at Fort Severn where a famine cannibal subsequently became violently insane and was executed by his family; they later expressed fear that he might become reanimated as a cannibal spirit or "Witik" (Bishop 1975, 243). In the late 1700s, Thompson (1962, 103) translated the verb "Nee weet to go" (Cree *niwīhtikōwiw* 'I am a wihtikow') as "I must be a Man eater." Richardson in 1819 described the Saskatchewan Cree concept of windigo as "a devil into which those who have fed on human flesh are transformed" (Franklin 1923, 1:119).

Windigo Disorders

By defining the windigo condition as "a sort of mania, or fever, a distemper of the brain" ("Windigo Cures and Precautions"), Nelson anticipated anthropological discussion of "windigo psychosis" as a culturally specific mental disorder. The conventional anthropological explanation, expressed most forcefully by Teicher (1960), has been that the socially shared belief in the reality of windigo transformation produced among Algonquians a distinctive mental disorder characterized by a craving for human flesh, even in the absence of famine. Alternatively, both the belief system and the individual cases of mental disorder have been explained in terms of culturally mediated characteristics of Algonquian personality (Hay 1971; Parker 1960). The basis for the analysis of "windigo psychosis" has been a corpus of reported cases in which Algonquians expressed either verbally or in actions a compulsion to commit cannibalism. Since the possibility of windigo transformation was culturally perceived as real in Algonquian societies, some scholars (Bishop 1982; Marano 1982) have questioned the relevance of the term "psychosis" to these disorders; others have noted that if the term is retained, the criteria for its use need to be more carefully specified (Brown 1982; Hurlich 1982).

Nelson's firsthand descriptions of persons who defined themselves as windigo or who were so categorized by others are relevant to Louis Marano's (1982) thesis that windigo psychotics who either expressed cannibal compulsions behaviorally or experienced them ideationally never existed. A corollary of this view is that all instances of Algonquian cannibalism resulted from famine and that reports attributing cannibal urges to executed windigos were the fabrications or hallucinations of the survivors. Nelson's secondhand reports by Crees and Saulteaux of cannibalistic threats uttered by persons defined as windigo appear to dispute this view, although they also raise the question of how such sources of information should be assessed. Nelson relates, for example, an instance in which a Saulteaux alarmed his daughter with his incipient windigo behavior: "One night towards the latter end of December, he began staring at his daughter with extraordinary intenseness: 'My daughter! I am fond of thee! I love thee extremely. . . . Yes! I love thee – I think I could eat a piece of thee, I love thee so much'" ("Windigo Possession, Lake Winnipeg"). Several similar descriptions of windigo behavior received from Indians exist (cf. Thompson 1962, 193; Teicher 1960, 95, 100; Flannery et al. 1982, 73; Brown 1971, 21). The argument against the psychological or behavioral reality of an Algonquian cannibal syndrome points out the lack of reliable, eyewitness accounts of such behavior from Europeans (Marano 1982). However, the few available examples of such testimony (Henry 1901, 201; Marano 1981, 166–68; Vandersteene 1969, 56–57; Thompson 1962, 103) coincide closely with the Algonquian accounts. There are also a number of cases in which sufferers reportedly translated cannibalistic impulses into threatening actions when conventional foods were available (Smith 1976, 22; Bishop 1981, 398; Teicher 1960, 49). It is, in any event, clear from Nelson's account that persons sometimes defined themselves, and were defined by others, as incipient windigos in contexts where conventional food was available (cf. Thompson 1962, 194).

Nelson's manuscript, along with other sources, suggests that the experience of famine cannibalism may have been a significant component in the development of windigo behavioral disorders: "I have seen several that had been reduced to this disturbing alternative, and tho' many years after, there appeared to me a wildness in their eyes, a confusion in their countenances much resembling that of reprieved murderers" ("Sources and Forms of Windigo"). These observations parallel others noting dissociation, anxiety or depression among survivors of famine cannibal incidents (Isham 1949, 227; Hearne 1911, 86; Thompson 1962, 104). The guilt and anxiety of the survivors of such tragedies were doubtless aggravated both by the suspicion and ostracism that they felt from the community and by the cultural premise that famine cannibals were likely to become windigos. The demented Cree executed by his family at Fort Severn in 1772 (Bishop 1965, 243) had previously committed famine cannibalism, as had the Ojibwa cannibal observed by Alexander Henry the Elder (1901, 201) who rejected conventional food and remarked alarmingly on the plumpness of his hosts' children. The Cree "Wiskahoo" (Thompson 1962, 103), who defined himself as a windigo and was eventually executed as one, had been on the verge of famine cannibalism in the past, a circumstance that perhaps precipitated his disorder.

Nelson's manuscript makes clear, however, that windigo murder and famine cannibalism were extremely infrequent, even during food crises ("Sources and Forms of Windigo," cf. Graham 1969, 155). Given the sensational character of the subject, it is worth noting also that windigo disorders themselves were rare (Fogelson 1965, 88) and terminated far more typically in cure than in execution or in murder and cannibalism.

Nelson's eyewitness description of windigo symptoms parallels and confirms conventional elements in Indian accounts: sufferers rejected food and requested their own executions. The persons observed by Nelson appeared to alternate between manic and depressive states: "Their eyes (for I have seen people who are thus perplex'd) are wild and uncommonly clear – they seem as if they glistened. It seems to me to lodge in the head. They are generally rational except at short, sudden intervals when the paroxysms cease [seize] them: their motions then are various and diametrically contrary at one time to what they are the next – Sullen, thoughtful, wild look and perfectly mute: staring in sudden convulsions, wild incoherent and extravagant language" ("Windigo Dreams"). One commonly reported windigo symptom absent from Nelson's account is the hallucinatory perception of human beings as animals. Landes (1938, 216) suggested that this was a conventional assumption about the disorder, ascribed to but not demonstrably experienced by the sufferers. Possibly sufferers spoke metaphorically of their intended victims as animals.

Origins of Windigo Behavior

Nelson described three types or forms of human windigo which had distinct origins. The first involved transformation of a famine cannibal into a compulsive seeker of human flesh, while the other two involved predestination by either the northern nonhuman windigo giants or the malign spirits Ice and North. Nelson's manuscript is especially detailed with respect to the latter two forms which were associated by boreal Algonquians with the vision fast and the spirit guardian relationship.

Nelson discussed first the idea that individuals who eat human flesh in a famine crisis may thereafter develop a compulsive craving for it and develop into windigos. Degeneration into a windigo is sometimes represented by Algonquians as the inevitable consequence of famine cannibalism (cf. Merasty 1974, 1; Preston 1978, 62), and the idea existed among Ojibwa and Cree at least as early as the second half of the eighteenth century (Hearne 1911 [1795], 85–86; Henry 1901 [1809], 199). Other sources indicate that not all windigos were thought to originate as famine cannibals and not all cannibals were thought inevitably to become windigos (cf. Isham 1949, 100-1; Thompson 1962, 103-4; Honigmann 1956, 41; Flannery et al. 1982, 59). But the eating of human flesh was understood as a sufficient if not necessary condition. Consumption of human flesh was understood to produce the superhuman strength which allowed the windigo to overcome its human victims (Speck 1935, 37). As the self-diagnosed windigo in one of Nelson's stories put it: "For if you do not kill me until I have eaten of human flesh, you'll perhaps not be able to do it afterwards" ("A Windigo Execution"). Such a belief may possibly help to explain the ritual exocannibalism directed by Algonquians against the French (Henry 1901, 102-8) and the Inuit (Drage 1968, 2:46).

Nelson, like other non-Indians, felt the need to explain windigo disorders within the framework of a secular folk psychology and one of his theories prefigures some of the premises of behaviorism: "Any kind of animal substance at such times [famine contexts] must come very grateful to the stomach; and hence it is I believe that those who have once preyed on their fellows, ever after feel a great desire for the same nourishment, and are not so scrupulous about the means of procuring it" ("Sources and Forms of Windigo"). Like Nelson, Henry the Elder (Henry 1901, 201) attempted a rational explanation for the supposed cannibal impulses expressed by a former famine cannibal, suggesting tentatively that the sufferer's exclamations over the plumpness of his host's children expressed only innocent "admiration." Nelson, however, went on to discuss the second and third forms of windigo, both of which he describes as "delegated." Adopting the perspective of his informants, he described the disorder in these contexts as the result of "witch or wizardisms" or "denunciations from their gods" ("Sources and Forms of Windigo").

Nelson's "delegated" condition of windigo appears analytically separable from the idea of possession, in the sense of the physical inhabitation of the victim by a malignant spirit. Crees in northwestern Manitoba use the verb *pīhciskōw-* to refer to possession of this kind, and it remains a conventional explanation of windigo. As Johnny Bighetty put it: "Some kind of spirit goes into them up there in the Northwest Territories and they go crazy" (Brightman 1977-79; cf. Teicher 1960, 101; Thompson 1962, 103, 194). Other Cree explanations, however, parallel Nelson's emphasis on the critical relationship in Algonquian thought between waking experience and the beings and events experienced in dreams and especially in the vision fast at puberty. To Nelson's Saulteaux and Cree informants, the windigo condition and the famine cannibalism incident that catalyzed it were prefigured in dream experiences with specific malevolent beings who functioned as spirit guardians. Among Ojibwa-speaking groups, these beings were the nonhuman windigo giants in the north (cf. Landes 1938, 214). Also "delegated" in Nelson's idiom was a third form of windigo caused by dreaming of the evil beings, Ice and North; these associations are probably Cree rather than Ojibwa. A number of accounts identify the spirit associated with windigo transformation, either by possession or external control, as the "Devil" or as Macimanitōw (Thompson 1962, 194; Vandersteene 1969, 56; Marano 1981, 167; Dusenberry 1962, 160), suggesting a further connection of the windigo complex with a major evil deity, although as noted before, some European observers may have conflated more than one such deity into the Devil.

The dream experiences that prefigured the windigo state in Nelson's account appear to approximate those associated with the pawākan [Cree] or spirit guardian relationship. Landes (1938, 214) described the Ojibwa belief that human windigos possessed one of the giant nonhuman windigos as spirit guardians. A similar explanation was given by the Plains Cree, "Waypust" (Preston 1978, 62), although the guardian was described only as "an evil spirit." Waypust added that the malign entity might deceive the visionary by appearing in another form. This observation is congruent with Nelson's example of the prefiguring dream, and also with conventional Cree understandings of dreams in which persons, actions, and objects appear in disguised form. Nelson's account exemplifies also the idea that events which transpire in dreams may be subsequently reproduced, sometimes many years later, in the dreamer's waking life. In one dream ("Windigo Dreams"), which would readily permit analysis as objectifying anxiety over cannibalism, the dreamer was exhorted by Ice to eat human body parts disguised as animal flesh. Alerted to the trick, the dreamer refused each offering and therefore, by his own account, escaped degenerating into a windigo in later life. The refusal of the meat appeared to effect or parallel the rejection of the Ice being as a guardian spirit.

An alternative vision experience leading to windigo was recognized by Montana Cree: Macimanitōw, the evil deity, might send a fasting youth a particular animal spirit as a helper, and later in life the visionary would become windigo if he ate meat from the corresponding species (Dusenberry 1962, 160). Here, the taboo against cannibalism was extended to encompass the relationship between human and animal guardian.

Nelson also reported the belief that a windigo condition might be induced not by beings disposed to be hostile to humans, but rather by the individual's normally supportive spirit guardian if the latter became angry with its human dependent for neglecting sacrifices or making disparaging remarks ("Windigo Cures and Precautions"; cf. Preston 1978, 62; Landes 1938, 214). A recent Cree explanation of windigo as a condition that develops in those who have died from freezing (Brightman 1977–79) was not attested in Nelson's manuscript.

Pragmatics of Windigo

The windigo complex called forth a variety of purposeful actions on the part of boreal Algonquians. Nelson's account contains valuable information on cures for windigo and sheds some light on factors that might prompt individuals to simulate a windigo condition.

Nelson's statements about cures are of special interest in the light of Lou Marano's thesis (1982) that windigo fears functioned to induce the elimination of individuals who were burdensome and threatened the group's ability to survive or threatened to discharge latent aggression upon them. Nelson's comments are consistent with much case evidence in noting the rarity of such stressed reactions: "They are in general kind and extremely indulgent to those thus infected: they seem to consider it as an infliction [affliction?] and are desirous of doing all they can to assist" ("Windigo Cures and Precautions"). Of methods for curing windigo, other sources have noted administration of hot grease (Rohrl 1970) and an attempt at exorcism using the shaking lodge (Teicher 1960, 100); Nelson added that proximity to a hot fire, administration of spirits, and the warm temperature of summer were understood to effect cures.

In his two narratives describing windigo executions, Nelson recorded that an axe was used and that in one case the body was burned. Axes occur with considerable frequency both in folk narratives and in accounts of executions as the instruments used to kill windigos. An entry in the Nelson House District Report of 1815 (HBCA B.141/e/1) stated that axes were used to kill cannibals because the latter were "unworthy of being killed by the gun." More probably, as Nelson states, guns were considered unreliable and the use of the axe was enjoined both to "kill" the incipient windigo and to inflict corporal damage that would prevent subsequent resurrection after the nominal death. Cremation of the body was intended to serve the same preventive function, particularly by melting the windigo's supposed heart of ice. Corpses of slain windigos were also sometimes shackled with trap chains, beheaded, or subjected to other mutilations that expressed the fears of the executioners that the deceased might become reanimated (Teicher 1960, 93–103; Duchaussois 1923, 294).

The contextual factors determining whether persons defined as windigo were given treatment or summarily executed remain to be specified. As noted before, famine cannibals often were ostracized (Hearne 1911, 85–86n; Graham 1969, 155), and some were killed, probably when their behavior was interpreted as showing windigo tendencies. Cures were evidently not attempted on those who had already become cannibals defined as windigo; windigos who had not committed cannibalism might be either cured or executed. In two cases, those of "Moostoos" (Teicher 1960, 93–103) and François Auger (Marano 1981, 166–71), attempts at cure were judged unsuccessful and preceded execution. It is doubtful that either famine or windigo cannibals were ever precipitously executed without perceived evidence that they represented a continuing threat to others. A significant exception to this generalization could occur if windigo accusations served to rationalize collectively the murder of a mentally deranged or physically disabled peron who had not expressed specific windigo behavior or threats (cf. Marano 1982).

One passage in Nelson's manuscript is of particular interest in relation to pragmatic aspects of the windigo complex. One of Nelson's informants suggested that another Cree might be misrepresenting himself to Nelson as a windigo, his probable motive being to impose upon or frighten others. In another instance, the desire to secure a remedy of high wines (double-distilled spirits) was suggested as a possible motive for misrepresentation ("Windigo Cures and Precautions"). Some individuals may have simulated a windigo condition in order to control others or to elicit supportive behavior from relatives. More tragically, the suicidally inclined might identify themselves as windigo to provoke execution. Additional practical manipulations of windigo beliefs are exemplified by cases where "windigo scares" were purposely started in order to gain access to trapping land (Flannery et al. 1982, 75) or to frighten competing fur traders of mixed parentage (Godsell 1938, 109).

The Symbolic Structure of the Windigo Complex
Nelson's windigo stories and observations are rich in material on the symbols and cultural logic underlying the complex. Most clearly expressed are associations with freezing, winter, ice and the North. The evil spirit entities that "delegate" the windigo condition are the giant cannibals of the north (Ojibwa), and beings associated with ice and with the northern direction and wind (Cree). Nelson noted also the idea that the human windigo, as his or her condition deteriorates, develops a frozen heart or other internal organs (cf. Cooper 1933, 21). This internal freezing was of practical significance both in curing and executing windigos; it was thought necessary to melt, eject, or otherwise eliminate the internal ice in order to produce a cure or a successful execution. The significance of hot bear grease (cf. Cooper 1933, 22; Rohrl 1970), and presumably also of the alcoholic drinks mentioned by Nelson ("Windigo Cures and Precautions"), derives in part from their ascribed capacity to melt the windigo's frozen viscera. It is probable also that the definition of bear grease as the exemplar of appropriate food and of bears as human-like animals is relevant; the idea that grease would induce vomiting of the internal ice suggests a conceptual antagonism between the substances.

Since it was believed that slain windigos might become reanimated if the internal ice were not destroyed, hot tea or water was sometimes poured into the opened chest cavities of executed sufferers (Teicher 1960, 96; Duchaussois 1923, 293–94). Nelson's observations that the warm weather of summer was thought to produce recovery (or remission?) is paralleled by the Ojibwa belief that humans might alternate seasonally between normal and windigo conditions, becoming cannibalistic only in winter (Laidlaw 1927; Landes 1938, 222). The idea that a windigo condition is prefigured when children eat ice or snow is also widely distributed (Cooper 1933, 22–23).

Cooper (1933, 21, 23) was the first to elaborate a combined ecological and psychological explanation both of the windigo belief system and of windigo as a culturally specific form of insanity. He suggested that the cannibalistic urges experienced by sufferers were "directly traceable" to a conflict between the threat of crisis cannibalism during food shortages and the rigid proscription of such cannibalism among Algonquians. In somewhat similar terms, Landes (1938, 214) related the disorder to the fear engendered by actual or potential starvation. While starvation and famine cannibalism are dominant symbols in the windigo complex, it is not possible, however, simply to deduce the origin, persistence, or characteristics of the belief system from ecological coordinates. Ojibwa and Cree conceptions of windigo are organized in terms of strong metaphorical and metonymic associations linking winter, the north, ice, starvation, cannibalism, insanity, and human identity. This cultural logic has surely had a powerful effect on how boreal Algonquians have experienced, categorized, and reacted to mental disorders. The distributional problem of why Algonquians but not other boreal forest inhabitants possessed the windigo complex was noted as early as the late eighteenth century by David Thompson (1962, 194) and remains to be satisfactorily elucidated. It is characteristic of Nelson that this problem engaged his attention. He formulated it in terms of the contrast between the universally human and the culturally specific. The specificity of the windigo disorder led him ultimately to credit the explanations of his Algonquian informants:

There is such a singular, strange, incomprehensible contradictoriness in almost all these cases, and many I have heard, that I do most verily believe they are denunciations, witch or wizardisms: in any other manner they are not rationally to be accounted for, *unless we suppose all those who feed upon human flesh to be thus possest – then it is natural to man in those cases; but why then not the same with us as with these people?* ("Sources and Forms of Windigo"; emphasis added).

MEDICINE: HEALING AND SORCERY

When speaking English, boreal forest Algonquians and other North American Indians often use the word "medicine" to characterize persons, objects, and activities associated with healing and sorcery. Although Cree and Ojibwa healers knew and used many effective plant medicines (cf. Densmore 1928, 299–305; Smith 1932, 348), Nelson correctly followed the categorizations of his informants by discussing medicine in all its dimensions as a facet of Algonquian religion. In this discussion, "medicine" refers in the narrow sense to healing, and "sorcery" to magico-religious techniques for causing misfortune to others. "Hunting medicine" and "love medicine" are related topics conceptually associated with sorcery by Algonquians. The exact semantics of the relevant Cree and Ojibwa terms vary by area and dialect and have yet to be worked out adequately for even a single speech community.

Disease Theory and Healing Techniques

From the point of view of Western categorization, Crees and Ojibwas treated illness with combined "empirical" and "magico-religious" techniques; particular courses of treatment might emphasize one or the other approach or combine them either concurrently or in succession. This distinction is probably not relevant to the traditional Algonquian perspective. As with such techniques as singing or sucking with tubular bones, the effectiveness of medicines presupposed or was derived from experiences or communication with spirit beings. Botanical medicines, for example, might be understood as antagonistic to an alien agent producing illness in the patient's body (Hoffman 1891, 159). The interpenetration of empirical and magico-religious concepts is exemplified in Nelson's discussion of the relations of songs to healing; each medicine revealed to humans in dreams had its own song which was sung when the plant or other substance was collected and administered. Nelson also made clear that the effectiveness of the medicine depended upon the performance of the song and the simultaneous attendance or influence of the curer's spirit guardian: "When they [healers] sing, those of their familiars who instructed the song . . . attend, invisibly of course, and perform that which he promised this (medecine, supposing it is one) should effect" ("Songs: Their Transmission and Uses"). Songs might also be sung when medicines such as roots were removed from the earth and tobacco offerings were placed in the hole (Densmore 1928, 325; Smith 1932, 349). Ultimately, as Nelson observed, medicine knowledge was thought to derive from the benevolent creator being or the transformer (cf. Smith 1932, 349) who introduced it to benefit mankind. Landes (1968, 58) distinguished medicines derived from the spirit guardian from salable "magics" that operated impersonally and mechanically, but suggested that these were continuous rather than discrete categories.

Techniques of treatment depended, of course, upon diagnosis, and the latter distinguished between effective and ultimate causes of health disorders. Serious or protracted illness was often attributed to the presence of an alien object in the patient's body. Alternatively, soul loss, or, more rarely, physical possession by a spirit were identified as effective causes of illness. The ultimate causes were said to be human sorcerers, malevolently intentioned spirits, or the patient's own earlier misconduct. Despite popular stereotypes to the contrary, not all illness or injury was ascribed to spiritual or magico-religious causes. Concomitantly, many of the botanical and other medicines used in the treatment of common, predictable, or minor disorders were probably understood to be effective independently of immediate ritual or magical influences.

Nelson distinguished between botanical and "mineral" medicines, the latter including varieties of stone, soil, bone, and shell. Botanical medicines typically were boiled while the others were pulverized and dissolved in water; some medicines combined both classes of ingredients. A sizeable literature describes the medicinal uses of specific plants by Ojibwa (Gilmore 1933; Reagan 1921a, 1921b, 1928; Stowe 1940; Hoffman 1891, 198–201; Densmore 1928, 336–67; Smith 1932, 352–92; Black 1980) and Cree (Beardsley 1941; Strath 1903; Corrigan 1946; Holmes 1884; Leighton 1985). Considerable variation existed within and among communities with respect to medicinal uses of particular species and to their combinations, proportions, preparations, dosages, and administration. Medicines were usually administered either internally as beverages or externally as poultices. Nelson observed one treatment in which the healer masticated a botanical medicine and then blew vigorously on the patient in order to introduce the remedy into his body. This technique alternated with that of sucking the afflicted part of the body in order to remove the intrusive disease agent, conceived of as a small tangible object like a bone, stone, worm, maggot, wood fragment, or metal splinter. If the injury or illness was not localized, the sucking and blowing techniques were applied to the pit of the stomach or the temples. A detailed account of the preparation and administration of botanical and other medicines by Minnesota Ojibwa was prepared by Densmore (1928, 325–35). In sorcery certain objects and botanical substances were thought to be effective without necessary physical contact with the victim, but it is not clear that similar techniques were used in curing.

Medicine Dreams and Visions
Although knowledge pertaining to medicine might in theory be revealed to anyone in a dream or vision experience, all Cree and Ojibwa groups recognized one or more categories of professional healers whose vocation derived from the special character of their dreams and practical instruction by others. Some Ojibwa groups distinguished as many as four categories of healers, although the differences between them were variable

(Cooper 1936; Landes 1968, 47–50; Hoffman 1891, 156–59). Nelson (1811, 35) was aware that medicines and their associated songs were often bought and sold; visionary revelation and instruction for a price were complementary sources of a healer's repertoire of materials and techniques: "It is surprising to see what a stress these people lay upon their medicines – they sell nothing to each other whatever, but their medicine they sell amazingly dear; they say it is **"life"**, and any person who is desirous of getting himself cured or healed will begrudge no price to obtain the proper means; but as they sell their medicines they sell their song with it – for each medicine, that is root or herb, has its song."

Consistent with the definition of medicine knowledge as private property, the visionary or dream inspiration of specific medicines and techniques exhibited a high degree of individualism and variation. Such aspects of curing as the identification of medical uses for specific plants or the compounding of plants for a new medical purpose are understood by Crees to derive from dreams or from their interpretation (Brightman 1977–79). Even the Ojibwa Midewiwin, or Grand Medicine Society, an esoteric association concerned with healing and sorcery, did not transmit a uniform complex of knowledge to each initiate (cf. Landes 1968; Hoffman 1891). Some regularized instruction accompanied initiation and advancement through each grade, but most medical knowledge was less standardized.

Although the Midewiwin was a repository of knowledge of herbs, it did not have a pharmacopoeia accessible to every member. The remedies are individual, not general, and an individual when questioned invariably replies, "I can tell you about my own medicines. I do not know about other people's medicines nor their uses of the same plant." Thus it is frequently found that different people have different names and uses for the same plant (Densmore 1928, 322–23; cf. Smith 1932, 345).

In addition to the standardized Midewiwin teachings, a body of medical knowledge for treating common complaints was accessible to everyone. However, new elements must also have been introduced into Algonquian medical systems through individual innovation or modification and through diffusion. The innovations were, of course, culturally patterned, but maintained diversity and variation in contrast to standardized knowledge disseminated through purchase, instruction, and initiation.

Probably all boreal Algonquian societies identified one or more particular spirit or animal beings with medicine, and the ability to cure successfully and legitimately was thought to derive from visionary communication with the appropriate being. Among some Southwestern Ojibwa, for example, Thunderbirds and Bear were identified as the spirit guardians of shamans (Densmore 1928, 324; Landes 1968, 47–50). Nelson devoted a long passage in his manuscript to such a "Medicine owner" whom he called "Esculapius," using the Latin name for Aesculapios, the Greek god of medicine and healing. The account of the underground abode of the medicine owner with its adjacent rivers and lake parallels in certain features the puberty vision of a Lake Nipigon Ojibwa (Morriseau 1965, 65–67), but Nelson did not make clear whether his description came from Cree or Ojibwa sources. The beliefs Nelson described are of sufficient theological and symbolic complexity to suggest affinity with the Ojibwa Midewiwin society or cognate Cree organizations. Nelson had attended the "Mee-tay-wee" at Jack Head on Lake Winnipeg (Brown 1984, 204), but unfortunately mentioned the rite only in passing, as a ceremony requiring initiation ("Skepticism, Belief, and Innovation").

As with other spirits, communication with "Esculapius" was approached through fasting, dreaming, and concentration: "when they want to dream of these things . . . they must fast and lay down to sleep, keeping their minds as free as possible from any other thoughts whatever, and wholly bent and employed on that particular one alone" ("Medicines and the Abode of Esculapius"). Nelson observed, "it is not every *Indian* that is favored with these dreams," suggesting that shamanistic specialization was limited to those who subjectively experienced the appropriate dreams and publicly validated them through successful cures.

Nelson's report of the medicine vision may be a composite or a first-person account by a single informant. During the vision, the dreamer, or the dreamer's soul, left the site of the fast and travelled to the medicine owner's abode. The spirit dwelt inside a mountain from which forty rivers with colored water issued to converge in a large lake on a plain at the foot of the mountain. The different water conditions in the rivers (turbulent, placid, etc.) symbolized or prefigured variations in human health and longevity. The underground dwelling possessed six doors, each oriented to a different direction. After being greeted by "Esculapius," the dreamer was admitted through a door positioned exactly in the midst of the rivers with twenty on either side. Inside the mountain dwelt "doctors" from every society in the world; the informant's description was such as to permit Nelson's identifying French, English, German, Hebrew, and Greek physicians among them. Nonbotanical medicines such as stones, bone, and shell were kept in the cavern where the dreamer was instructed in their use. Outside the cavern, along the watercourses and on the side of the mountain, every medicinal plant in the world was found in abundance. There the dreamer was taught the identification of botanicals, their uses, methods of preparation and combination, how to collect them, and the songs to be sung with their collection and use or when teaching their uses to others. Nelson was told that the dreamer retained so vividly the details of these instructions that he could recognize particular medicinal plants immediately, even if he had never encountered them before in waking life.

Nelson's manuscript indicates that other beings besides "Esculapius" could provide medical knowledge. Spirits identified with particular plant species, for example, appeared during visionary dreams ("Roots and Herbs"). Alternatively, the dreamer's personal guardian spirit revealed the identity and uses of medicines together with the requisite rituals ("Songs: Their Transmission and Uses"). Ultimately, as Nelson noted, knowledge of medicine was thought to have derived from the benevolent creator being, or from the transformer who introduced it to benefit mankind (cf. Smith 1932, 349).

Sorcery

Techniques and concepts of what was called sorcery were similar in many respects to those of healing, and the two were often associated in practice. Like medicinal knowledge, knowledge of sorcery derived ultimately from spiritual sources and could be bought and sold under appropriate circumstances. Serious health disorders, whether caused by illness or injury, were often ascribed to the actions of sorcerers, and medical treatment was sometimes specifically or exclusively directed toward identifying and defeating or destroying such enemies. Individuals who were successful healers were thought to be at least potentially capable of sorcery (Landes 1968, 58–59).

Nelson's manuscript contains information on several distinguishable classes of sorcery. It alludes briefly to the technique of sucking an intrusive disease object from the patient's body; such objects were sometimes thought to be sent and implanted by sorcerers with the assistance of their spirit guardians ("Songs: Their Transmission and Uses"). The Lac la Ronge conjuring episode with which the manuscript begins exemplifies another form of sorcery: a monster was called up from the underwater depths to stalk and destroy the victim ("Conjuring at Lac la Ronge, December 1819").

Cree and Ojibwa concepts of the soul are closely implicated in conventional ideas of sorcery. The exteriorized soul of a sorcerer was thought to function as an agent of illness or injury, and the theft of a victim's soul was a form of sorcery resulting in madness or death. Some Ojibwa communities shared an explicit belief in two souls or differentiated spiritual components with distinct functions and attributes (Schoolcraft 1848, 127; Jenness 1935, 18–20; Vecsey 1983, 59–62). Manitoba Crees explicitly recognize only a single soul anatomically associated with the heart, although concepts of multiple afterlives are implied by their simultaneous beliefs in ghosts, an afterworld in the west, and the aurora borealis as the dancing souls of the dead (Brightman 1977–79). Nelson mentioned only a belief in a single soul which was associated with the heart and had the size and shape of an egg yolk ("The Soul"). The use of the soul as an agent of sorcery is exemplified in Nelson's story of an elderly woman subjected to "soul darting." In this narrative, a sorcerer was thought to have exteriorized his soul in the form of a small bean-like object. It penetrated the head of an elderly woman, afflicting her with unconsciousness and eventual aphasia. Her son extracted the bean from her temple by sucking and imprisoned it in a tobacco box from which it then escaped ("Soul Darting"). The identification, in this story, of the sorcerer's soul as the intrusive object in the victim's body is an unusual element. More typically, sorcerers were thought to metamorphosize either their body or their soul to assume the forms of bears, owls, fireballs, and other frightening objects (Vecsey 1983, 147–48).

The involuntary absence of the soul from the body was thought to produce derangement and eventual death. Consequently, according to Nelson's informants, sorcerers could harm their victims by stealing and imprisoning their souls or by physically crushing them. Both the sorcery and the retaliatory attack on the sorcerer were effected with the shaking lodge (cf. Hallowell 1955, 175; Morriseau 1965, 72, 76–77) and it was thought that the stolen soul could be liberated from the lodge where it was imprisoned.

One of Nelson's informants offended a sorcerer and subsequently dreamed that his soul was being drawn into the shaking lodge by his enemy's spirit guardians. The absence of the soul from his body resulted in derangement and convulsions. Through the intervention of a benign spirit, the sorcerer was compelled to release the soul and it flew back to the body and re-entered it. During the dream, the victim's identity and self-awareness remained with the soul; he experienced sensations of flight and observed the shaking lodge of the conjuror. It is interesting to remark, however, that if Nelson translated correctly, the narrator used the pronoun "I" to refer both to his body and his soul while the two were separated ("The Soul").

Just as healers compounded botanical medicines, sorcerers were thought to prepare poisons which they deceitfully administered to victims in food or in the guise of remedies. There seems little reason to doubt Algonquian testimonies that such practices occurred, although accusations probably vastly outnumbered factual cases. Such poisons, like other means of sorcery, could be bought and sold. Among the Southwestern Ojibwa, their uses were said to be taught during initiation into the higher grades of the Midewiwin (Landes 1968, 59). Although much is known about Ojibwa and Cree medicines, virtually no information is on record about the ingredients of poisons and consequently of their actual or imputed toxic properties.

Nelson's two examples of poisoning both concern botanicals apparently used specifically by rejected suitors to avenge themselves on women. As with medicines used in healing, nominally magical techniques alternated with or supplemented actual administration. In the first case, the root of a thistle-like plant which was given in tobacco to a woman during menstruation reportedly produced a blackened complexion and facial hair when accompanied with a verbal spell. That some such disorder, whether purposely induced or not, afflicted Cree women at Lac la Ronge was suggested by Nelson's eyewitness testimony about women whose complexions became "of a *nasty* black with abundance of hair growing out on the face" ("Sexual Sorcery").

The second example concerned an unidentified root, perhaps baneberry (one of the *Actaeas*), which was used medicinally as an astringent for wounds. One of Nelson's informants mixed it with vermillion (a red-orange dye) and sprinkled it in pulverized form at a site where his victim had urinated. The powder supposedly produced an excessive menstrual flow that eventually threatened her life. Not wishing to cause her death, he appealed to the old man who had taught him this procedure and was told to give the victim a length of the root to eat as an antidote. The root's magical strength appears to have been derived, in this instance, from its use as an astringent and perhaps as a regulator of excessive menstrual flow; it was said to produce the opposite of these curative effects when administered to a healthy individual. The idea that sorcery could be effected in such a way parallels Cree mythological references to impregnation when men urinate at sites earlier used by women (Brightman 1977–79). The story also exemplifies the premise that some poisons or sorcerous medicines could work their evils without being physically administered (cf. Densmore 1928, 327–28; Smith 1932, 427); they could, for example, be worn by the sorcerer in the proximity of the victim or placed where the latter would step on them.

Some techniques of sorcery employed images of the victim, although botanical substances were usually used in conjunction with them. Nelson described the use of an animal hide image cut into the shape of a human figure. A powdered root was placed on the image and ignited, the burning of the leather prefiguring the death of the victim or injury to the part of the body the sorcerer desired selectively to injure. Nelson's informants stated that these medicines depended on the assistance or power derived from the sorcerer's spirit guardian, and were otherwise ineffective.

Another form of sorcery was intended to starve or discourage the victim by making it impossible for him to hunt or trap successfully. Nelson recorded two techniques for effecting such results. In some instances, the sorcerer was thought to deploy his spirit guardians to frighten game away from the victim. In others, a root, possibly from the giant hyssop (*Agastache foeniculum* [Pursh] Ktze) was mixed with other ingredients and placed on drawings of the animals the sorcerer intended to disperse. As with other varieties of sorcery, conventional controls and countermeasures existed. Nelson related two stories of bewitched hunters who overcame sorcery by treating their guns with sweetflag and lye, respectively. In other cases, the curse was imposed only for a limited time which had to expire before hunting prospects would improve (cf. Landes 1968, 23). Nelson perceptively summarized the Algonquian perspective on such conflicts which predicted resolutions or interpreted them after the fact in terms of the relative power attributes of the antagonists: "this depends entirely upon the precautions the *bewitcher* has taken, the Power, influence, or number of his Dreamed: as also on the other hand of the Dreamed, their power, influence &c, of the *bewitched*" ("Hunters Bewitched and Restored"). Botanical and other substances were often employed to counteract different forms of sorcery (Densmore 1928, 327–28); these typically were worn as amulets or kept in the home.

The motivations for sorcery in Nelson's narratives were romantic or sexual rejection, wife stealing or alienation, alleged unwillingness to sell medicines, insults to the sorcerer's medicines, and conspicuous differences in hunting success. Sorcery often provoked defense or retaliatory measures. Sorcerers could control the scope of their revenge, as when placing a curse on a hunter for a predetermined period of time or directing injuries to particular parts of the body.

In Manitoba Cree communities today, sorcery is usually discussed as an intentional act but sorcerers are also sometimes thought to be possessed or controlled by malignant spirit guardians from whom the impulses to commit sorcery derive (cf. also Landes [1968, 59] on Ontario Ojibwa). In Nelson's cases, it is interesting that sorcery crossed the local ethnic boundaries; métis as well as Indians both used and feared sorcery and one of the Hudson's Bay Company's Canadian employees also defined himself as a victim.

Medicine for Hunting and Love
Medicines used to exert influence over hunting and over sexual or romantic relationships were conceptually associated and often employed the same botanical ingredients. Cree verbs referring to hunting and trapping often metaphorically connote sexual activities; more generally, hunter–prey and male–female relationships are conceived of as similar and can represent each other in the contexts of myths, dreams, rituals, and jokes (Brightman 1977–79). Both love and hunting medicines are included within the broader domain of sorcery or "bad medicine," the common element being the effect of the medicine in subverting the autonomy and welfare of other animate beings (Black 1977b; Landes 1968, 65).

Nelson described a technique for influencing hunting success by using a powdered plant medicine, probably giant hyssop. Three moose were outlined on a piece of birchbark and powder applied to the head and heart of each. The bark was then fastened with sinew to a stick planted in the ground and allegedly wound itself tightly while the hunter sang. The hunter preceded these actions by invoking his spirit guardian, requesting that it render the moose foolish and easy to stalk and kill. In general, Algonquian hunting medicines emphasize the adversarial aspects of the human–animal relationship, in contrast to the complex ritual rules that express respect for slain prey. Similar techniques among Southwestern Ojibwa involved piercing the heart of the animal's image and placing medicine on the puncture (Hoffman 1891, 221–22; Smith 1932, 350). The technical parallel with sorcery intended to harm or kill a human victim is obvious (cf. Vecsey 1983, 147–48).

Giant hyssop was probably also an ingredient in love medicines described by Nelson. Nelson's métis informant Baptiste (probably the HBC canoeman Baptiste Paul listed in HBCA B.89/a/7, p. 60) related two instances of its use. In one, the medicine apparently induced confusion and sexual availability, and in the other a rejected husband used it to regain the affection of his straying wife ("Love Magic"). The medicines were administered to the sleeping victims, apparently as a salve. Other forms of love medicine employed wooden images, the victim's hair, and other substances together with botanicals, but did not involve contact (cf. Morriseau 1965, 56; Landes 1968, 65–67). As with stories describing uses of plant poisons, it is difficult to establish how frequently love medicines were actually used and even more difficult to specify their psychological or physical effects. Nelson was told that these effects ranged from arousing spontaneous desire to incurring hypnotic dependency and sexual aggressiveness. Together with the descriptions of sorcery used by rejected suitors, Nelson's account of love medicine reveals ambivalent and hostile aspects of male–female relations in communities where women were simultaneously pressured to reject premarital experimentation and to accept suitors for fear that refusal would provoke love medicine or other sorcery (Hallowell 1955, 229–300; Landes 1938, 43, 57–63).

Confession

Although serious health disorders were primarily blamed on human or nonhuman antagonists, some illnesses and accidents were understood as consequences of the sufferer's own incorrect actions or those of his or her senior relatives. It is often not clear whether such misfortunes were seen as automatic consequences or bad conduct or as mediated by spirits.

Nelson recorded the terms "on-gee-nay" (Ojibwa) and "Oh-gee-nay" (Cree) which referred to a patient's being "afflicted or chastised for his own sins, or those of some of his or her near relatives" ("Deviance, Confession, and Expiation"). Disorders which were attended by unusual circumstances or did not respond to conventional treatment were sometimes interpreted as punishment for such concealed or forgotten offenses. Public confession was thought either to remove the affliction or to be a preconditon for its treatment by other means (cf. La Barre 1964). Confession was prompted during shaking lodge performances when the spirits exhorted patients to confess or would help them to remember the forgotten offenses (Hallowell 1955, 256, 267–75; Dunning 1959, 80).

Although antagonistic spirits might punish diverse and not always predictable aspects of human behavior, certain offenses were expected to provoke retribution through illness. Murder, incest, deceit, physical cruelty, other-than-heterosexual activity, and the practice of sorcery could all bring on punishment by disease (Vecsey 1983, 148–50).

Nelson's accounts of confession were obtained second-hand, and related little about the circumstances other than that the sufferers confessed publicly to their families and others and that the confessions were detailed and devoid of circumlocution or evasion. Sexual misconduct ranked high among transgressions thought to provoke disease (Hallowell 1955, 256), and it was presumably such content that provoked the pious horror Nelson expressed when writing on the subject. An apparent crime admitted in some confessions was bestiality which was practiced, according to Nelson's sources, by some Crees and Ojibwas out of inclination and by the Athapaskan-speaking Beaver Indians to the west to dispell sorcery (cf. Hallowell 1955, 295). Nelson mentioned also incest and murder, and referred cryptically to yet another offense so distasteful that he refused to identify it.

Another confession described to Nelson exemplified the belief that sorcery eventually brings reflexive illness or injury upon the user and his or her relatives (Landes 1968, 59–60). Deaths, illness, and other misfortunes suffered by sorcerers were sometimes interpreted as chastisement from spirits for abusing their powers (Morriseau 1965, 77). As noted earlier, "bad medicines" associated with sorcery were associated, as were cures, with visionary revelation and with initiation or purchase. For example, "Esculapius," the medicine owner described by Nelson, presided also over the ingredients of sorcery.

Sometimes Esculapius will not instruct his votary in their (i.e. plants used in sorcery) use, satisfying himself with telling them they are all bad *medecines*, or perhaps not mentioning them at all. To others again, he explains every circumstance &c, relating to them; but with a most strict injunction never to employ them at his *Peril* "unless you wish to die: I teach you all these things because I love you, and know your heart to be compassionate: but *mind my words*, if you ever employ them with an ill or evil *view*, thou shalt die. Other *indians* as well as thyself love life – it is sweet to every body; render it therefore not a burden or a disgrace; and I *hate* those who thus abuse my confident affection ("Medicines and the Abode of Esculapius").

The apparent paradox of a benign spirit disseminating knowledge of sorcery is explained by the ethical principle that sorcery is legitimate if used in self-defense or in response to an injury provoked by another (Landes 1968, 80). The paraphrased speech of "Esculapius" makes clear that spirits punished aggressive sorcery with death (cf. Morriseau 1965, 78), and Nelson added that dreamers were sometimes forbidden to teach sorcery techniques to others. However, it was thought that other malign spirits taught and encouraged aggressive sorcery without moral qualifications. Consequently, fear of sorcery and intimidation by shamans were and are sources of anxiety in boreal Algonquian communities, whatever the actual incidence of sorcerous practices. Persons possessing knowledge of sorcery were sometimes expected to use it aggressively despite the moral condemnation of the spirits and the associated disease sanction. One confession recorded by Nelson was that of a Cree sorcerer who interpreted his decline as a consequence of the disease sanction or the reflexive return of his bad medicine. Having initially travelled to Lac la Ronge to receive instruction in the local healing medicines, he had also gotten involved in learning the evil techniques of sorcery. "I burned with anxiety to becoming as knowing as themselves and I was gratified. Had I rested here, all had yet been well; but in learning their medecines I also learned of them those vices, those sins, that by *their practice* have reduced me to this wretched situation" ("Deviance, Confession, and Expiation").

The concept of a disease sanction for transgressions and the spirits' condemnation of aggressive sorcery as recorded by Nelson demonstrate the clear ethical content of boreal Algonquian religion (cf. Vecsey 1983, 148–50), a characteristic sometimes erroneously attributed only to the religious traditions of literate state societies. On this topic, as on many others concerning Cree and Northern Ojibwa religion and thought, George

Nelson advances our knowledge more than any other single pre-twentieth-century source.

A FINAL NOTE

The discussions in this section seek to provide historical and comparative contexts for the stories and information that Nelson wrote down in 1823. They survey dozens of sources, written and oral, ranging from the 1600s to the present. They help to show that the Lac la Ronge Crees participated in rich and complex cultural traditions whose broad patterns, though locally variable, spread across vast areas of northeastern and subarctic North America. Lac la Ronge was not an isolated or static community. Nelson conveys, even as an outsider, something of its dynamism, its responsiveness to changing conditions, and the extent to which it was in touch with both the Indian worlds around it and the fur traders who sojourned among its inhabitants.

Other kinds of context, however, are lost in the writing-down processes that both Nelson and we have undertaken. When dealing with ceremonies, stories told, and customs observed, we have all tried to convey actions and interactions that happened in real life. We cannot restore their total setting or their vibrancy, or even the languages in which the participants communicated, except to a limited degree.

Some might say that therefore we should not try, or that, rather than render imperfect images, comparisons, and analyses, we should leave Nelson's text in the obscurity that covered it from 1823 to the present. And there is also the question of media transfer – the losses and distortions that arise when stories and ceremonies are taken from a living oral context and placed in the new and foreign settings of the printed page and comparative study.

It is our feeling that this material, whatever its deficiencies and difficulties of transmission, is far too valuable to be left inaccessible and unknown. It comes from a time before the missions, treaties, reserves, and residential schools which brought such drastic discontinuities into native communities and such disruptions of their cultural heritages. It reaches back to a more open time, so it appears, of trust and sharing and conversations between some native people and a rather unusual person who cared about what they were saying and listened as well as he could.

When the Reverend Stan Cuthand agreed to read the Nelson manuscript and to compose his commentary for Part IV of this book, he found that various aspects of the text fascinated, stimulated, and at times disturbed him. He was interested in many aspects of what Nelson had recorded from the distant past, and supportive of that effort to preserve. Story telling, as he writes, takes more time than many people have today, and so there is value in having the stories handed down in writing, to "remind us of half forgotten tales, ideas, and concepts."

Stan Cuthand's thoughtful and evocative response is both a valued contribution to discussion and a powerful statement about his own life in two worlds. If Nelson's writings stir more voices to speak and more people to remember and respond, in whatever directions they may choose, the conversations of 1823 may be revived to reach once again beyond the printed page. As Nelson said in beginning his text, we "leave every one to make his own remarks and to draw his own conclusions."

I V

Overleaf: NbNc-1, Hickson–Maribelli Site Face xxvii (detail)

ON NELSON'S TEXT
BY STAN CUTHAND

While I was growing up I lived in two worlds. At school (Little Pine Day School, Little Pine Reserve, near North Battleford, Saskatchewan), I lived in the precise factual world of the Anglican church. We learned by rote and memorized names and dates. It was a world of battles and British history, of Admiral Horatio Nelson and the Duke of Wellington and the certainty of one God.

But when I was at home, I lived in the free and allegorical world of the Cree. It was a world peopled by the heroes of the plains and the mythic beings of Cree spirituality, the free roaming buffalo hunters and the great tribal warriors. And unlike the Duke of Wellington and Admiral Nelson, the war heroes were still members of the community.

As a young boy, I felt these old warriors were guardians of our heritage and lifestyle. It was they who objected when the school officials cut the braids of children whose families had maintained their traditions. At Sundances and community celebrations, these elders would get up and tell the stories of their battles and the daring horse stealing which went on between the tribes. Their stories included the famous battles of men long dead. Their stories were the military history of our people, just as the stories of Admiral Nelson are to the British.

I remember many times hearing the story of my paternal grandfather, Misatimwas, who was a war chief when Poundmaker was the civil chief of the Cree. In the battle of Cutknife Hill during the rebellion of 1885, he was shot and wounded in the abdomen. Chief Fine Day later told this story:

During the rebellion I saw a man get cured with a Bear skin. He was "Misatimwas," or Hunting Horse. I don't think that Bear skin was used in the fighting because it was too awkward. Misatimwas was dying – wounded in the belly. His guts were coming out. He told them to cut it off but no one had the courage to do it, so he did it himself. The Bear hide was hanging in the tipi where he lay. Misatimwas drank a lot of water all the time. His father took down the Bear hide near morning, when Misatimwas was just about dead. The old man started to speak to the hide and covered his son with it – head to head – and sat behind the heads. He took a rattle and started to sing a Bear song. The fire went out and it was pretty dark. Before long we saw the bear hide moving and we heard a Bear squealing. The old man kept on singing. We could hear the bear all the time, coming down. I don't know if the sound came from the hide or from the man's body.

Misatimwas was so low that he didn't want any more water. When the fire blazed up Misatimwas motioned me to come closer. "If I see the Sun coming up, I'll live." I could hardly hear him. His father asked what he said and I told him. Misatimwas sank lower. It seemed as though the Sun wouldn't come up soon enough. I listened to his breath and the others were watching for the Sun. They finally saw it, but I thought that Misatimwas had fooled himself – that he was going to die anyway. But when the Sun was quite high he drew a deep breath. Not long after he breathed good – called for water and was well. I saw this with my own eyes. He was Jose Cuthand's father (Fine Day, *My Cree People*, 1973, quoted in Wiebe and Beal 1985, 104–106).

In my youth, the religious, philosophical and moral history of the Plains Cree was explored in the winter. This was the time for invoking the names of the *Ātayōhkanak*, the mythical beings who would be called to the shaking tent. It is these beings about whom George Nelson writes.

The superheroes like Pine Root and Beaded Head were the original beings of the earth. They were not human beings although they behaved and acted as human beings. They also performed extraordinary feats of spiritual power and thought. They were the ones who prepared for the coming of mortals to the earth. These heroes transformed themselves into stars, plants and animals and eventually peopled the world as we know it. There is an on-going conflict between the gods and other supernatural beings like the Thunderbird, the Great Serpent, the Wīhtikōw, and the Pākahk. This struggle is a preparation for future generations who may get to live in an ideal world where only good remains.

In the period when the world was being peopled by mortals, the stories of the trickster grew up. There are many names for this same kind of character in Cree and in other languages; Wīsahkēcāhk, Cahkāpēs, and Ayās in Cree, Nannabush of the Ojibway, Nāpi of the Blackfeet and Iktomi of the Assiniboine, are all personages to which the trickster stories are attributed. I was told by John Ratt, Sr., of Sucker River (a small village twenty miles north of the town of La Ronge) that he knew of a storyteller who told Wīsahkēcāhk stories for four days straight and concluded by saying that the stories are endless. I believe there once were literally hundreds of trickster stories. In La Ronge some of these stories were also told by Mrs. Mary Jane Bell, who used the name Cahkāpēs for the trickster.

Some Wīsahkēcāhk stories tell of how he recreated the world after the flood. In one he has the misfortune to fall off a cliff and as he is going down he says, "I made this earth; may it be a soft landing." Wīsahkēcāhk has many foibles including pride and a rather nasty sense of humor and he does not have the stature of a god.

There are many famous story tellers whom I knew in my youth. Pound-maker, the second, used to come to our house in the winter to tell stories. On one occasion, when my brother's child died, he came with his blankets and moved in. He told stories all night long to keep the parents going. He had a lot of funny stories too. He wasn't a somber story teller.

There were also grandmothers who were very good story tellers. While the elders (men) told stories of the Ātayōhkanak to gatherings, the grand-mothers spoke of the same beings to the extended family as a means of pointing out a moral to the young.

In the 1930s, when I was twelve or thirteen, my cousins attended a shaking tent (kosāpahcikan) which was performed at Manitou Lake about sixty miles (100 kilometres) east of Saskatoon. The "conjuror" was Maskosis (Little Bear). They told me that Maskosis was tied up very tightly by his wife. His fingers were laced together, his wrists were tied and his toes were also laced. He was sitting at the far end of a completely darkened great lodge, well away from the shaking tent. The shaking tent was a small box, just large enough to hold a man, made of square sharpened poles very strongly secured in the ground, with bells on the tops of the poles. Initially, in the darkness, my cousins could hear him singing where he had been tied up and then suddenly his voice started coming from the shaking tent. On that occasion there was a very funny visit from Wīsahkēcāhk who came early and fooled Little Bear. My cousin spoke to Wīsahkēcāhk. It was in one way not unlike a seance, in that one could inquire about long dead relatives. In former times it had a lot more to do with struggles between different medicine men as Nelson describes.

Manitou Lake, the site of this shaking tent performance, was considered to be a sacred place and many young men went there on vision quests. In about 1889, my grandfather, Misatimwas, and another young man, Pāpāsces, slept on the beach there for four nights. On the second night Pāpāsces descended to the depths to commune with the spirits.

LAC LA RONGE

By the time I went to Lac la Ronge in 1944, I was pretty thoroughly indoctrinated by the Anglican Church. I had graduated from Emmanuel College in Saskatoon and was sent out by Bishop Henry Martin to serve as priest based in La Ronge. In spite of my education in the Anglican church, I was surprised at the degree of acculturation of the La Ronge Cree. I felt that they had accepted even more of what the church said than I. I suppose it is not surprising because they had been converted to Christianity in 1847, at least sixty years before my family. I was also preceded by several very strong minded priests, such as Harry Hives and Ahab Spence.

On one occasion when I was travelling across Lac la Ronge in a canoe, I started singing a Cree song. There are taboos against singing Sundance songs on a cloudy day and against singing of spirits one really wouldn't want to invoke in the middle of the lake – like the Great Serpent, but this song did not offend any of these taboos. However, my companions Joel and Dan McKenzie urged me to stop. I never heard anyone sing Cree songs in La Ronge.

It seems to me that in La Ronge the church probably used the people's fear of the Wīhtikōw to reinforce its teachings, but it is also possible that the many native priests involved in the church before my time used the church to neutralize their existing fears.

In any event the people of Lac la Ronge did not expect me to be interested in Indian myths and it was not until I had been there for some time that I finally went to chief Nehemiah Charles, who was a lay reader in the church, and asked him to tell me a good story. He told me about the tribe of cannibals, which Nelson calls the Hairy Hearts (in my experience Wīhtikōw can refer both to a community of cannibals and to a free-roaming individual spirit Wīhtikōw). The cannibal tribe were in a camp on the shore of the lake and they were drumming and singing. It was said that anyone who heard the music would be drawn toward it and would be killed by falling on a stake as he approached the camp fire. One man wanted to hear the music but not get killed and he had some personal power. As he was coming up to the campfire he was killed, but he transformed himself into a spark of flame and so he escaped.

I realized then that the Cree myths were hidden from people like me but were still being told. Once people realized that I was interested, I heard many stories. My experience was probably not unlike Nelson's in that once the people knew of his interest, they were happy to tell him the stories which he later related to his father.

Among the stories told in La Ronge, some of the characters were the same but there were several differences. The Woods Cree were not familiar with the buffalo and I heard no stories about Kisēnāpēw-mostos (Kind-old-man-buffalo), one of the guardian spirits of the Plains Cree. Before I went north, I had never heard of the Crazy Woman. Nor was I familiar with the Great Lynx. But in Stanley Mission, on the Churchill River about fifty miles north of the town of La Ronge, the children used to play a game called Misipisiw. It was a tag type game in which the child who was the Great Lynx would throw the other kids into the water. To them the word meant "to be feared."

I believe that the Cree in the La Ronge area have many more Wīhtikōw stories than the Plains Cree. I knew of the mythical being, the Wīhtikōw, but to the northerners, the Wīhtikōw was not just a mythical being. It was a malevolent spirit which was very much alive and sort of lying in wait all the time. Mrs. Matthew Charles of La Ronge used to tell me that the dogs would bark all night around a house if there was an unbaptised child because the Wīhtikōwuk were hanging around. Christianity held the Wīhtikōw at bay.

The Anglican Church inadvertently reinforced some myths. Once I was visiting Chief Nehemiah Charles during a thunder storm. Although it was hot and muggy, he refused to have the door open because he was concerned about Thunderbirds. When I suggested that they were only mythical beings, he said he could prove they existed because they were referred to in the Bible. He found a section of the scripture which said in English, "and the thunder shall come"; in syllabics it read "and the thunderbird shall come."

I should have suspected that there was a heavy undercurrent of Cree myths because Chief Nehemiah Charles was terrified of water and whenever he had to cross the river he took many people with him.

Over the years I was told a number of stories about the vision quests of La Ronge area Cree. They set out on very arduous solo journeys and suffered from isolation and physical discomforts in the hope that the spirits would see their suffering and come to them to give them powers to prophecy, to live a long life, to heal the sick or to have power over evil spirits and to know the mysteries of the unknown spirit world. John Roberts of Lac la Ronge told me of a man who paddled a small canoe along the shores of Lac la Ronge, naked and sitting on grass. This man's vision quest was never to step on land until his return to his original embarkation point. (Lac la Ronge is more than 30 miles in diameter.)

John Ratt at Sucker River, twenty miles north of La Ronge on the lake, told me of another man who sought to know the mysteries of a rolling rock on the Churchill River. This was a large boulder the Crees believed had moved from one side of the river to the other. He went there with the Hudson's Bay Company freighters who were travelling up the river on their way west and he stayed there several weeks until they returned. He slept on the rock every night and every morning found himself sleeping on the ground. His quest was to discover the power behind this unusual event and to commune with the spirit of the rock, but when he returned home he felt that he had not succeeded. The vision quests of some men were motivated by a desire to have power over other people or to manipulate the spirits to destroy another medicine man. These vision quests did not always succeed and some were self-destructive.

Nelson speaks of some of his acquaintances being bewitched by medicine men. I had no experience of this before going to La Ronge although I had heard some stories. One day a man came running towards me with his brother-in-law in hot pursuit and threatening to do terrible things to him. The second fellow was living with his mother-in-law and could offer no explanation of why he was doing this. His brother-in-law said that the woman had bewitched him and so I sent him away to Little Hills (near La Ronge). By the way the young man acted, I believed that he had been bewitched. That woman was a medicine person.

The spirits were invoked by medicine people for revenge or protection too, at times. But it is said that you have to believe in order to be affected so sending destructive medicine did not work on missionaries, although it was no doubt tried.

There were medicine people in La Ronge who were well known for their ability to heal the sick. Mrs. David Patterson and Mr. Jerrimiah McKenzie both had a wide reputation for their healing powers.

THE CONTEXT OF CREE MYTHS

There is a very strong relationship between Cree myths and Cree society. The stories of the mythical beings reinforced socially beneficial behavior. This is something which George Nelson, in describing Cree spirituality, does not touch on to any great extent.

For instance, the stories and ceremonies surrounding Pākahk, the skeleton being, reinforce sharing of food and all material goods. Pākahk is the helping spirit of the hunters to both Plains and Woods Cree. At Little Pine Reserve, a Mahtāhitōwin Dance or "Gift Exchange Dance" was held in the fall, to honour Pākahk. We went many times to this celebration as children, and were included in the ceremony of gift-giving and receiving. The ceremony began at the central teepee with a dance which included the passing of bladders full of grease, a favorite treat of Pākahk. As the ceremony continued everyone became involved. We wandered from teepee to teepee formally exchanging gifts after a brief formalized dance with gestures. It sometimes happened that you were eventually given back something which you had given away earlier. And the thing to do was to try and be the last one to give a gift. This ceremony reinforced the ethic of sharing and at the same time it seemed to me to serve the same purpose as a lawn sale in redistributing stuff one had either grown out of or didn't presently need.

(The teachers at the school didn't like the ceremony because we were so tired after four nights of dancing that we couldn't do our work. They even took it upon themselves to berate my father for giving away a hay rake and a wagon one year. He told them it was none of their business.)

In some places, gift giving is institutionalized around an image set up where one could bring a gift and receive a gift. The image is called a Manitōhkan and I remember one such idol at the Little Hills reserve. People would pick up something from the gifts scattered around the Manitōhkan and then they would leave another gift or some tobacco, just as they would when collecting medicines. On Lac la Ronge, I was once travelling by canoe with Dan McKenzie, and as we passed by a steep cliff he asked to stop and get some medicine. We drew up to the cliff at a place where there was a hole scooped out of red rock. While Dan dug out more of the red rock he said, "Now you should sing." When he had as much medicine as he wanted, he left some tobacco in the hole in exchange.

I was told that it was possible to be bewitched and become a Pākahk, roaming the land. This might happen if a person deceived another, abused another's family or property, or insulted him. The injured party would go to a medicine man and pay the medicine man to bewitch the offender. But among the Plains Cree this is not to be confused with the original mythical being for whom the Gift Exchange Dance was held. It is also said that if you starve or freeze to death in the winter you will become a Pākahkos (the diminutive of Pākahk), a small creature about four feet high with long icy fingers and a little rifle. In the winter you can hear him in the bush shooting. The people say "there's Pākačkos," when the trees pop in the very cold weather. The possibility of turning into such a being is used to motivate children to keep the fire going in the winter.

A lot of Cree myths, but particularly the Wīhtikōw, reinforce a taboo against cannibalism which, as Nelson points out, the Cree abhorred. In my experience the Wīhtikōw was given different names in different parts of the country and I have heard Bush Cree story tellers use Nelson's term O-may(i)-mi-thay-day-ace-cae-wuk to refer to the mythic beings, the Wīhtikōw. In my experience the word taken literally would mean "those who cause bad hearts by noise" (however, I have travelled to northern Manitoba – the Pas – where they say it means "hairy chests" as Nelson does), and in one story the cannibals challenged a group of Cree to a battle. The Wīhtikōwuk made a terrible noise which froze the people with fear. But one man, with the support of a stronger spirit, was able to recover from this noise and challenge one of the Wīhtikōwuk to a life or death hand-to-hand fight. In the course of the fight they went way up in the air. The Wīhtikōw was eventually defeated.

Nelson describes how a person can become a Wīhtikōw, with ice in his heart, and how that person will sometimes ask to be killed. A Cree medicine man named Wandering Spirit [Kāpapāmahkākēw] was hanged in 1885 for the murder of an Indian agent, Mr. Tom Quinn, in the Frog Lake Massacre during the Rebellion of 1885 (Wiebe and Beal 1985). His followers were convicted of the murder of an old woman of the tribe. The old woman had put a blanket over her head and said to Wandering Spirit, "Kill me now for when I get up I will have too much power and you will not be able to stop me." She knew that she was becoming a Wīhtikōw. Wandering Spirit authorized his followers to kill her as she requested although he hated to do it. Her killing was witnessed by two women, Theresa Gowanlock and Theresa Delaney, who were hostages taken during the Frog Lake massacre [cp. Charette 1980, 136–38].

I feel a clear distinction is made between the people who become Wīhtikōwuk or Pākahkwak and the original powerful spirits. The former are related to but not identical to the mythical beings, Pākahk and Wīhtokōw, who are supernaturally powerful.

There are also spirits which are relatively benign and comical. The Mīmīkwīsiwak or Mēmēkwēsiwak (Plains Cree) occupy coulees and river banks in the prairies. Sam Moostos from Fort à la Corne, saw a Mēmēkwēsiw standing in the water of the North Saskatchewan River and yelled with fright. When his mother came, it ducked under the water but you could still see the ripples. Others have seen them at Gordon's Reserve, near Punnichy. They are harmless little people and friendly to humans but they can play tricks on some people who are non-believers. In the north I heard many stories of the Mēmēkwēsiwak. They were reputed to live in caves near Nistowiak Falls, at the north end of Lac la Ronge where it empties into the Churchill River, and many people had gone to see them. I was never able to make the trip although I wanted to go.

REFLECTIONS

I have to admit that at first this text by George Nelson distressed me because so many terrible things happen in it. Yet I have no reason to doubt that he saw what he describes. It is possible that he did not understand the background of these stories in the context of the Ātayōhkanak, because it is almost another language which is used to describe the spirit world, but even so the events and stories he relates are compelling.

Today there are many elders who are trying to bring back Indian religion and who want to emphasize the harmony of man and nature. Nelson's text shows a starker reality. That harmony is the ideal we all strive for, but the struggle to attain harmony is what many of these stories are about. The struggle and even the horrible conflict between good and bad make some of the best stories. I don't want to see our history or Cree mythology romanticised. George Nelson's text is like a voice out of the past reminding us of our spiritual history.

Story telling takes time. I heard a great many of the stories from La Ronge while on dogsled trips of many days' duration or while sitting and passing the time among friends. That kind of time is not available to many of us now and so it is necessary to commit some of these stories to paper as Nelson has done. His text may remind us of half forgotten tales, ideas, and concepts, so that they can be saved for another generation.

ON THE ETHICS OF PUBLISHING HISTORICAL DOCUMENTS

BY EMMA LAROCQUE

When I first read George Nelson's journal, I reacted to it in much the same way I have reacted to a host of fur trade journals, missionary writings, and other "original" sources on Indians. Like these sources, the Nelson journal raises layers of issues, ranging from the "mild" problem of inaccurate ethnography to the very grave problem of entrenched ethnocentrism, not only in the primary sources but in subsequent scholarly works as well. As these problems are finally being exposed and challenged, especially by the growing number of concerned scholars, native and non-native alike, questions are being raised regarding ethics and objectivity in scholarship. The members of the Board of Manitoba Studies in Native History faced such challenges when they considered this manuscript for publication.

First, the problem of ethnocentrism. This problem is so immense, so all-embracing, so far-reaching, yet so typical that it is extremely difficult to attempt to respond, especially in a few pages! Whatever particular merits there are in Nelson's journal, it is, in the final analysis, informed by a Eurocentric perception of Indian life. It is written within a framework I have come to call "the dichotomy of civilization versus savagery" which is pervasive in scholarly and popular literature on native peoples (LaRoque 1983).

There have been many theories and controversies since 1492 about the nature of the Indian. But the most persistent and common belief has been the European idea that humanity moved from the depths of savagery to the heights of civilization. This belief in cultural hierarchy is ethnocentric in its basis for, historically, Europeans categorized themselves as "the civilized" and the Indians as the "savages." "Civilization," and its antithesis "savagery," was (and still is) invariably measured by white European standards. The underlying assumption was that, as savages, Indians could not be as developed, organized, or ordered as Europeans, and from this has come a cluster of ideas, images, and terminology that has set Indians apart in an inferior status. This dichotomy of white civilization and Indian savagery has resulted in gross distortions about Indians in literature, historiography, and ethnography.

The Nelson manuscript may be praised for its attempts at fairness and its ethnographic detail. Given his era, Nelson is remarkably open-minded and seems to have been genuinely interested in presenting correct information. He also criticized his own society, albeit from a primitivist perspective. As to the information it contains, the journal is both marvellous and problematic. It is marvellous in that the information regarding the shaking tent ceremonies (which Nelson reduces to "conjuring") is largely consistent with what is generally known about these ceremonies. Yet, it is precisely at this point that Nelson reveals his quintessential Eurocentrism: because the "civilized" Nelson views Indian culture as "savage," he judges, belittles, and thereby reduces the rich, intricate, and multi-faceted aspects of Indian world views, religions, and mythologies to "witchcraft," "sorcery," "conjuring," "shamanism," and so forth. In doing so, Nelson typifies the double standard inherent in structuring white "civilization" as a diametric opposite to Indian "savagery." In fact, what really happens from such a "civ/sav" dichotomy is a *double* double standard by which white and Indian virtues and vices are judged. That is, the same traits or behaviors (good or bad) or organizational systems may be evident equally in white and Indian peoples and cultures, but whites, no matter how bad or good, are always civilized, and Indians are always savage. To be sure, offending whites are freely criticized, but the condemnation is never extended to all whites. On the other hand, all Indian behavior is deemed savage, and an Indian exhibiting "civilized" or Christian characteristics is seen as an exception. Indians are judged as a sub-genus to the white to the point that even "acceptable" Indian ways have to be set apart or used as a castigation of white civilization. Hence, the Noble Savage of primitivist construct.

In this framework Indian life cannot be judged at face value; it is scaled according to the civ/sav stratification. Savagery is seen as a psychosocietal, static condition – the antithesis of the highest human condition, civilization. Even in warfare, the "civilizers" made a clear-cut distinction between a supposed civilized and savage warfare. American ethnohistorian Francis Jennings notes the assumption that civilized warfare is rational, purposeful, and essentially non-violent, whereas savage warfare is irrational, aimless, and bloodthirsty (Jennings 1975). As Hollywood has so plainly presented it: cowboys "scout," Indians "lurk"; cowboys "battle," Indians "massacre" (LaRoque 1975).

Similarly, tendentious words and classifications are used to describe Indian forms of religio-mythic expressions. For example, white Christians "worship" and "pray"; Indians engage in "ceremony" or "ritual" and "conjure." Yet, when the biased definitions are put aside, Indians and whites are doing essentially the same things: both are entertaining notions of the supernatural. Scientifically, it can be said that both are in the arena of "magic"; that is, both believe in the possibilities of "an extraordinary power or influence seemingly from a supernatural source." But because Indians are supposedly within the confines of a savage state, they remain "superstitious" while civilized Europeans have "great religions."

The implication here is radical. Our larger scholarly task is not merely to sort out ethnographic detail (though, heaven knows, this too is very important since Indian ethnography has been mutilated by so many well-meaning scholars!), but also to accept native thought and organization as of equal worth to European thought while acknowledging the differences. For this to take place, we must dismantle the civilization/savagery dichotomy which is rooted so deeply in Euro-white cultural myth. This will entail dismantling traditional and judgmental thought and classification. It will mean the elimination of terms such as "sorcery," "conjuring," "witchcraft," and "primitive." In short, we must overturn the ethnocentrism inherent in Western thought and scholarship concerning notions of development, order, organization, and society.

What then is the worth of this manuscript? The editorial board of this series, led by the native members, struggled through a number of concerns. It is true that this manuscript does make, with qualifications, a substantial contribution toward a greater understanding of Indian life and thought in the 1800s. But because of the cumulative effect of biased (and often racist) scholarship on native peoples, this journal, if read in ignorance or with an ethnocentric bias, might contribute to a further defamation and belittlement of native life and thought. We chose to publish it, to open it to scrutiny. But manuscripts such as this should raise questions regarding ethics and balance in scholarship. Must we print everything we find in the archives? What happens when it is anti-Indian? Would we publish anti-semitic documents or material that defames another ethnic group? Many original sources contain such inflammatory material on Indians that they qualify as hate literature. The portrayal of Indians has ranged from that of inhuman, flesh-eating, cruel, howling savages (in portions of the Jesuit *Relations*) to that of "poor blind unfortunate creatures" in Nelson's journal. And what about the perpetuation of demeaning images of women? This journal in spots refers to "sluts" or "bitches." While it is not immediately clear what Nelson meant by these references, I am not comfortable with the overall presentation of women in this manuscript. Yet, we continue to publish and to use these sources in the name of scholarship. Such questions must be faced whenever the wider circulation of an "original source" is contemplated.

That these primary documents have contained deplorable material on native peoples seems to have largely escaped the eyes of most scholars. The insistent focus on culture and anthropology has served to distract or dilute the uncomfortable issues inherent in much of the literature on native peoples. But how far can we take such "scholarship"? Wherein lies our responsibility to combat slander, pornography, racism, hate, or plain ignorance in literature? It happens that, comparatively speaking, the Nelson journal is moderate in its approach to native peoples, but it is still constructed around the civilization (Christian)/ savagery dichotomy with its tendentious terminology and classifications. Do we risk, one more time, perpetuating this framework? In exchange for what? A few more morsels of raw ethnography to satisfy our unsatiated intellectual appetites? Yet, what else do we have? We are faced with the task of extricating "truth" from sources immersed in murky ambiguity, at best.

Finally, apart from the all-encompassing issue of the civ/sav framework, how may Nelson's cultural contribution be assessed? Very briefly, what amazes me about this manuscript is that my Plains-Cree Métis community in northeastern Alberta was still living and reciting in the 1950s and 1960s essentially the same religion, legends, and myths discussed in the manuscript! This shows me that a lot of cultural knowledge is extant in the native community and that scholars of native culture are not solely dependent on the problematic original sources; that cultural information can be received and tested against the living knowledge of many native persons. There is now a growing number of native scholars and they may best be able to synthesize living knowledge of their culture with research in academic disciplines.

On the issue of culture itself, I would caution that, while Nelson has a good grasp of some of the central Algonquian beliefs and myths, he is limited by his lack of comprehensive, contextual, and regional knowledge of Cree and Ojibwa languages, legends, myths, and religion(s). While Nelson understood the literal meaning of many words, he missed the nuances in translating Indian words, phrases, myths, personae, and concepts into English.

To Nelson's credit, he does try to compare the Indian world view and stories with those of others around the world. He did sense, even with his prejudices, that there is a universality in Indian myths and legends as well as in Indian religions. Here, a comparative literary perspective on mythology and symbolism may be useful, including motifs of good and bad twin sets, male-female tension/balance, male-female symbolism, the flood or catastrophe, the creator or transformer (re-creator), the "trickster" (a mirror to society, to human foibles), and the good-evil deity(ies). It is important that in our quest for specific ethnographic details we not isolate the Indian *weltanschauung* from other universal human motifs.

Nelson clearly struggled within himself on matters related to the apparent power of Indian thought and beliefs. What was obscure to him was that the architecture of his struggle was framed by his engagement in the Western dichotomization of white "civilization" over Indian "savagery."

REFERENCES

Ahenakew, Edward
1929   Cree Trickster Tales. *Journal of American Folklore* 42:309–53.
1973   *Voices of the Plains Cree*. Toronto: McClelland and Stewart.
Allouez, Claude
1899   Relation of 1669–1670. In Reuben G. Thwaites, editor, vol. 54.
Archives nationales du Québec, Montréal
1802   Engagement de George Nelson en qualité de commis à messrs. Alexander
        Mackinzie [sic] and Co. No. 1151 (54), notarial records of H. Crebassa.
Aubin, George F.
1982   Ethnographic Notes from Golden Lake. *Papers of the Thirteenth Algonquian
        Conference,* edited by William Cowan. Ottawa: Carleton University.
Bacqueville de la Pothèrie, Claude C. Le Roy
1931   Letters of La Pothèrie [1700]. *Documents Relating to the Early History of Hud-
        son's Bay*, edited by J.B. Tyrrell. Toronto: Champlain Society.
Baraga, Frederick
1966   [1878] *A Dictionary of the Otchipwe Language Explained in English*. Minneapolis:
        Ross and Haines (1st ed. 1853).
Bardon, Richard, and Grace Lee Nute
1947   A Winter in the St. Croix Valley, 1802–1803. *Minnesota History* 28:1–14,
        142–59, 225–40.
Barnouw, Victor
1977   *Wisconsin Chippewa Myths and Tales and their Relation to Chippewa Life*.
        Madison: University of Wisconsin Press.
Bauer, George W.
1971   Cree Tales and Beliefs. *Northeast Folklore* 12:1–70.
1973   *Tales from The Cree*. Cobalt, Ontario: Highway Book Shop.

Beauchamp, W.M.
1888   Onondaga Tales. *Journal of American Folklore* 1(1):44–48.
Beardsley, Gretchen
1942   Notes on Cree Medicines, Based on a Collection Made by I. Cowie in 1892. *Papers of the Michigan Academy of Science, Arts and Letters* 27:483–96.
Bell, R.
1897   The History of the Che-che-puy-ew-tis. *Journal of American Folklore* 10:1–8.
Bishop, Charles A.
1974   *The Northern Ojibwa and the Fur Trade.* Toronto: Holt, Rinehart and Winston.
1975   Northern Algonquian Cannibalism and the Windigo Psychosis. *Psychological Anthropology*, edited by T.R. Williams. The Hague: Mouton.
1981   Territorial Groups before 1821: Cree and Ojibwa. *Handbook of North American Indians*, vol. 6, *Subarctic*, edited by June Helm, 158–68. Washington, D.C.: Smithsonian Institution.
1982   Comment on "Windigo Psychosis" by Lou Marano. *Current Anthropology* 23(4):398.
Black, Mary B.
1977a   Ojibwa Taxonomy and Percept Ambiguity. *Ethos* 5:90–118.
1977b   Ojibwa Power Belief System. *The Anthropology of Power*, edited by Raymond Fogelson and R.N. Adams. New York: Academic Press.
Black, Meredith Jean
1980   Algonquin Ethnobotany: An Interpretation of Aboriginal Adaptation in Southwestern Quebec. *Canadian Ethnology Service Paper 65.* Ottawa: National Museum of Man Mercury Series.
Blackbird, Andrew J.
1887   *History of the Ottawa and Chippewa Indians of Michigan and Grammar of their Language, and Personal and Family History of the Author.* Ypsilanti, Michigan: Ypsilantian Job Printing House.
Bloomfield, Leonard
1930   Sacred Stories of the Sweet Grass Cree. *National Museum of Canada Bulletin 60*, Anthropological Series 11. Ottawa.
1934   Plains Cree Texts. *Publications of the American Ethnological Society*, vol. 16. New York.
1957   *Eastern Ojibwa*, edited by C. Hockett. Ann Arbor: University of Michigan Press.
Boas, Franz
1940   *Race, Language and Culture.* New York: Free Press.
Boulanger, Tom
1971   *An Indian Remembers.* Winnipeg: Peguis.
Brightman, Robert A.
1977–79 Fieldnotes on Rock Cree, unpublished.
Brinton, Daniel
1885   The Chief God of the Algonkins in his Character as a Cheat and Liar. *American Antiquarian*, 7(3):137–39.

Brown, Jennifer S.H.
1971   The Cure and Feeding of Windigos: A Critique. *American Anthropologist* 73:20–22.
1977   James Settee and His Cree Tradition: An Indian Camp at the Mouth of Nelson River Hudson's Bay. *Actes du huitième congrès des algonquinistes*, edited by William Cowan. Ottawa: Carleton University.
1982   Comment on "Windigo Psychosis" by Lou Marano. *Current Anthropology* 23(4):399.
1984   "Man in his Natural State": The Indian Worlds of George Nelson. *Rendezvous: Selected Papers of the Fourth North American Fur Trade Conference, 1981*. St. Paul: Minnesota Historical Society.
Burgesse, J. Allan
1944   The Spirit Wigwam as Described by Tommy Moar, Pointe Bleu. *Primitive Man* 17:50–53.
Chamberlain, Alexander F.
1890   The Thunder-Bird Amongst the Algonkians. *American Anthropologist* 3:51–54.
1891   Nanibozhu among the Otchipwe, Mississagas, and other Algonkian Tribes. *Journal of American Folklore* 4:193–214.
Charette, Guillaume
1980   *Vanishing Spaces: Memoirs of Louis Goulet*. Winnipeg: Editions Bois-Brûlés.
Chabot, Richard, Jacques Monet, and Yves Roby
1972   Robert Nelson. *Dictionary of Canadian Biography* 10:544–47. Toronto: University of Toronto Press.
Christ Church (Anglican), Sorel, Quebec
1787ff.   Baptismal, Marriage, and Burial Registers. Archives of the Synod of the Diocese of Montreal.
Clay, Charles
1938   *Swampy Cree Legends*. Toronto: Macmillan.
Coleman, M. Bernard, Ellen Frogner, and Estelle Eich
1962   *Ojibwa Myths and Legends*. Minneapolis: Ross and Haines.
Cooper, John M.
1933   The Cree Witiko Psychosis. *Primitive Man* 6:20–24.
1934   The Northern Algonquian Supreme Being. *Catholic University of America Anthropological Series*, no. 2, 1–78.
1936   Notes on the Ethnology of the Otchipwe of Lake of the Woods and Rainy Lake. *Catholic University of America Anthropological Series*, no. 3.
1944   The Shaking Tent Among Plains and Forest Algonquians. *Primitive Man* 17(3–4):60–84.
Corrigan, C.
1946   Medical Practice Among the Bush Indians of Northern Manitoba. *Canadian Medical Association Journal* 44:220–23

Coues, Elliott, ed.
1897   *New Light on the Early History of the Greater Northwest: The Manuscript Journals of Alexander Henry and of David Thompson.* 3 vols. New York.

Couillard-Després, A.
1926   *Histoire de Sorel de ses origines à nos jours.* Montreal: Imprimerie des Sourds-muets.

Curtis, Edward
1928   *The North American Indian*, vol. 18. New York: Johnson Reprint Co.

Danziger, Edmund J., Jr.
1978   *The Chippewas of Lake Superior.* Norman: University of Oklahoma Press.

Davidson, D.S.
1928   Some Tête de Boule Tales. *Journal of American Folklore* 31:262–74.

Denig, Edwin T.
1952   Of the Crees or Knisteneau. *Bulletin of the Missouri Historical Society* 9(1):37–69.

Densmore, Frances
1928   Uses of Plants by the Chippewa Indians. *Annual Report of the Bureau of American Ethnology* (1926–27) 44:275–397.

Dewdney, Selwyn
1975   *The Sacred Scrolls of the Southern Ojibway.* Toronto: University of Toronto Press.

Dickason, Olive Patricia
1984   *The Myth of the Savage and the Beginnings of French Colonialism in the Americas.* Edmonton: University of Alberta Press.

Dion, Joseph F.
1979   *My Tribe the Crees.* Calgary: Glenbow Museum.

Dixon, Roland B.
1909   The Mythology of the Central and Eastern Algonkins. *Journal of American Folklore* 22:1–9.

Drage, Theodore Swaine
1968   [1748–49] *An Account of a Voyage for the Discovery of a Northwest Passage.* 2 vols. New York: S. R. Publishers.

Duchaussois, Pierre
1923   *Mid Snow and Ice: The Apostles of the Northwest.* London: Burns, Oates, and Washbourne.

Dunning, R.W.
1959   *Social and Economic Change Among the Northern Ojibwa.* Toronto: University of Toronto Press.

Dusenberry, Verne
1962   *The Montana Cree: A Study in Religious Persistence.* Uppsala: Almqvist and Wiksells Boktryckeri Ab.

Edmunds, R. David
1984   *Tecumseh and the Quest for Indian Leadership.* Boston: Little, Brown.

Ellis, Henry
1967 [1748] *A Voyage to Hudson's Bay by the Dobbs Galley and California, in the Years 1746 and 1747* . . . New York: Johnson Reprint Co.
Fisher, Margaret W.
1946 The Mythology of the Northern and Northeastern Algonkians in Reference to Algonkian Mythology as a Whole. *Man in Northeastern North America*, edited by F. Johnson. *Papers of the Robert S. Peabody Foundation for Archaeology* 3:226-62.
Flannery, Regina
1939 The Shaking Tent Among the Montagnais of James Bay. *Primitive Man* 12(1):11-16.
1940 The Cultural Position of the Spanish River Indians. *Primitive Man* 13:1-25.
1944 The Gros Ventre Shaking Tent. *Primitive Man* 27:54-59.
Flannery, Regina, Mary E. Chambers, and Patricia A. Jehle
1982 Witiko Accounts from the James Bay Cree. *Arctic Anthropology* 18(1):57-77.
Fogelson, Raymond D.
1965 Psychological Theories of Windigo Psychosis and a Preliminary Application of a Models Approach. *Context and Meaning in Cultural Anthropology*, edited by Melford Spiro. New York: Free Press.
Fortune, Reo F.
1932 Omaha Secret Societies. *Columbia University Contributions to Anthropology*, vol. 14. New York: Columbia University Press.
Franklin, John
1823 *Narrative of a Journey to the Shores of the Polar Sea in the Years 1819, 1820, 1821, and 1822.* London.
Gatschet, Albert S.
1899 Water Monsters of American Aborigines. *Journal of American Folklore* 12:255-60.
Gilmore, M.R.
1933 Some Chippewa Uses of Plants. *Papers of the Michigan Academy of Science, Arts and Letters* 27:119-43.
Goddard, Ives.
1974 An Outline of the Historical Phonology of Arapaho and Atsina. *International Journal of American Linguistics* 40:102-16.
Godsell, Philip H.
1938 *Red Hunters of the Snows.* Toronto: Ryerson.
Graham, Andrew
1969 [1767/1791] *Andrew Graham's Observations on Hudson's Bay, 1767-1791*, edited by Glyndwr Williams. London: Hudson's Bay Record Society.
Granzberg, Gary
1980 Television and Traditional Cree Culture. Selected Papers from the Fifth Annual Congress of the Canadian Ethnological Society, edited by J. Ryan. *Canadian Ethnology Service Paper 62*, 128-37. Ottawa: National Museum of Man Mercury Series.

Greenberg Adolph, and James Morrison
1982   Group Identities in the Boreal Forest: The Origin of the Northern Ojibwa. *Ethnohistory* 29(2):75-102.
Hallowell, A. Irving
1926   Bear Ceremonialism in the Northern Hemisphere. *American Anthropologist* 28:1-175.
1936   The Passing of the Midewiwin in the Lake Winnipeg Region. *American Anthropologist* 38(1):32-51.
1942   The Role of Conjuring in Saulteaux Society. *Publications of the Philadelphia Anthropological Society*, vol. 2.
1955   *Culture and Experience*. New York: Schocken Books.
1976   *Contributions to Anthropology: Selected Writings of A.I. Hallowell*, edited by Raymond Fogelson. Chicago: University of Chicago Press.
Hay, Thomas H.
1971   The Windigo Psychosis: Psychodynamic, Cultural, and Social Factors in Aberrant Behavior. *American Anthropologist* 73:1-19.
Hearne, Samuel
1911   [1795] *A Journey from Prince of Wales's Fort in Hudson's Bay to the Northern Ocean*, edited by J.B. Tyrrell. Toronto: Champlain Society.
Henry (the Elder), Alexander
1901   [1809] *Travels and Adventures in Canada and the Indian Territories between the Years 1760 and 1776*, edited by J. Bain. Boston: Little, Brown.
Hewitt, J.N.B.
1925   Ethnological Researches Among the Iroquois and Chippewa. Explorations and Field-Work of the Smithsonian Institution in 1925. *Smithsonian Miscellaneous Collections* 78(1):114-17.
Hindley, John I.
1885   *Indian Legends. Nanabush, the Ojibbeway Saviour*. (No publisher given, cited in Chamberlain 1891.)
Hoffman, William J.
1891   The Midewiwin or "Grand Medicine Society" of the Ojibwa. *Annual Reports of the Bureau of American Ethnology* 7:143-300.
Holmes, E.M.
1884   Medicinal Plants Used by the Cree Indians. *Pharmaceutical Journal and Transactions* 15:302-04.
Honigmann, John J.
1956   The Attawapiskat Swampy Cree: An Ethnographic Reconstruction. *Anthropological Papers of the University of Alaska* 5(1):23-82.
1981   West Main Cree. *Handbook of North American Indians*, vol. 6, *Subarctic*, edited by June Helm, 217-30. Washington, D.C.: Smithsonian Institution.
Howard, James H.
1977   *The Plains Ojibwa or Bungi*. Lincoln, Nebraska: J and L Reprint Co.

Hudson's Bay Company Archives (HBCA), Provincial Archives of Manitoba, Winnipeg

    A.34/1, fo.55, 1823, employment records.

    B.4/a/5, Fort Alexander journal, 1822–23.

    B.89/a/7 Ile à la Crosse journal, 1822–23.

    B.89/a/7, Ile à la Crosse journal, 1823–24.

    B.89/e/1, Ile à la Crosse, district report, 1823, by George Keith.

    B.106/d/16, unsigned account book attributed to Lac la Ronge, 1822–24.

    B.141/e/1, district report, Nelson House and Deer Lake Districts, 1815.

Hurlich, Marshall
1982   Comment on "Windigo Psychosis" by Lou Marano. *Current Anthropology* 23(4):400.

Isham, James
1949   [1743–49] *James Isham's Observations on Hudson's Bay, 1743 and Notes and Observations on a Book Entitled "A Voyage to Hudson's Bay in the Dobbs Galley, 1749,"* edited by E.E. Rich. London: Hudson's Bay Record Society.

Jarvenpa, Robert
1982   Intergroup Behavior and Imagery: The case of Chipewyan and Cree. *Ethnology* 21(4):283–99.

Jenness, Diamond
1935   The Ojibwa Indians of Parry Island: Their Social and Religious Life. *National Museums of Canada Bulletin 78*, Anthropological Series 17. Ottawa.

Jennings, Francis
1975   *The Invasion of America: Indians, Colonialism and the Cant of Conquest.* New York: W.W. Norton and Company.

Johnson, Nick
1974   Bits of Dough, Twigs of Fire. *Arts Canada*, Thirtieth Anniversary Issue, nos. 184–87: 60–69.

Jones, Peter (Kahkewaquonaby)
1861   *History of the Ojebway Indians, with Especial Reference to their Conversion to Christianity.* London.

Jones, Volney H.
1965   The Bark of the Bittersweet Vine as an Emergency Food among the Indians of the Eastern Great Lakes Region. *Michigan Archaeologist* 11(3–4):170–80.

Jones, William
1905   The Algonkin Manitu. *Journal of American Folklore* 18:183–90.

1917–19 Ojibwa Texts. *Publications of the American Ethnological Society* 7, part 1, 2 vols. Leyden: E.J. Brill.

Josselin de Jong, J.P.B. de
1913   Original Odzibwe Texts. *Beiträge zur Volkerkunde.* Leipzig: Herausgegeben aus Mitteln des Baessler-Instituts 5.

Kelsey, Henry
1929   [1683/1722] *The Kelsey Papers*, edited by Arthur G. Doughty and Chester Martin. Ottawa: Public Archives of Canada.
Kinietz, Vernon W.
1947   Chippewa Village. *Bulletin of the Cranbrook Institute of Science* 25:1–259.
1965   *The Indians of the Western Great Lakes, 1615–1760*. Ann Arbor: University of Michigan Press.
Kohl, J.G.
1985   [1860] *Kitchi-Gami: Life Among the Lake Superior Ojibway*. St. Paul: Minnesota Historical Society Press.
LaBarre, Weston
1964   Confession as Cathartic Therapy in American Indian Tribes. *Magic, Faith, and Healing*, edited by A. Kiev, New York: Free Press.
Lahontan, Louis Armand, Baron de
1905   [1703] *New Voyages to North America*, edited by Reuben G. Thwaites. 2 vols. Chicago.
Laidlaw, George
1927   Ojibwa Myths and Tales. *35th Annual Ontario Archaeological Report*, 1924–25.
Landes, Ruth
1938   *The Ojibwa Woman*. New York: Norton.
1968   *Ojibwa Religion*. Madison: University of Wisconsin Press.
LaRoque, Emma
1975   *Defeathering the Indians*. Agincourt: Book Society of Canada.
1983   "The Métis in English Canadian Literature." *Canadian Journal of Native Studies* 3(1):85–94.
Leighton, Anna L.
1985   Wild Plant Use by the Woods Cree (nihīthawak) of East-central Saskatchewan. *Canadian Ethnology Service Paper 101*. Ottawa: National Museum of Man Mercury Series.
Le Jeune, Paul
1897   Relation of What Occurred in New France in the Year 1637. In Reuben G. Thwaites, editor, vol. 12.
LeMercier, François
1899   Relation of 1666 and 1667. In Reuben G. Thwaites, editor, vol. 50.
Linderman, F.B.
1920   *Indian Old-Man Stories*. New York: John Day Company.
Lips, Julius
1947   Naskapi Law (Lake St. John and Mistassini bands). Law and Order in a Hunting Society. *Transactions of the American Philosophical Society* 37(4):379–492.
Long, John S.
1986   "Shaganash": Early Protestant Missionaries and the Adoption of Christianity by the Western James Bay Cree, 1840–1893. Ed.D. dissertation, University of Toronto.

Lyons, Ponsonby A.
1878   Encyclopaedia. *Encyclopaedia Britannia*, vol. 8, 190–204 (ninth edition). London.

Lytwyn, Victor P.
1986   *The Fur Trade of the Little North: Indians, Pedlars and Englishmen East of Lake Winnipeg, 1760–1821*. Winnipeg: Rupert's Land Research Centre, University of Winnipeg.

Maclean, John
1897   *Canadian Savage Folk: The Native Tribes of Canada*. Toronto.

McNeice, Gladys
1984   *The Ermatinger Family of Sault Ste. Marie*. Sault Ste. Marie: Creative Printing House.

Marano, Louis
1981   Windigo Psychosis: The Anatomy of an Emic-Etic Confusion. Ph.D. dissertation, University of Florida.

1982   Windigo Psychosis: The Anatomy of an Emic-Etic Confusion. *Current Anthropology* 23(4):385–97.

Marshall, Peter J., and Glyndwr Williams
1982   *The Great Map of Mankind: British Perceptions of the World in the Age of Enlightenment*. London: J.M. Dent and Sons.

Mason, Leonard
1967   The Swampy Cree: A Study in Acculturation. *National Museum of Canada Anthropology Papers* 13. Ottawa.

Masson, Louis F.R., ed.
1889–90 Les bourgeois de la Compagnie du Nord-Ouest. 2 vols. Quebec.

Merasty, Marie
1974   *The World of Wetiko: Tales from the Woodland Cree*, edited by C. Savage. Saskatoon: Saskatchewan Indian Cultural College.

Morriseau, Norval
1965   *Legends of My People the Great Ojibway*. Toronto: McGraw-Hill Ryerson.

Nelson Family Papers
1765   Indenture of William Nelson to Thomas Head, schoolmaster, 29 December 1765. Montreal: McCord Museum.

Nelson, George
1805–06 Journal, Lac du Bon[n]et. Nelson Papers, Metropolitan Public Library of Toronto.
1811   River Dauphine, letter-journal. Ibid.
1816   Letter, 8 July 1816, to William Morrison. Selkirk Papers, Public Archives of Canada, MG2, A1, vol. 28:8638. Ottawa.
1820   Copy of letter to the agents of the North West Company, 14 June, Cumberland House. George Nelson Papers, Metropolitan Toronto Library. (In code, deciphered by Sylvia Van Kirk.)
1823   Untitled manuscript, miscellaneous. George Nelson Papers, Metropolitan Toronto Library.

1825ff. Unpublished reminiscences. George Nelson Papers, Metropolitan Toronto Library.

Nicks, Trudy
1980   The Iroquois and the Fur Trade in Western Canada. *Old Trails and New Directions: Papers of the Third North American Fur Trade Conference*, edited by Carol M. Judd and Arthur J. Ray. Toronto: University of Toronto Press.

Norman, Howard
1982   *Where the Chill Came From.* San Francisco: North Point Press.

Paget, Amelia
1909   *People of the Plains.* Toronto.

Parker, Seymour
1960   The Witiko Psychosis in the Context of Ojibwa Personality and Culture. *American Anthropologist* 62:603-23.

Pearce, Roy Harvey
1967   *Savagism and Civilization: A Study of the Indian and the American Mind.* Baltimore: Johns Hopkins Press (1st ed. 1953).

Pentland, David
1978   A Historical Overview of Cree Dialects. *Papers of the Ninth Algonquian Conference*, edited by William Cowan. Ottawa: Carleton University.

Perrot, Nicholas
1911   Memoir on the Manners, Customs, and Religion of the Savages of North America. *The Indian Tribes of the Upper Mississippi Valley and Region of the Great Lakes*, edited by E.H. Blair, vol. 1. Cleveland.

Petitot, Emile
1886   *Traditions indiennes du Canada Nord-Ouest.* Paris.

Preston, Richard
1975   Cree Narrative: Expressing the Personal Meanings of Events. *Canadian Ethnology Service Paper 30.* Ottawa: National Museum of Man Mercury Series.
1978   Ethnograhic Reconstruction of Witigo. *Papers of the Ninth Algonquian Conference*, edited by William Cowan. Ottawa: Carleton University.

Radin, Paul
1914a   Some Myths and Tales of the Ojibwa of Southeastern Ontario. *Memoirs of the Canada Department of Mines, Geological Survey, Number 48*, pp.1-83.
1914b   Some Aspects of Puberty Fasting Among the Ojibwa. *Museum Bulletins of the Canada Department of Mines, Geological Survey, Number 2*, pp.69-78.
1914c   Religion of the North American Indians. *Journal of American Folklore* 27:335-73.
1936   Ojibwa and Ottawa Puberty Dreams. *Essays in Anthropology Presented to A.L. Kroeber.* Berkeley: University of California Press.

Radin, Paul, and A.B. Reagan
1928   Ojibwa Myths and Tales. *Journal of American Folklore* 41:61-146.

Rasles, Sébastien
1900   "Letter . . . to his Brother." In Reuben G. Thwaites, editor, vol. 67.

Ray, Arthur J.
1974   *Indians in the Fur Trade: Their Role as Hunters, Trappers and Middlemen in the Lands Southwest of Hudson Bay 1660-1870*. Toronto: University of Toronto Press.

Ray, Verne F.
1941   Historic Backgrounds of the Conjuring Complex in the Plateau and the Plains. *Language, Culture, and Personality: Essays in Memory of Edward Sapir*, edited by L. Spier, A.I. Hallowell, and S. Newman, 204-16. Menasha: Sapir Memorial Publication Fund.

Reagan, A.B.
1921a   Some Chippewa Medicinal Recipes. *American Anthropologist* 23:246-49.
1921b   Some Plants of the Bois Fort Indian Reservation and Vicinity in Minnesota. *Transactions of the Illinois State Academy of Science* 14:61-70.
1928   Plants Used by the Bois Fort Chippewa. *Wisconsin Archaeologist* 7:230-48.

Rhodes, Richard
1985   Trends in Linguistics, Documentation 3: Eastern Ojibwa-Chippewa-Ottawa Dictionary. Berlin: Mouton.

Richards, J. Howard, and K.I. Fung, eds.
1969   *Atlas of Saskatchewan*. Saskatoon: University of Saskatchewan.

Richardson, Boyce
1975   *Strangers Devour the Land*. New York: Alfred A. Knopf.

Ritzenthaler, Robert E.
1953   Chippewa Preoccupation with Health: Change in a Traditional Attitude Resulting from Modern Health Problems. *Bulletin of the Milwaukee Public Museum* 19:175-258.

Robson, Joseph
1965   [1752] *An Account of Six Years Residence in Hudson's Bay from 1733 to 1736 and 1744 to 1747*. Toronto: Johnson Reprint Co.

Rogers, Edward S.
1962   The Round Lake Ojibwa. *Occasional Paper 5, Art and Archaeology Division, Royal Ontario Museum*, University of Toronto.

Rohrl, Vivian
1970   A Nutritional Factor in Windigo Psychosis. *American Anthropologist* 72:97-101.

Rossignol, Marius
1938   Religion of the Saskatchewan and Western Manitoba Cree. *Primitive Man* 11(3-4):67-71.
1939   Property Concepts of the Cree of the Rocks. *Primitive Man* 12(3):61-70.

Rousseau, Jacques
1953   Rites païens de la forêt québecoise. *Cahiers des dix* 18:129-55.

Rousseau, Jacques, and Madeleine Rousseau
1947   La cérémonie de la tente agitée chez les Mistassini. *Actes du vingt-huitième congrès international des americanistes* 38:307-15.

Russell, Frank
1898   *Explorations in the Far North.* Iowa City.
Savard, Rémi
1979   Contes indiens de la Basse Côte Nord du Saint Laurent. *Canadian Ethnology Service Paper 51.* Ottawa: National Museum of Man Mercury Series.
Schaeffer, Claude E.
1969   Blackfoot Shaking Tent. Glenbow-Alberta Institute, *Occasional Paper Number 5.*
Schmidt, Wilhelm
1933   *High Gods in North America.* Oxford: Clarendon Press.
Schoolcraft, Henry Rowe
1839   *Algic Researches.* 2 vols. New York.
1848   The Indian in his Wigwam, or Characteristics of the Red Race of America. Buffalo, New York.
1860   Of Nanibozho and the Introduction of Medical Magic. *Archives of Aboriginal Knowledge* 1. Philadelphia.
Scoggan, H.J.
1957   Flora of Manitoba. *National Musem of Canada Bulletin 140.* Ottawa.
Semmens, John
1884   *Mission Life in the Northwest.* Toronto.
Simms, S.C.
1906   Myths of the Bungees or Swampy Indians of Lake Winnipeg. *Journal of American Folklore* 19:334–40.
Skinner, Alanson
1911   Notes on the Eastern Cree and Northern Saulteaux. *Anthropological Papers of the American Museum of Natural History* 9(1):1–177.
1915   Associations and Ceremonies of the Menomini Indians. *Anthropological Papers of the American Museum of Natural History* 13:167–215.
1916   Plains Cree Tales. *Journal of American Folklore* 29:341–67.
1928   Bungi Tales (Part 2 of Sauk Tales). *Journal of American Folklore* 41:147–71.
Smith, Huron H.
1932   Ethnobotany of the Ojibwe Indians. *Bulletin of the Milwaukee Public Museum* 4(3):327–525.
Smith, James G.E.
1975   Preliminary Notes on the Rocky Cree of Reindeer Lake. *Contributions to Canadian Ethnology*, edited by D.B. Carlisle. *Ethnology Service Paper 31*, 171–89. National Museum of Man Mercury Series. Ottawa.
1976   Notes on the Wittiko. *Papers of the Seventh Algonquian Conference*, edited by William Cowan, Ottawa: Carleton University.
Speck, Frank G.
1915   Myths and Folklore of the Timiskaming Algonquian and Timagami Ojibwa. *Canada Department of Mines Geological Survey, Memoir 71*, Anthropological Series 9.
1925   Montagnais and Naskapi Tales. *Journal of American Folklore* 38:1–32.
1935   *Naskapi.* Norman: University of Oklahoma Press.

Steager, Peter
1976   The Child Who Was Not Born Naturally. *Papers of the Seventh Algonquian Conference*, edited by William Cowan. Ottawa: Carleton University.
Steinbring, Jack H.
1981   Saulteaux of Lake Winnipeg. *Handbook of North American Indians*, vol. 6, *Subarctic*, edited by June Helm, 244–55. Washington, D.C.: Smithsonian Institution.
Stevens, James R.
1971   *Sacred Legends of the Sandy Lake Cree*. Toronto: McClelland and Stewart.
1985(ed) *Legends from the Forest Told by Chief Thomas Fiddler*. Moonbeam, Ont.: Penumbra Press.
Stocking, George W., Jr.
1987   *Victorian Anthropology*. New York: Free Press.
Stowe, G.C.
1940   Plants Used by the Chippewa. *Wisconsin Archaeologist* 11:8–13.
Strath, R.
1903   Materia Medica, Pharmacy and Therapeutics of the Cree Indians of the Hudson Bay Territory. *St. Paul Medical Journal* 5:735–46.
Swindlehurst, Fred
1905   Folk-Lore of the Cree Indians. *Journal of American Folklore* 18:139–43.
Tanner, Adrian
1973   The Significance of Hunting Territories Today. *Cultural Ecology*, edited by Bruce Cox. Toronto: Collier.
1979   *Bringing Home Animals: Religious Ideology and Mode of Production of the Mistassini Cree Hunters*. New York: St. Martin's Press.
Tanner, John
1956   *A Narrative of the Captivity and Adventures of John Tanner (U.S. Interpreter at the Saut de Ste. Marie) during thirty years residence among the Indians in the Interior of North America*. Minneapolis: Ross and Haines (1st ed. 1830).
Teicher, Morton I.
1960   *Windigo Psychosis: A Study of a Relationship between Belief and Behavior among the Indians of Northeastern Canada*. Seattle: University of Washington Press.
Thompson, David
1962   *David Thompson's Narrative, 1784–1812*, edited by R. Glover. Toronto: Champlain Society.
Thompson, John B.
1976   Wolfred Nelson. *Dictionary of Canadian Biography* 9:593–97. Toronto: University of Toronto Press.
Thwaites, Reuben G., ed.
1896–1901 *The Jesuit Relations and Allied Documents*. Cleveland.
Tyrrell, J.B.
1931   *Documents Relating to the Early History of Hudson's Bay*. Toronto: Champlain Society.

Umfreville, Edward
1954   [1790] *The Present State of Hudson's Bay*, edited by W.S. Wallace. Toronto: Ryerson Press.
Vandersteene, Roger
1969   Some Woodland Cree Traditions and Legends. *Western Canadian Journal of Anthropology* 1(1):40–64.
Van Kirk, Sylvia
1984   George Nelson's "Wretched" Career, 1802–1823. *Rendezvous: Selected Papers of the Fourth North American Fur Trade Conference, 1981*. St. Paul: Minnesota Historical Society.
1985   (with Jennifer S.H. Brown). George Nelson. *Dictionary of Canadian Biography* 8:652–54. Toronto: University of Toronto Press.
Vecsey, Christopher
1983   *Traditional Ojibwa Religion and its Historical Changes*. Philadelphia: American Philosophical Society.
Vincent, Sylvie
1973   Structure du rituel: La tente tremblante et le concept de mista.pe.w. *Recherches amérindiennes au Québec* 3(1–2):39–68.
1977   Structures comparées du rite et des mythes de la tente tremblante. *Actes du huitième congrés des Algonquinistes*, edited by William Cowan. Ottawa: Carleton University.
Voorhis, Ernest
1930   *Historic Forts and Trading Posts of the French Régime and of the English Fur Trading Companies*. Ottawa: Department of the Interior.
Waisberg, Leo G.
1975   Boreal Forest Subsistence and the Windigo: Fluctuation of Animal Populations. *Anthropologica* 17:169–85.
Wales, William
1771   Journal of a Voyage . . . to Churchill River, on the North-west Coast of Hudson's Bay . . . in the Years 1768 to 1769. *Philosophical Transactions*, vol. 60. London.
Warkentin, Germaine
1983   Exploration Literature in English. *The Oxford Companion to Canadian Literature*. Toronto: Oxford University Press, 242–49.
Wiebe, Rudy, and Bob Beal
1985   *War in the West: Voices of the 1885 Rebellion*. Toronto: McClelland and Stewart.
Wilson, James S., and James Light
1980   Archaeological Resource Survey of Lac la Ronge Provincial Park, Northern Saskatchewan. *SRC Technical Report Number 104*. Resources Branch, Department of Northern Saskatchewan.
Wolfart, H. Christoph
1973   Plains Cree: A Grammatical Study. *Transactions of the American Philosophical Society* 63(5):1–90.
Young, Egerton R.
1893   *Stories from Indian Wigwams and Northern Camp-Fires*. Toronto.
1903   *Algonquin Indian Tales*. Toronto.

INDEX

- wrongly identified as Supreme
Being 35-36, 43, 125-126
wind in shaking lodge 44
windigo 85-91, 167, 196
- associated with cold and starvation 170
- baiting, trapping and killing
of 86-87
- cures and precautions
against 93-94, 168, 169
- dreams of 90
- execution of 89-90, 92-93,
168-169, 196
- misrepresentation of self 169
- origins of 165-168
- as Macimanitōw (evil deity) 161
- as pawākan 142, 167
- symbolism of 170
windigo, examples of 86-87, 89-90,
90-93, 162, 163-164, 167
- at Lake Winnipeg 91-92
- at Lac la Ronge 89-90
windigo, kinds of 88-90, 159
- dream-predestined cannibals 90-94,
142, 159, 166-167
- famine cannibals 88-89, 162, 164,
165
- non-human giants 86, 88, 159-160,
167
- people who starved to death 159
- spirit-bewitched cannibals 90,
91-92, 165, 166, 167, 168
windigo complex 85, 91, 159, 163-165
- explanations of 170
- geographical distribution of 171
- infrequency of 164-165, 168
windigo concept, history of 161-162,
192-193

Wīsahkēcāhk *see* Wee-suck-a-jock
Wisconsin 4, 5, 9-10, 58, 60
Wolf (spirit) saves traveller's life 84,
144
Wolverine (spirit) 40, 114, 134
women
- associated with Nelson 9-10, 13,
14, 20, 51-52, 60
- in myths 44-45, 48-49, 78, 80,
86-87, 94-95, 113, 121-122, 124,
129, 135, 137, 138
- in religious ritual 54, 64, 140, 155
- in stories told to Nelson 29, 64-65,
66, 67-68, 69-71, 72, 74, 89-90,
91, 94, 99, 101, 177, 178-179,
180, 181, 202
- *see also* Crazy Woman; Nelson,
marriages of
worship, Indian modifications in 81-82

XY Company (Sir Alexander Mackenzie
and Company) 3, 5, 9, 10

www.ingramcontent.com/pod-product-compliance
Lightning Source LLC
Jackson TN
JSHW011934131224
75386JS00041B/1381